SUPERCORPORATE

CULTURE AND ECONOMIC LIFE

SUPERCORPORATE

Distinction and Participation
in Post-Hierarchy South Korea

MICHAEL M. PRENTICE

STANFORD UNIVERSITY PRESS
Stanford, California

STANFORD UNIVERSITY PRESS
Stanford, California

Printed in the United States of America on acid-free, archival-quality paper

Library of Congress Cataloging-in-Publication Data

Names: Prentice, Michael M., author.
Title: Supercorporate : distinction and participation in post-hierarchy South Korea / Michael M. Prentice.
Other titles: Culture and economic life.
Description: Stanford, California : Stanford University Press, 2022. | Series: Culture and economic life | Includes bibliographical references and index.
Identifiers: LCCN 2021046766 (print) | LCCN 2021046767 (ebook) | ISBN 9781503629479 (cloth) | ISBN 9781503631878 (paperback) | ISBN 9781503631885 (ebook)
Subjects: LCSH: Quality of work life—Korea (South) | Work environment—Korea (South) | White collar workers—Korea (South) | Corporations—Korea (South)—Employees. | Hierarchies—Korea (South) | Personnel management—Korea (South)
Classification: LCC HD6957.K6 P74 2022 (print) | LCC HD6957.K6 (ebook) | DDC 306.3/6095195—dc23
LC record available at https://lccn.loc.gov/2021046766
LC ebook record available at https://lccn.loc.gov/2021046767

Cover design: Black Eye Design
Cover art: iStock
Typeset by Motto Publishing Services in 10/14 Minion Pro

Acknowledgments

The first seed of this project was sown in the small offices of a marketing company in New York City where I worked shortly after graduating from college. It was at that distinctly new American office environment—with its open office layout, congenial atmosphere, and large open conference room with glass doors—that I also came to work with men and women across the world in their own office worlds in South Korea. The New York office came to play a role as a Western marketing expert in the complex ecosystem of large South Korean conglomerates and their brand-conscious media agencies. While the company played the role of outside expert in these relationships, I found myself impressed by the South Korean partners we interacted with on late-night conference calls, through emails, or on occasional business trips. One moment stuck out in particular: one of the partners of the New York firm had just received a PowerPoint file from an advertising agency in Seoul with whom we were collaborating. He printed out copies of the document and told me and another colleague, "*This* is a perfect document," with the implication that we should read it and produce documents just like that. With the partner's words, the presentation itself, written in perfect English and laid out on ten cleanly organized slides, took on a quasi-magical quality to me as a young office worker struggling over the art of PowerPoint slide design and logical sequencing. The document, surely long forgotten now, laid out a simple and self-evident structure for a new approach to corporate brand strategy, and it did so without the use of a presentation or any explanation. Each slide seemed perfectly crafted both in wording and graphics. It inspired my first interest in the ways that South Korean office workers produced office documents.

The second seed for this project emerged when I encountered shareholding charts that were first produced in 2012 by the Korean Fair Trade Commission.

These charts, which at first glance appeared to be electric circuit diagrams, displayed to the public the complex internecine shareholding relations among the largest conglomerate entities in South Korea at the time. Released annually for the largest groups by assets, the charts shed light on the ways that conglomerate relations were premised on complex and crisscrossing ownership across subsidiaries. The charts also revealed certain mysteries such as the way that obscure subsidiaries or holding companies could be said to be the head companies for a large group or the way that a corporate owner might only own 0.1 percent stock while also being the central node across dozens of companies. For a long time, I believed that the mysteries of the charts could ultimately be explained by a logic known to corporate insiders and that the mechanisms of corporate obfuscation could be unwound to reveal more obvious truths behind them about how corporate control operated. I believed that I might enter the South Korean corporate world and uncover (or at least be able to explain) these complex phenomena.

These two encounters were both born from an interest in exploring some of the mysteries of the South Korean corporate world at a time when I became interested in office cultures outside the US. While both experiences propelled me to pursue a PhD and attempt to work within the South Korean corporate world for research, such encounters were in many ways prefigured by two ways of thinking about East Asian capitalism from the West. In thinking about documents, I was influenced by ideas of South Korea as a zone of elite professionalism that could replicate the objects of Western capitalism better than those in the West could. Little did I know at the time of the complex workplace relationships behind documents and the ways that South Korean employees would equally find their own work lives weighed down by the politics of perfecting documents. In thinking about shareholding, I would find out by talking to many people in these worlds that shareholder charts were not treasure maps holding secrets to uncovering some mechanism that would explain all other phenomena; they were also complex political artifacts that revealed ongoing tensions between state regulators, international finance, and corporate ownership. Moreover, as I would come to discover, the internal worlds of conglomerates do not revolve solely around chairmen or their retention of power; they are far from the day-to-day thoughts of most corporate workers. There are also many other lines, visible and invisible, that connect organizations and the men and women within them.

I was fortunate to come to know a number of people, both within universities and in corporations, in South Korea, the US, and the UK, who could disabuse me of some of these pretenses, romantic or otherwise, and who encouraged me to understand multiple ways of looking at corporate life and its articulations with other aspects of South Korean society. One of the first lessons was that simply describing something as corporate in English does not cover the heterogeneity of organizational life in South Korea. My fascination with all things corporate took me to some unexpected places—an old rubber manufacturer in a forgotten part of central Seoul, a military helipad on the top of a corporate tower, a steel factory in Pohang, a shipbuilding yard on Geoje Island, and a BBQ restaurant in downtown Detroit—that did not always contribute to data in a hard social scientific sense. Such encounters helped me to understand the broader worlds that I was attempting to describe. South Korean economic life can often appear neatly encased in high-rising office towers, difficult for outsiders to access, but there are many interesting and dynamic places worthy of study.

Countless people in South Korea aided me in attempts to study different aspects of corporate life. I was fortunate to work at four different companies in Seoul between 2011 and 2015 and have benefited from the tutelage of bosses and fellowship of coworkers. To those who offered employment and institutional support, I would like to thank Rudy Lee, Jaehang Park, Nelson Hur, Kim Keun han, Jimmy Chung, Kim Kyung-gyu, Dawna Cha, and Randy Ringer. I learned a great deal from colleagues at the time and I owe a special debt of thanks to Sora Lee, Minjoo Oh, Eunyoung Park, Inyoung Kim, Seulgi Kim, Jason Hwang, Sean Hong, Katie Noh, and Lynn Lee. During my research, I also benefited from interviews with a number of professionals who shared their time and expertise with me: Shin Ho-cheol, Zee Minseon, Katie Byun, Jane Kim, Lee Seong-yong, Choi Yukyung, Gaz Shin, Kim Seong Hoo, Kim Seung-kyeung, Park Tae-jeong, Park Tae-woon, Jeong In-sub, Kim Kyuhwan, Lee Ju-bok, Yang Jae-man, Park Seong-su, Park Chan-yong, Baik Wangyu, Heo Chang-wook, Lee Sangjae, Yoon Seong-wook, Chris Woo, and Kim Hong-tae.

The main material for this study would not have been possible without the lengthy participation from members of the pseudonymous Sangdo holding company with whom I worked for a year in 2014 and 2015. There are many people I would like to directly thank and moments for which I would like to express my appreciation, but doing so would hurt the confidentiality that ethnographic research is built on. I would like to offer my appreciation to those who are known only by their pseudonyms. In particular, I owe a debt of thanks to a member of the owning family of Sangdo, who allowed me to work inside Sangdo for one year as an intern and contract worker. In particular, I would like to thank members of the human resources team with whom I spent nearly every day for a full year and who have remained in contact with me in years since. I also would like to thank the retiring and incoming CEOs, the executives, and the team managers who allowed me to speak with them and learn about their professional worlds and histories of work. I was able to meet employees from nine different departments who allowed an interloper to talk to them about their own work worlds. I was also introduced to and had some fortunate interactions with many interesting people across Sangdo who showed me just how large and diverse the world of Sangdo was and the great responsibility it is to attempt to capture its dynamics.

Any ethnographic account of living persons must safeguard the trust of those who participate in research, which may involve critical accounts of places they work and live, by safeguarding their anonymity. The ethics of organizational anonymity are double-edged, as readers might expect more critical accounts from inside capitalism's hallowed spaces from which to build new kinds of critique of the privileged, but the risks to such actors are of no less concern. Indeed, the researcher may need to go to extra lengths due to the multiple indirect and associational risks that contemporary office life brings, where responsibility—legal, moral, or otherwise—can be distributed across many people. Risks to corporate organizations might affect not just research participants but all who work in or depend on such workplaces. Furthermore, workplaces such as Sangdo's are unique places with their own histories, structures, and layouts. Any overly specific mention—of where a building is located or what products a company makes—might allow readers in the know to connect the dots, which might have unknown harms, including relations among those who still work together. I have anonymized not only names of people and workplaces but also numerical figures, team structures, and basic company information. In any ethnographic writing there is a tension between overgenericization and overspecification, and this book attempts to capture the nuances of those at the Sangdo Group and elsewhere in South Korea with sufficient care to their anonymity and minimal generalization.

To those I can thank by name, my time in South Korea was aided by cama-raderie and support from the wider community of anthropologists and other scholars in Seoul who provided an intellectual home during my fieldwork. This includes the close-knit and supportive community of linguistic and cul-tural anthropologists in Seoul, including Wang Hahn-Sok and Kang Yoonhee at Seoul National University, Linda Kyung-nan Koh at Hankuk University of Foreign Studies, and the late Roger Janelli at Indiana University who of-fered their support over many years. Nicholas Harkness at Harvard Univer-sity has offered insightful advice on occasions too numerous to mention. I also benefited from support from Jung Hyang-jin, Oh Myeong-seok, and Han Kyung-gu from Seoul National University and Yoon Sung-joon from Kyonggi University. I owe a special debt of thanks to Kim Jae-il from Dankook Univer-sity who made some key introductions on my behalf.

I was fortunate to come to know many friends, graduate students, and professors who both lightened and deepened my time in Seoul: Dong-ho Park, Yeon-ju Bae, Kim Seong-In, Heangin Park, Myeongji Lee, Haewon Lee, Caroline Lee, Jay Cho, Heejin Lee, John Lee, Holly Stephens, Daniel Kim, Jeong-su Shin, Gayoung Chung, Jonghyun Park, Vivien Chung, Jenny Hough, Xiao Ma, Javier Cha, Sandy Oh, Jaymin Kim, Sara McAdory-Kim, Chi-hoon Kim, Sunyoung Yang, Susan Hwang, and Irhe Sohn. I was fortunate to be at the Institute of Cross-Cultural Studies at Seoul National University where I bene-fited from advice from many senior anthropologists. Research assistants Han-kyeol Chung (in Seoul) and Mina Lee and Heejin Kwon (in Ann Arbor) were exceptionally helpful as I connected the dots during and after my research. A special debt is owed to Inbae Lee and Sean Park who have been unofficial re-search assistants and friends for many years.

At the University of Michigan, the Nam Center for Korean Studies was a home away from home and a model of an interdisciplinary community of scholars. I want to thank Nojin Kwak, Youngju Ryu, David Chung, Do-hee Morsman, Jiyoung Lee, Adrienne Janney, and the late Elder Nam and his fam-ily who provided institutional support to activities at the center that I was for-tunate to overlap with during periods of its growth.

At the University of Michigan, I benefited from the tutelage of many fac-ulty members. I thank, in particular, members of my dissertation commit-tee Barbra Meek, Erik Mueggler, Michael Lempert, Juhn Ahn, and Gerald Davis. They each offered the right mix of encouragement and challenge that motivated me during my research and writing. Matthew Hull has had a remarkable ability to help me realize how much there is at stake even in the smallest of bureaucratic forms or events, not only in my own project but in anthropology and the social sciences more broadly. Our conversations always provided new motivation and desire to explore and think more deeply.

This book was based on research funded by various grants and institutions: Foreign Language and Areas Studies (FLAS) grants via the University of Michigan, a Korea Foundation predoctoral fellowship, and a SeAH-Haiam Arts & Sciences summer fellowship. Research in South Korea was aided by a Korea Foundation language grant, a Fulbright-IIE research grant, a Wenner-Gren dissertation fieldwork grant, and a Rackham Centennial Award. The dissertation writing stage was supported by the Rackham Humanities Research Fellowship, a Social Sciences Research Council Korean Studies Dissertation Workshop, and the Core University Program for Korean Studies through the Ministry of Education of the Republic of Korea and Korean Studies Promotion Service of the Academy of Korean Studies (AKS-2016-OLU-2240001). My postdoctoral fellowship at Harvard University was funded by the Korea Foundation.

I have been fortunate to work in a number of academic institutions including Harvard University, Brandeis University, the University of Manchester, and the University of Sheffield. Colleagues, friends, and staff are too many to name. In the UK, I am thankful to have spent the pandemic knowing close friends were nearby: Jini Kim, Meghanne Barker, Juan Manuel del Nido, Scott McLoughlin, Sabine Mohammed, Deborah Jones, Jean-Christophe Plantin, and Chip Zuckerman. Hyun Kyong Chang has been the best person with whom to spend the pandemic, and ever after.

I would like to thank Ilana Gershon for first introducing me to Stanford University Press. Marcela Maxfield and Sunna Juhn have both been diligent and patient in guiding the manuscript through writing, review, and publication.

Sections of Chapter 2 were originally published in Korean as "Resisting Organizational Flatness: Titles, Identity Infrastructures, and Semiotics in Korea Corporations," in *Lingua-Culture in Contemporary Korean Society*, edited by Yoonhee Kang and published in 2022 by Seoul National University Press (pp. 453–78). A revised version of Chapter 3 originally appeared in the article "Old Spirits of Capitalism: Masculine Alterity in/as the Korean Office" in *Anthropological Quarterly* 93 (2): 89–118.

The manuscript was fortunate to receive funding for a book workshop from George Washington's Institute for Korean Studies. Jisoo Kim, Roy Grinker, Hirokazu Miyazaki, Alexander Dent, Joel Kuipers, and Yonho Kim each provided comments that helped me raise the stakes of the book and refine its arguments.

For more than fifteen years, I have been fortunate to rely on the tutelage of Shirley Brice Heath, my undergraduate advisor at Brown University. Shirley has taken many young scholars under her wing over her illustrious career and I am fortunate to have remained under her watchful eye. As much as she impresses with her sage advice, those fortunate to be her students also derive inspiration from the way she models her own conduct as a rigorous researcher and ever-curious scholar.

This book is dedicated to my parents, Nat and Anita Prentice, who have witnessed and withstood the ups and downs across the full arc of this project. A book surely must be dedicated to the parents who would make a trip to South Korea where they would tour a remote shipyard on the whim of their son, play virtual golf, and score higher than I ever did on late-night karaoke. As a return gift to them, I have written the book with them as imagined readers so that they might reap some reward for their years of support.

Romanization

This book follows the Revised Romanization (RR) format of Korean language romanization. Exceptions to the use of RR are the following: personal names that have their own spellings, company names, and legacy terms found in English dictionaries, including chaebol, hangul, kimchi, and the Korean won.

Hard to map in any system for native English speakers are vowels. Vowels represented with single characters (*a, e, i, o, u*) map onto basic cardinal vowels. Double-vowel representations are less intuitive but can be pronounced in the following way:

ae	[ɛ] or "eh"		*wi*	[wi] or "wee"
eo	[ə] or "au"		*oe*	[we] or "way"
eu	[ɯ] or "uh"		*ui*	[ɯi] or "ee"

SUPERCORPORATE

Introduction

THE 2014 ANNUAL EMPLOYEE SURVEY of white-collar workers at the Sangdo Group, a pseudonym for a mid-level South Korean industrial conglomerate, contained some surprising, but not unexpected, responses. After thirty-seven questions about their workplace satisfaction and team behaviors, employees were given the opportunity to leave an evaluation in their own words. Around 10 percent of the more than 1000 respondents offered their own diagnoses of life in the Sangdo Group. One wrote starkly, "The attitude of an oppressive boss: the boss who says unconditionally 'just do it,' psychologically and physically, causes employee stress." Others complained about work itself: "meaningless overtime, never-ending meeting reports, ever-changing requests from management." Others attacked Sangdo's "military culture," its "drinking-heavy culture," and its "Korean-style management culture." Some were more constructive and proposed solutions of their own, such as the implementation of "performance-based pay," "360-degree feedback," "concentrated work time," and "flexible working hours." The longest response, at nearly two pages, addressed the unknown surveyors directly, saying that if the Sangdo Group could develop a shared vision of where it was going, all employees could be united, and all other problems would simply be solved in turn. To the human resources (HR) team that created the survey, these results were not entirely unexpected, reflecting familiar gripes and suggestions seen on prior surveys and overheard in offhand complaints.

One set of results, however, revealed a discrepancy that was not so easy for the HR team to explain. In questions about their desired workplace, the South Korean employees responded, seemingly paradoxically, that they wanted both greater collaboration with coworkers and greater individual distinction and recognition for their own work. To the HR team that reviewed the results, these should have been exclusive positions. In fact, the questions were specifically included in the survey in part to distinguish different styles or types of employees, such as those who might seek teamwork and cooperative relations compared with those who were more interested in their individual advancement. However, when more than 90 percent of respondents across Sangdo's dozen subsidiaries said that their desired workplace combined both cooperation and distinction, the HR team had difficulty reconciling the apparent contradiction. One employee wrote, for instance, "I want to have positive discussions about the future of the company with other employees where we can freely talk to each other," while another wrote that "we need fair evaluations (*gongjeonghan pyeong-ga*) that give equal respect between employees." Employees expressed a desired for the creation of new "systems" (*siseutem* or *jedo*) that could be implemented to properly sort out inter-employee distinctions without bias, while they also expressed a desire for more freedom to interact and share ideas with others through "mutual communication" (*uisasotong*) that would overcome "one-way" (*ilbanghyang*) styles of communicating.

This book considers a dilemma in the hopes and aspirations surrounding white-collar office work in contemporary South Korea. White-collar office work, particularly at large corporations or within conglomerate organizations, has been long admired as a place of security and stability—regular or standard jobs (*jeong-gyujik*) which accrue greater benefits and garner recognizable social prestige. However, there are subtle fault lines in the image of standard work in a twenty-first century South Korea that might imagine itself as post-hierarchical. By post-hierarchical, I refer to the notion that South Korea as a nation is continuously distancing itself from the militarized and top-down form of industrialized modernity that marked the latter half of its twentieth-century journey. This period was marked by various impositions of formal hierarchy that might have seemed necessary in the context of South Korea's massive socioeconomic transformations from a country of largely agricultural workers ravaged by the Korean War to a highly corporatized society operating some of the world's largest industrial enterprises in chemicals, steel, semiconductors, pharmaceuticals, and others. Two economic dictatorships, rigid gender and seniority norms, and forms of interactional control all could be argued to serve in the name of national development. These have variously been seen as the products of traditional norms, compressed industrialization, pressures from being on a capitalist periphery, or Cold War extremes. Whether necessary sacrifices or unnecessary cruelties, whether the product of South Korean society or geopolitics, the question at the heart of this book is this: what form of work comes in the wake of seemingly negative forms of hierarchy? There is considerable ambiguity around what a post-hierarchy South Korea should look like. For some, post-hierarchy represents a breakdown of vertical workplace norms and structures where employees of different ages and abilities might freely communicate regardless of their ranks, cooperate with others, and have positive team experiences free from traditional social pressures. For others, post-hierarchy represents fair and neutral evaluation where individuals' skills, achievements, and work efforts can be properly recognized and distinguished, free of concerns around age, gender, or seniority that interfered with individual merit and marked South Korean office systems of the past. Differentiating from the forms and legacies of the past, particularly the culture of male managers from a previous generation who are often seen as the residue of such problems, is not so difficult. It is in those times, people, and practices that negative forms of hierarchy still reside. A more basic problem lies in what role office or professional work should have, either in better articulating individual differences or in working to eradicate them.

This story about the place of office work in South Korea reflects tensions around contemporary ideas and ideals of participation vis-à-vis distinction. Is participation, as the anthropologist Christopher Kelty observed, a matter of losing oneself in the crowd or the masses to be as one with others, or is it a matter of participating so as to ultimately distinguish oneself from the crowd?[1] These are in some sense unresolved contradictions at the heart of many contemporary modern organizational questions. While the spread of neoliberal thinking and policies around the world since the 1970s has led to a dramatic restructuring and rethinking of work where questions of distinction and participation have seemingly been shaped for many of us (by the market, by economists, or by financial institutions), there are other places in the world where large organizations continue to be aspirational sites for economic mobility and idealized forms of small-scale social interaction with others—where issues of deciding about how to distinguish from and how to participate with are still being decided. A view of twenty-first century South Korean office life reveals an intensification of both interpersonal difference-making and communal cooperation within the space of large organizations. The former occurs through things like formal testing, work tracking, individual feedback mechanisms, annual evaluations, pay bands, and gradated bonuses. These distinctions have become relevant variables in civil society, where the distinctions of one's employment help to indicate one's relative trajectory in life. A middle-class South Korean might be able to distinguish between a full-time engineer at Samsung Electronics in the city of Suwon and a sales representative at Samsung Fire Insurance in Daejeon. At the same time, there are various programs and policies that emphasize cooperative work while de-emphasizing individual distinctions. These include new organizational forms around first-name policies, 360-degree feedback, team- or cell-based work units, small group meetings, hobby groups, town hall meetings, and "mutual communication" mantras.

This book investigates the tension between distinction and participation as idealized but ultimately ambiguous and competing futures amid post-hierarchical narratives in contemporary South Korea. The book is based on an ethnographic account of the Sangdo Group, a pseudonym for a mid-level South Korean conglomerate made up of roughly a dozen companies and one holding company involved in the steel and metals industries. I conducted ethnography in one small corner of Sangdo where I worked as an intern at Sangdo for twelve months between 2014 and 2015 as part of my doctoral research in anthropology. My research was conducted far from the large factories and hot forges of the South Korean steel world; rather, it was within the buttoned-up head office of the Sangdo holding company located at the top of the forty-story Sangdo tower in an area of Seoul (key identifying details of the group have been omitted). There, I was embedded in a small HR team that was attempting to bring changes to the workplace systems of the wider conglomerate that was seen as old-fashioned, male-dominated, and seniority-driven. How to create a post-hierarchical workplace at Sangdo—one that was more than just a rejection of hierarchy—was not always entirely clear in practice. As the employee survey revealed, some employees wanted more technocratic management, separate from the problems of human interference; others had a feeling of being deprived and isolated (*baktalgam*) precisely in their work and thus wanted more human engagement. These two drives ultimately led to different kinds of contradictions in practice: if distinctions are often measured in forms of rank and achievement, and such ranks and achievements are always relative to others, how can workplace distinction claim to be nonhierarchical? Furthermore, if HR managers can impose new forms of participation or workplace organization, however enlightened or global, on others, are they simply echoing top-down forms of social control in the name of change? This book traces how managers in the HR department (and other managers) understood these tensions and wrestled with creating new programs that might foster positive workplace environments for teams to work together and enable employees to be fairly distinguished in their work while avoiding the reimposition of hierarchies of old.

A generation of social scientists has looked at formal workplace distinctions with a critical eye.[2] Over the course of the twentieth century, there have been many dehumanizing or alienating varieties of organizational systems around the world that categorize people based on how efficiently they carry out tasks, their level of communication skills, or even what other people think of them. Likewise, scholars have also been rightly skeptical of ersatz models of corporate culture, produced in HR departments and elaborated in manuals, that are used for kitschy campaigns and recruitment efforts promoting idyllic communitarian values that might elide more pernicious forms of distinction below the surface that arbitrarily define human value or are meant to divide labor forces through interpersonal competition over scarce posts.[3] Human resource policies in South Korea are no exception and have been the site of domestic critiques for many years, from cruel practices of excluding those on the outskirts or bottom of the labor system, to aggressive neoliberalizing evaluation policies that attempt to deduce the quality of persons through arbitrary standards like English language proficiency even for those within full-time positions.

Despite these historical criticisms surrounding corporate employment, corporations (or imagined corporate life) in South Korea have remained ever popular. They have been sites of frequent change and reform to problems of both distinction and participation, places where bad policies might be eradicated and new ideas tested, where issues of economic democratization (*gyeongje minjuhwa*) might be realized. I describe this phenomenon in the book as the "supercorporate ideal." The supercorporate ideal can be defined as the broader promise of corporations to realize and channel post-hierarchical forms of both interpersonal distinction and positive social interaction. The term supercorporate captures the sense that large corporate organizations cannot be reduced to sites of pure economic or organizational function alone, nor are they solely the objects of control by owners or capitalist institutions. Rather, they are loaded with broader sociocultural significance. The aura of corporate work captures a sense of class mobility for individuals and for national development. Gaining employment, being promoted, and being affiliated with a large corporation remain key markers of success in middle-class South Korea. Likewise, the success of individual corporations in terms of higher revenues or global recognition remains a key measure through which South Korean ideas of development are still tracked, even in a seemingly postdevelopment twenty-first century. Like broader narratives of national industrial-capitalist achievement, the attainment of corporate work provides an important frame for narrativizing the mobility of families through individual success. In this sense, the notion of supercorporate moves beyond only the function of individual corporate organizations or conglomerates within commodity or financial markets to understand them as part of a culturally narrated field.

A key aspect of the supercorporate ideal, particularly marked in South Korea but certainly not absent elsewhere, is that corporations are sites where fair distinctions can be organized and recognized through a technocratic assemblage of different techniques and policies. That is, corporations are not just sites that people gain access to or that elites maintain their control over; they are also fundamentally sites where people might desire to become stratified. Managerial grades, company brands, professional categories, and other signifiers or distinctions comprise basic sets of signs for marking normative urban middle-class career aspirations. Some of these are clearly elaborated, such as core ranks in the corporate ladder or the grades given during annual evaluations; others are more diffuse, such as prestige areas of work, bonuses, or benefits. In this sense, corporate organizations are sites of assembling forms of meaning that go beyond what is necessary for organizational, economic, or market function in the strictest senses. A basic function of what corporations are expected to do—not necessarily as actors themselves, but as sites in society—is to offer a constellation of legible forms of quantitative and qualitative distinction through which the aspirational middle classes can come to recognize themselves and others.

This is a supercorporate "ideal," however, because the actual organization of distinctions never appears to be as clean as it appears on television, in management plans, or even in critical accounts of capitalism, where corporate ways of sorting people seem to work hyperefficiently. This is because the full spectrum of participatory life in contemporary office work is mediated by much more than corporate techniques; office life is awash in numerous genres of communication, documentation, and interaction, some of which are related to formal work but many of which are simply part of the wider context of social life in an organization. If certain kinds of social markers, such as being hired on a managerial track at a large conglomerate, convey one set of socially legible signs, then things such as being consigned to photocopying, coffee pickups, or ghostwriting PowerPoint presentations for one's boss also generate their own set of emergent distinctions not readily visible to those on the outside. Office workers, even those in privileged roles, must exist in working environments not of their own making, learning and mastering various genres of documentation, technological platforms, and corporate procedures while also navigating organizational structures, special management projects, and interoffice politics. In this sense, the heterogeneity of modern office work, particularly in large corporate organizations, creates its own messy topography at the office level that does not always align cleanly or clearly with broader social distinctions. This is because work practices generate their own localized orders of meaning, participation, and distinction. While some of these resonate or align with external distinctions such as one's rank (and, perhaps, relative salary or office size) or perhaps feel more participatory than others (a town hall meeting with the CEO), the potential field of signs at work and how they come to be recognized is emergent, expansive, and full of misalignments. Seemingly small or unimportant encounters over how work is done, what is said in meetings, or how one coworker addresses another can cause dissonance against other signifiers that corporate systems or techniques are supposed to reinforce and make stable.

As much as management systems might attempt to delimit distinction or participation through formal efforts, both are part of an active field where meaning can never be settled or fixed. At times, failures can appear to recall negative elements of hierarchy of the past, such as bosses who are prone to shouting. At other times, hyperdistinction can appear to roil the social life of an office by breeding too much concern about interoffice competition. This book argues that corporate life in South Korea is a site of unstable distinctions in which efforts to continually remap or redefine the lines of office life to enact a supercorporate ideal always appear to fail in doing so. This has less to do with cultural, generational, or even managerial problems, as much as those might appear to be coherent explanations; rather, it concerns the difficulty of stabilizing seemingly post-hierarchical forms of individual distinction and collective participation within any given corporate organization compared to the ideal that corporate organizations represent from the perspective of middle-class aspirations.

The broader South Korean labor market is a contentious zone of classification struggles, with many labor battles revolving around the rightful inclusion of certain categories of labor, such as dispatch work (*pagyeonjik*), irregular work (*bijeong-gyujik*), or contract work (*gyeyagjik*), into standard labor where economic benefits, job stability, and social recognition might be better guaranteed.[4] The labor issues of the men and women I worked alongside at Sangdo were in contrast much different, reinforced to some degree by the comforts of being a full-time or regular worker at a recognizably large corporate group (*daegieop*) where the realities of production were largely experienced through reports and spreadsheets. Nevertheless, large corporate work environments are also marked by a number of other concerns around distinction making, reflecting the seemingly fragile positions of those who might otherwise be considered insiders. There were concerns at Sangdo, for instance, that many workers in the broader conglomerate—those working in regional sales offices or doing back office IT work—were themselves being denied the benefits and privileges that other office workers had. The relative status of regional sales employees compared with headquarters accountants might escape the attention of the general public in terms of broader labor inequities, but their relative differences are followed rather closely by employees themselves and those who attempt to manage them. This book, too, takes seriously that the opportunity to distinguish oneself through the markers of corporate employment is an important premise and promise of modern corporate work and that the ethics and logistics of managing where distinctions are drawn and how employees work together are complex matters.

Understanding such uneven labor terrains internally was an implicit goal of the annual employee survey launched at the end of 2014. The manager of the HR team, Jang, was convinced that the survey would reveal the inner workings of Sangdo's many distributed workplaces where younger employees were imagined to be toiling under tyrannical bosses, long hours, and unevenly enforced labor policies. The HR team in the holding company, at a remove from these worlds but organizationally above them, Jang believed, could provide one avenue for channeling the collective dissatisfactions of the workforce. By collecting employee responses and then converting them into hard numbers and statistical correlations, the HR team could make apparent the dynamics that would allow them to improve the Sangdo workplace across South Korea that they might never have even visited. The survey was one example of a new turn in Sangdo's group management via the holding company, where a bevy of new experts had been recently hired to bring outside knowledge and leadership to the group's subsidiaries and their distributed offices and branches.

Though not a household name in South Korea, the Sangdo Group at the time was undergoing considerable changes to its visibility on the Seoul landscape as well as its group structure. In the early 2010s, the conglomerate became formally centralized in a newly built office tower. What had been a small holding company that existed largely as a secretariat for the chairman next to much larger and relatively autonomous subsidiary organizations was expanding to become a new expert hub overseeing the multinational group. New expert teams had been created in HR, strategy, performance management, legal affairs, and public relations and mid- and upper-level managers brought in bearing accounting degrees, consulting backgrounds, or long tenures at more prestigious conglomerates. These expert groups each addressed different scales of the conglomerate group's distinctiveness as a group: the strategy team was created to analyze new markets into which the subsidiaries could expand. The public relations team oversaw the multiyear revitalization of the corporate brand, including the introduction of shared company values and internal branding. The HR team also carried out many projects addressing the very infrastructure of personnel distinctions: benefits policies, promotional exams, executive reviews, employee training and internal education, and work-tracking systems.

From a one-floor office on the top of the Sangdo tower, these teams might have appeared to some as an elite group of experts attempting to impose new managerial ideals on unique and rather distinct subsidiary organizations. Critiques of managerial idealism are often premised on the fact that managerial programs are out of step with human values because of their (overly) rational designs, noble intents, or class distance.[5] This book takes corporations (and the people that comprise them) as relatively sincere sites of ethical engagement along the lines of what Hegel might have described about corporations two hundred years ago in his *Philosophy of Right*. Hegel identified corporations as key sites for the exploration of the ethical life (*sittlichkeit*) in ways that other kinds of social forms (such as the market or the state) might not make possible. To Hegel, corporations were one form of ethical community building within capitalism, membership in which could indicate that "one is a somebody."[6] Of course, Hegel could not have in mind the widespread growth of the modern managerial corporation of the twentieth century focused on large-scale industrial production, imbricated in global commerce, and seemingly disembedded from its local contexts. I would suggest, though, that for many South Korean white-collar employees and managers who approached their work with the promise of fairness, morality, and recognition, navigating corporate life's ideals and the complex realities of everyday office life remain objects of ethical concern.

If Hegel saw in the nascent idea of a corporation an opportunity for freedom, which for him was the "natural right to exercise one's skill," this book points to a different kind of (possible) freedom for contemporary times: that of participating in corporate stratifications.[7] By stratification, I do not refer to a romanticized view of human inequity; rather, I refer to the promise of gradated or stratified qualities of persons organized by or at least concentrated in modern corporate organizations. These qualities might articulate how people track and recognize career progressions and where one might ostensibly be free of forms of social control or evaluation elsewhere (by the state, the family, or society). To achieve recognized ranks such as a full-time junior employee (*sinipsawon*) or team manager (*timjang*) is a way of indicating that one is important in South Korea where large corporations remain waypoints for the mobile middle classes. This promise is not always fulfilled, and it is complicated by a number of factors in practice. The ideal—or the promise—might be considered a form of freedom and it is something that continues to make office life a continually reworked site of reform and reflection in contemporary South Korea.[8]

Supercorporate South Korea

There was a time in the mid-twentieth century when the stability of large organizations was believed to be an important achievement of capitalism. Corporate organizations were not only embedded within communities but also provided long-term institutional trajectories for individuals' life paths, labor harmony, and community investment. In the 1970s, beginning in the United States, new criticisms around the rigidity and staidness of bureaucratic and hierarchical organizations paved the way for new ideas about the primacy of markets and finance where individuals did not necessarily need to rely on inefficient managerial pathways or be beholden to the oppressive norms of workplaces. Sociologist Gerald Davis has described this as a shift from a "society of organizations" to a "portfolio society." In a society of organizations, "corporations were essential building-blocks that shaped the daily lives of their members," but under a portfolio society, "the organization man has been replaced by the daytrader."[9] This shift dovetailed with the great dehierarchicalization of American workplaces, what is euphemistically referred to as delayering, or the obliteration of middle management as an organizational function and a viable career path. What was really happening was that new kinds of institutional actors such as investment banks, hedge funds, and other financial institutions were converging on corporate organizations in a new constellation of both control and distinction that would greatly reorganize capital and labor in the US, the West, and beyond.

The appeal of working for large industrial corporations and attaining middle- or upper-management status still occupies a key position in the cultural imaginations of places such as South Korea and Japan where large corporate groups and large managerial-track recruitment systems still occupy central positions as prestige sites in broader cultural and economic imaginaries.[10] In Japan, a range of scholars over a long period have discussed the role of corporations in mediating Japan's narrative of capitalist modernity and postwar normalization, particularly around the figure of the salaryman. The salaryman narrative persists even amid changing conditions that render the dream of proverbial lifetime employment more difficult to attain.[11]

The aspirational aspects of South Korean corporate life have often been overshadowed by the attention paid to the country's turbulent and contested political economy over the past fifty years, particularly the attention on the chaebol and the role of the developmental state. The term chaebol represents a class of conglomerates owned and managed by dynastic family lineages that occupied center stage in the depictions of South Korean economic growth in the 1970s, 1980s, and 1990s. The classic industrial chaebol combined ambitious or politically well-connected capitalist leaders who led and oversaw new industrial enterprises in tandem with government plans, licenses, loans, and otherwise favorable treatment.[12] This form of state–corporate capitalism in which the state nurtured the environment for large corporate enterprises to grow was a particular creature of the developmental state—sometimes referred to as Korea, Inc.–which was believed to help South Korea aggressively accelerate its industrialized modernity. By the mid-1990s, the developmental state had largely retreated from its commanding role over the banks and

capital investments, leaving large chaebol groups to expand into many different industries, carrying high debt loads in the process. The economic and so-
cietal trade-offs of this over-expansion culminated in a debt panic that trig-
gered the Asian Financial Crisis of 1997. Debt ratios had skyrocketed and
necessitated significant intervention and industrial reorganization from both
the state and the International Monetary Fund (IMF).

The end of the twentieth century might have appeared to sound the death
knell of South Korea's particular brand of big corporate capitalism and pave
the way toward new capitalist models in which aspects of South Korean organizational life might dissolve, such as the role of unions, family corporate ownership, or a seniority-based promotion system. While there have been significant changes in the new millennium, particularly around the diminished role
of organized labor, the twenty-first century has seen no turn away from big organizational life. Even as the role of the state has receded to a largely regulatory and promotional role, and foreign and institutional investors have taken
out larger stakes in South Korean companies, big domestic organizations remain a prominent fixture on the economic landscape. Likewise, full-time or
regular employment on managerial tracks have also remained key endpoints
for fulfilling educational trajectories and marking forms of social distinction. A testament to the appeal of large corporate life has been the growth of
new groups much different from those of the industrial era yet which replicate similar organizational models. These include tech giants such as Naver
and Kakao, video game company Nexen, and cosmetics company Amore Pacific. Even state-linked entities such as Korea Telecom (KT) and steel giant
POSCO (formerly state owned) remain popular sites for professional middle-
class employment.

The chaebol phenomenon has garnered attention from outsiders largely for
its three irregularities vis-à-vis Western capitalism: the continuation of family ownership and control, the conglomerate form itself, and close integration
with state development goals. (Each of these aspects were at various points
heralded or seen as economic paragons in the West but have long become bo-
geymen.) It is not hard to find South Koreans who are critical of aspects of the
corporate system, such as the legacy of chaebol ownership or the high degrees
of capital concentration in conglomerates at the expense of minority shareholders or medium and small enterprises. Chaebol actors are frequently a target of public censure around the moral misconduct of owners, labor clashes,
outdated behaviors from older managers, or funds wasted on entertainment.

Such criticisms nevertheless reinforce the ideas that corporations and the dynamics of office life are objects of a public gaze and that good corporate organizations should be sites of both earnest governance and earnest recognition. In this sense, the position of large corporate employment and economic success as an index of both national development and individual aspiration remains much less questioned across the political spectrum.[13]

This is the premise of the popular novel *Kim Jiyoung, Born 1982* by Cho Nam-joo. The novel, originally published in 2016 and later translated into many languages and turned into a popular film, recounts the multiple sites of judgment that an aspiring working woman in Seoul faces from all corners of her social world. These judgments become heightened as Kim Jiyoung marries and has a child while continuing to work. This reflects the normative stricture that anthropologist Cho Han Hae-Joang has described in South Korea as "housewife-ization." Such a process took hold in the twentieth century in South Korea, and in many other places, when men became closely linked to the promises of modern work and women were linked to their husbands', and later children's, successes.[14] While Kim Jiyoung's struggle is reflected in the gender hierarchy that cuts across society, family, and organization, the ultimate desire for the main character, at least in her professional experiences, is not to leave such a system completely but to be able to participate in it. The novel suggests that Kim Jiyoung should be allowed to participate within the corporate world free of judgment, and moreover be rewarded for her talents and efforts in the prestige category of knowledge labor she works in (advertising planning). This reflects an underlying notion that it is not corporate systems per se where problems lie but rather the broader social hierarchies that inhabit them. In the novel, however, a nonjudgmental and understanding boss, professional recognition, and a new workplace serve as small spaces of liberation compared to other institutions and actors in society. The novel reflects one side of a supercorporate ideal that, while locating corporate work as a site of conflict, also imbues corporate work, once freed from problematic people and outdated ideas, with the potential to resolve such conflicts.[15]

If achieving positions or promotions can serve as markers of recognition as an insider, the position of insiders within their organizations is more muddied. This is partly because internal distinctions are mediated across a number of different zones or sites of interaction that array people in different roles. In the most formal sense, distinctions are grounded in HR techniques of categorizing, recording, and evaluating people. Areas of management such as human resource management (HRM) might attempt to measure employees along similar metrics in order to provide a basis for their rational distinction for review, promotion, or bonus. In theory, these systems might re-create legible external distinctions, keeping track of people and their relative degrees of difference across work tasks, responsibilities, and benefits. However, modern work and work life present a much more complex terrain of interactions across different kinds of practices that reflect how such abstracted qualities are also shaped by interactions with others.

Distinction and participation as abstract ideals can be understood as bundles of different qualities that cohere together to create an effect of their presence or absence across different spaces and times: the pleasure of friendly team relations, involvement in interesting projects, or the compliment of a senior executive on one's work. More than looking at the corporate system as a whole, abstracted from actual corporate reality, it is through everyday work encounters where aspects of distinction and participation become palpable to people. Different kinds of encounters can contribute to or break the promise of a positive workplace. For instance, assistant manager Jin-hee worked at a Sangdo subsidiary in Japan and I met her virtually through our work on a collaborative HR project. For her, the workplace in Japan was a place to restart a Korean corporate career in Tokyo after spending the early part of her postgraduate career doing volunteer work abroad. The Japan branch of Sangdo was largely filled with South Korean employees who could also speak Japanese with the subsidiary's clients there. She was aware of her lower salary relative to Japanese companies in Tokyo and of the fact that not many people knew about Sangdo or business-to-business steel sales. Jin-hee was nevertheless proud to be promoted after three years from an entry-level position (*sawon*) to a junior assistant manager position (*daeri*) in the branch. She took responsibility for a special project—linking the intranet system of the Japan office to the head office's system in Seoul and manually aligning the various database categories. At times, she was even able to meet with the subsidiary chief executive officer (CEO) on his visits to their branch from Seoul. Yet this combination of both distinction and participation in her work was partly dashed when a senior male executive did not address her by her new title after the promotion. Her confidence in the workplace was further weakened when the same senior executive cozied up to her at a company karaoke event after work, signaling that she was being treated more like female entertainment than as a permanent member on a managerial track. These events resonated with her own awareness of what such signs might mean in that context—a return to a more Korean-style workplace that she might not have expected in Tokyo and in her experiences up to that point. Seemingly discrete signs that emerge in the orbit of work (greetings, after-work events, and so on) can come together to reframe other qualities and associations around workplace distinctions, unsettling the official or seemingly materially important ones such as rank, salary, and one's responsibilities.

In this sense, a supercorporate ideal in South Korea does not reflect only the power or prestige of large corporations or the face-value of legible workplace ranks. Rather, it can be understood as the potential for alignments created within and across corporate life, shaped as much by the formal aspects of corporate systems as by the qualities of friendships and senior-junior relations that occur within any given team. The proper enactment of that assemblage might fulfill broader ideas about individual success as a personal or family mobility narrative; conversely, the misalignment of such might also confirm certain higher order narratives about individual failure, the problems of a certain office, or South Korea as a whole and the failure to properly achieve modernity. The important point is that the signs that come to recognize or interpret a supercorporate ideal in practice are neither reducible to formal programs nor are they necessarily things of the same quality everywhere in South Korea. Ongoing interpretations and narratives are part and parcel of corporate life itself; the same events may be interpreted by different people quite differently. In this regard, the work of people in professional areas such as HR or at the top of corporate groups is not simply to stand in for capital or management by imposing power or quelling resistance. It is partly to understand the points of friction in the rather unstable reality of distinction and participation in South Korea. More than hidden corporate agendas, it was the sheer unrealizability of perfect commensuration or perfect workplace satisfaction that represented the basic contradiction of corporate life to many HR workers I had the opportunity to speak with.

In practice, HR work in South Korea involves being conscious of what is seen as the abuse of participation, such as how bosses handed off work to their employees or to junior employees, who might not take vacation because of normative concerns. At another level, HR employees might have to be aware that any new ways of drawing distinctions had to carefully consider the effect or impact across other spaces of corporate life. As I describe in Chapter 2, experiments with flat organizational structures that rendered all employee titles as "managers" created problems at a number of South Korean workplaces in part because such flat structures leveled out other kinds of work distinctions that people relied on, such as knowing who their actual manager was.

If office life is a complex navigation between group participation and individual distinction, there was one site that threatened both: generational differences. Older male managers, as I discuss in Chapter 3, were seen to interfere with proper administration, humane treatment in the workplace, and equal gender opportunities. They are, in the context of this book, an embodiment of negative views toward hierarchy of the past. Partaking of broader narratives around generationalism (*sedaeron*) in South Korea, explanations from various corners of corporate life posited that older male managers were largely from another era and were responsible for workplace inequalities, understood in this case as the denial of both wholesome participation and fair distinction. The fact that negative aspects of hierarchies seem to continually reappear within corporate spaces does not necessarily rupture the mystique of corporate employment tout court; such appearances can actually enhance the ideas that some organizations are better than others or that there are certain areas that need to be reformed more dramatically.

Purifying and Managing Distinction and Participation

This book focuses on two different approaches to dealing with the complexity of distinction and participation and how they relate to the supercorporate ideal: attempts to purify distinction and participation and attempts to manage them. Purifying refers to the ways that actors attempt to simplify or consolidate interactions or differences between people to a core set of qualities, traits, or points. Managing refers to ways of mitigating or controlling the hazards of uneven distinction across the workplace such that only minimal or necessary distinctions might be made visible. If the idea of purifying captures the idea of getting rid of inappropriate stuff (or mediators, in more technical jargon) that complicate corporate life in order to make visible certain kinds of distinction or participation, the idea of managing acknowledges the complexity of corporate life itself, translating between or even concealing areas of difference that might create additional conflicts.

An example of purification came from an assistant manager, Baik, who worked on the strategy team at the Sangdo holding company. Baik had a deep interest in the global steel industry and Sangdo's place in it. According to him, for many decades South Korean steel companies occupied stable market niches for steel and metal products without overt competition, but Baik saw the ground changing beneath their feet. Challenges were on multiple fronts: state-sponsored steel overproduction in China had dampened prices globally, other South Korean conglomerates were seeking to move into some of Sangdo's unprotected industries, and the US was busy levying new import taxes on South Korean steel. To Baik, some of Sangdo's leaders were locked in an older mindset and unable to do what was necessary to change, such as merging subsidiaries, expanding into new markets, or implementing new production techniques in the factory to reduce storage time in the factories. In Baik's view, Sangdo was quickly falling in this new world order, and its relatively safe market positions in the South Korean pecking order might be threatened without drastic change.

One of Baik's projects on the strategy team involved piloting a new manufacturing method right on the factory floors of Sangdo's subsidiaries. Experimenting with a new management approach with a small group of strategists, Baik aimed to create a new system that would implement active error correction in the production process. A key part of this system focused on how reports were generated from the factory floor. One executive, Jung, who was leading the project with Baik, described it as a "one-page" system. In this system, data from the factory floor would be sent directly to subsidiary CEOs and then to the Sangdo chairman, skipping the layers of middle managers who might attempt to convert such data into PowerPoint presentations to impress their bosses who would in turn aim to impress their bosses. By the time the document would reach the decision maker, such as the CEO or chairman, the original information would be distorted. For Jung and Baik, a large-scale shift at the macro level, which would unsettle Sangdo's position in its markets, entailed rejiggering things on the literal ground floor. Their project partook in ways of thinking that were inherited from a long line of efficiency movements based on systematizing shop-floor measurement by purifying its modes of documentation. Through such an act of purification, other kinds of management practices, rooted in what they believed to be inefficiency created by managerial layers, could also be fixed in one fell swoop.

For the HR team with whom I spent the majority of my time at Sangdo, the problem was not necessarily in locating and eradicating signs of problematic practices but in managing how distinctions came to articulate within the office without upsetting interpersonal relations or office politics. In a quite literal way, HR managers had the greatest access to the details of educational and family histories, performance reviews, salary and bonus information, personal requests, and office incidents. Such records were kept tightly guarded even within the team (as a researcher, even I never saw where they were located) in part because of the revelation that overtly explicit distinctions between people might cause disruptions in team relations. Even the small revelation at the end of the calendar year that every member of one subsidiary received a gift certificate for 350,000 won (US$300) to be used on new domestic goods as a year-end bonus became a new axis of distinction because the holding company only received shampoo-and-conditioner sets. To those in the holding company, such a distinction conflicted with how they imagined their own positions as the experts in the conglomerate.

The employee survey, discussed more in Chapter 5, was a project meant to reveal negative effects of hierarchy across the conglomerate. Although the survey revealed a variety of opinions that vociferously argued for what should be fixed, the analysis and publication of the results became a site for carefully managing how the distinctions on paper might affect distinctions in other places, including the relationships between subsidiaries, the relationship between subsidiaries and the holding company, and the distinctions manifested by the experts at the holding company itself. For instance, many of the harshest complaints were not even shared directly with other subsidiary managers who were given only aggregated numbers that would provide a comparison of employee satisfaction rates relative to other branches and offices. Even the numbers of other subsidiaries were carefully anonymized to create an appropriate level of awareness while avoiding direct competitions. One subsidiary whose results were expected to be so low that they might upset the ownership and cause an internal scandal was simply left off the survey completely (and employees from that branch were prevented from filling it out).

A focus on purifying and managing distinctions across different sites of expertise captures the complexities of competing notions of how a super-corporate ideal can be achieved or perhaps threatened, where even the smallest difference that might distinguish people in the wrong way becomes an object of attention. This is not to say that such distinctions are immaterial in the grander scheme of things or are merely symbolic affairs. On the contrary, felt distinctions around even things such as office space, the opinions of others, terms of address, or time spent at work are each part of the broader assemblage of qualities of distinction and participation. These can never be reduced to a product of management alone but exist in a complex field shaped by the promise of what corporate work can do as a channel of social mobility qua organizational mobility. Large corporations with their internal divisions and interoffice relations are complex social and material environments that afford considerable kinds of distinctions in practice. For some corporations, the goal is to purify or reduce the number of distinctions by trying to simplify them, while for others the goal is to manage or conceal the possible outcomes of making corporate-centered distinctions that can cause their own set of problems.

Hierarchy and Distinction Reconsidered

By considering the criticism of certain kinds of hierarchy while also taking seriously the idea that better forms of distinction or participation are possible *within* corporations, this book reckons with broader ideas about ordered difference as a social phenomenon. Can one analyze distinction or participation within modern corporations without critiquing them as impositions in the name of capitalism? That is, can we see them as something other than new forms of social hierarchy that better mask their real effects? To frame the question in this way implies hierarchy might have a universal definition as a negative form of sociality. Hierarchy has largely become a neglected analytic concept in Euro-American thought, in part due to its connotations of fundamental differences between people and its almost obvious counter-position to positive liberal values such as egalitarianism, democracy, and fairness that presume no preordained order between individuals.[16] In particular, interpersonal distinction, as one kind of hierarchy, has also become cast as either a tool of capitalist control (a form of faux competition among workers) or as a meritocratic myth propagated by neoliberal schools of thought. To broach a topic like distinction in a place like South Korea poses its own risks as it can confirm either that the country is indeed a cutthroat capitalist society with an extreme form of capitalism vis-à-vis the West or that South Korea has not come to an awareness of other ways to find meaning in life outside of work. Without denouncing the origins of various forms of distinction, then, and their impact on South Korean society, this book might risk confirming the impression that there is some singular reason (based on cultural psychology or history) to explain why South Koreans might have bought into the idea of corporate-centered distinctions where others have abandoned them and sought new forms of freedom elsewhere in capitalism.[17] Likewise, to focus on the contradiction in modern South Korean work around competing ideas between work as a site of both distinction and participation might convey that there is something wrong with South Korean capitalism but not others.

To associate hierarchy or distinction with purely negative social forms narrowly associated with inequality or oppression reflects a blind spot regarding the sheer ubiquity of distinctions that are taken for granted across capitalist societies. A number of anthropologists have recently renewed attention to the way in which distinctions and other forms of hierarchy are thoroughly a part of Western societies that might ideologically consider themselves quite individualist or liberal. Cultural values such as egalitarianism, *laïcité*, or democracy that explicitly disavow other forms of hierarchy or distinction are themselves often deployed as superior to other kinds of values. Such measures may appear liberal or progressive in nature, but they can also be hierarchical impositions from outside. This point is reflected well in recent anthropological studies of global capitalist encounters, describing a new crop of Western manager-experts, keenly attuned to issues around formal hierarchy and authority, who have been at the vanguard of imposing new standards of supposedly egalitarian speaking or working that are putatively democratic in nature but which may simply create a new hierarchical order around their own values, downgrading local values in the process.[18]

The supercorporate ideal in South Korea often manifests in concerns over the proper function of corporations to sort out other citizens equitably where other institutions might be seen as corruptible or traditional. This is perhaps why South Korean corporate workers and social observers are keenly attuned to problems that might interfere with these goals: the strongest economic criticisms in South Korea are of those who access corporate positions by unfair means (through connections or nepotism), who abuse others in the office (through power-abusing acts known as *gapjil*), and who might manage systems of evaluation or administration only to help their friends or family. This is why I draw a contrast between criticisms of hierarchy in the workplace as a negative moral quality and rightful forms of distinction as a positive virtue. Criticisms of hierarchy reflect recognized forms of exploitation or abuse, such as from seniors to juniors and from large organizations to small ones. Distinction, however, can be better understood as a more appropriate way of measuring people and assessing their relative merit or capacity. There are plenty of ways one can find fault in even these seemingly "fair" forms of distinction as creatures of modern capitalism or as fantasies of evaluation.[19] However, as an ethnography, this book tries to avoid imposing its own value hierarchy (either cultural or intellectual) on South Korea or on the Sangdo office workers who allowed me to glimpse for one year the different kinds of considerations and calculations about others they made in the course of their own work.

Efforts to purify or manage distinctions in the Sangdo workplace reflect an engagement with the ethics of a certain kind of organizational governance at the interpersonal level: how should people cooperate in their work and how should they be distinguished from each other. This engagement includes looking at how HR managers might try to develop systems of evaluation that track, monitor, and tabulate how workers do vis-à-vis their peers, so that managers might not show bias or favoritism in their evaluations. It also means looking at where and how distinctions become manifest or are recognized in practice through pay bands, benefits, bonuses, vacation days, insurance policies, dress codes, and stock options, among others. These forms of distinction are never entirely within managerial control: as I describe in Chapter 6, even life outside the office can be rife with distinctions run amok as workers distinguish drinking quantities, consumer distinctions, or even their golf handicaps, adding to the complex bundle of associations that people can draw across corporate life. Many of the HR practices and concerns I describe emerged within a context where young people felt unfairly treated, where seniority was given precedent, and where after-work events were difficult to wrangle. While acts of purifying social relations might reflect grand or elaborate moves to target problems to allow for more fairly organized and distinguished office work, acts of managing distinctions reflect the ongoing ethical uncertainty of creating systems of distinction that might favor one kind of worker while disfavoring another. Nevertheless, it is clear that for those who buy into the supercorporate ideal, the promise of a positive workplace with good interactions and also of good distinctions—however those may be defined—always lies just beyond the horizon of even its harshest criticisms.

This book draws on the case of Sangdo and the notion of the supercorporate ideal to make two broad contributions. First, the book suggests that the issue of corporate distinction lies uncomfortably between globally circulating ideas of democracy and hierarchy (or democracy and bureaucracy) as two opposed poles of organizational form. This might make it appear that some places such as South Korea are premised on order and difference, whereas organizations elsewhere are not. For those in the West, where managerial hierarchies have long been dismantled and values around workplace democracy and flexible work reign, distinctions still matter greatly: workers distinguish themselves based on a company's values, how these values align with their own, and what difference they might be making in the world; these are all points of distinction, though by another kind of ideal.[20] Where these issues are often left to the decisions of workers themselves in the West, complex ethical issues around how to rank, evaluate, or distribute money in South Korea are often managed by professional teams of HR workers who carefully weigh the benefits and risks across large swaths of people. Nevertheless, the organization of distinction should be seen as one of the core features of contemporary corporate-capitalist societies, regardless of a particular organizational form.

Second, the book suggests how workplaces have become complex fields that complicate any singular or reducible ideal of distinction or participation in practice. The complexity of everyday work lives signals an expansion of communication and managerial technologies and the possible sites where people interact. It also reflects how many kinds of institutions or external organizations have taken an interest in articulating their own visions of what a supercorporate ideal should be. In South Korea, holding companies, investors, regulators, financial institutions, labor unions, and others express varying kinds of interest in the way corporate organizations distinguish and organize their workforces, reflecting different ideas or ideologies of how distinction or participation should be articulated. For external investors and management consultants, distinctions might be best reflected in terms of use-value or other commodity-linked qualities that can be tracked and inventoried without the need for human managers.[21] For labor unions, distinctions might be drawn around degrees of benefits, contract guarantees, and tenure-based rewards. For wealthy corporate owners, distinction might be reflected in comparisons with other corporate groups, fancy buildings, and other symbols that mark their corporate group as different from others. And for young office workers, distinctions might be premised on fair evaluations from their bosses and the freedom to go home on time. Each of these ways of thinking about distinction underscores how corporations are seen as important vehicles of both distinction and participation, the means and the forms of which have a variety of idealized configurations with the multiple signs that crisscross office life. While some of these actors might have an interest (financial or otherwise) in purifying corporate spaces to highlight one set or kind of distinctions, for some managers on the ground who dealt with the complexity of distinctions on a day-to-day level, such as the HR team at the Sangdo holding company whose perspective is the subject of the book, the risks of the wrong kinds of distinction were equally something to manage and contain. In this sense, this book is not an overview of the entire South Korean corporate world, nor does Sangdo represent a typical South Korean large organization, if some such organization could even be found. Rather, it is a way of thinking about how the ideals around the promise of corporate modernity come to bear on the realities of one particular organization in a time of change.

Overview of the Book

The accounts in this book largely revolve around the supercorporate ideal as it unfolded around a set of dynamics at the Sangdo Group during my research there: the holding company, its expert managers, and its efforts to guide, redefine, or manage the broader group from a distance. As I describe, beginning in Chapter 1, the Sangdo Group was not a conglomerate with established channels of top-down control but had an ambiguous relationship with intragroup management itself. I began research there during a time of transition when a new kind of vision for the conglomerate was taking shape in which the holding company would unite largely autonomous subsidiaries. This represented a direct confrontation not just surrounding different political tensions within the conglomerate but concerning the potential for an imposition of new ideals favored by urban Seoul elites. The case of this headquarters "in the making" reveals how a supercorporate ideal was nevertheless built out and translated through new kinds of spaces, projects, and techniques. The experience of managers throughout the book does not revolve around a familiar axis of control and resistance but around attempts to both purify and manage a supercorporate ideal within the complicated world of conglomerate life.

Chapter 1 discusses the creation of Sangdo as a unified conglomerate in the newly constructed Sangdo tower with the holding company at the top. The wider promotion of holding companies (*jijuhoesa*) in South Korea in the early 2000s was meant to unravel the hidden hierarchies that lay behind circular intraconglomerate shareholding arrangements; yet, somewhat paradoxically, holding companies have become new sites for central planning and owner consolidation. I describe how the advent of a new generation of ownership at Sangdo redefined the holding company as a strategy or planning office that would centralize what were largely autonomous subsidiaries. What was to the ownership an act of purification—by consolidating Sangdo subsidiaries under one roof with a reunified brand—was to the holding company managers a complex act of navigating new relationships and distinctions with the subsidiaries. Focusing on three professional areas within the Sangdo holding company—public relations, performance management, and HR—I show how expert teams had to translate new forms of distinction into relations with subsidiaries while also being cautious of what new hierarchies emerged.

Chapter 2 begins with a discussion of experiments in South Korea to radically upend corporate hierarchies through ideas of flatness. Almost all South Korean conglomerates and large organizations have experimented with some form of flattening since the year 2000 primarily as a way of reconsidering the role of interactional design and language policy. The chapter discusses the difficulty of translating the concept of flatness (as a spatial metaphor) into a complex infrastructure of identity markers premised on distinction, comprised of multiple forms of implicit and explicit gradation between employees. One reason that supposedly flat projects do not work is that they interfere with many of the distinctions that define the basic raison d'être of corporate labor for many workers: as a site for cultivating individual markers of mobility. More than just a preference for hierarchical forms of old, I discuss how even minor disruptions to these interalignments between employees can be sensitive and fraught topics.

In Chapter 3, I address how notions of hierarchy as a negative force from the past manifested in strong generational differences. I describe how the figure of the South Korean older male manager emerged in discussions around the office and in the media and is even covertly embedded in HR policy as a problematic figure. This figure was frequently blamed for ills in the office, from inefficiency to dissatisfaction. The life of such figures is significant as perceived personal attributes provided the inspiration for new kinds of office reform or efforts to fix problems caused by older male managers. Whether it is fair to locate problems in the older male manager figure or whether this reflects an ageist bias against older workers, the chapter focuses on the ways that the figure was one target from which to craft a new supercorporate ideal and the belief that getting rid of such figures would solve problems of both proper distinction and positive social interactions in the workplace.

Chapter 4 examines the implementation of the employee survey at Sangdo. A seemingly innocuous genre, employee satisfaction surveys operate as a key site for collecting the basic empirical evidence needed as grounds for corporate change. In doing so, they also create potential for a new kind of knowledge-based distinctions based on the surety of employee voices that can be converted into problems to be solved through action plans. I document the difficulties HR managers faced as they attempted to re-create the image of bad office cultures on the survey, yet were foiled when the numerical reality did not correlate to the image they hoped to present. This failure of numbers in turn threatened their own status as internal experts.

In Chapter 5, I examine one site where a different kind of supercorporate ideal was enacted: shareholder meetings. Shareholder meetings are quite unusual as state- and market-mandated forums that break the monotony of everyday office life and enact a flipped version of many forms of hierarchy and distinction. They are forums in which the minority shareholders seize power temporarily, a power communicated primarily through the right not only to speak but to publicly berate or accuse corporate executives. In South Korea, I describe how this power is exploited by different actors such as meeting extortionists (*chonghoe-ggun*), activist investors, foreign investors, and institutional investors, all of whom disrupt the parliamentary format of the meetings to enact new forms of distinction in which they can have greater external control to different ends. In turn, I describe how many employees are drawn into new participatory roles to protect the meeting from disruptive outsiders.

Chapter 6 turns to a site that is frequently a locus for complaint about South Korean office culture: after-hours socializing. After-hours work has often been imagined as a refuge from many of the formal demands of the working day and a site where unspoken aspects of office life can be resolved. I highlight how after-hours socializing in South Korea also operates as a zone with its own forms of distinction and participation. Activities such as going drinking together, singing, and playing games such as golf mediate work through forms of play or leisure; they are also sites of creating alternative distinctions, such as how much one could drink, how late one could stay out, and how well one could sing. These events also generate their own forms of normative coercion. Beyond the revelry that often contrasts with buttoned-up office life, I point to the ways that socializing itself is a complex site where employees must manage other peoples' preferences in ways that reflect the fact that team members and managers are still closely bound up within the nuances and calculations of distinction and participation among their own team members in ways that managerial systems can never fully separate.

In the Conclusion, I describe how some employees located hidden forms of distinction within the corporation itself: ties to Christianity and the military. Even passing mentions of comparison can reflect the way that corporations exist in the context of other institutions of which it is sometimes a model and other times a point of comparison. I suggest that the issue of locating difference is partly a creative act, not just an objective form or characteristic. This depends, in part, on how employees encounter or narrate forms of distinction for themselves.

In the Appendix, I discuss my own encounters as a researcher with different forms of distinction at Sangdo. These encounters greatly affected the ethnographic research process in three ways: First, how I was connected to the Sangdo conglomerate affected how others treated me and what I could access. Second, as an anthropology student I entered a space of experienced experts versed in organizational behavior, clear and transparent methods, and project timelines. Finding myself downgraded in rank and expertise, my own conceptions of what an anthropologist would or should be researching changed significantly in the field. Finally, I discuss how in the writing of this book, I became aware of my own distinctions in how I viewed corporate spaces as inherently sites of disingenuous control, as I moved toward focusing on the ethics and dilemmas of trying to remake corporations as spaces of both positive distinction and participation in a post-hierarchical South Korea.

1

A New Tower

HUNDREDS OF GLASSY OFFICE BUILDINGS dot the Seoul skyline much like the aristocratic towers of medieval Italian city-states: each represents a separate history, set of powers, and outlook on the city and world beyond. Adorned with oversized logos visible from afar, these tall buildings project individual corporate brands to the public at large, suggesting the outsized role that corporations play in South Korea's urban capitalist society. As much as they narrate the oft-told story of Seoul's and South Korea's twentieth-century economic journey as a collective entity, the buildings are just as much in competition with each other to demonstrate corporate wealth and prestige, to attract employees, and to convey a sense of organizational unity. While some towers bear big brand names such as Samsung or Kia, representing clear players on the national economic landscape, there are many others—with names such as Young Poom, Daelim, Samyang, and Taekwang—whose exact business many in South Korea would be hard-pressed to identify.

The forty-story Sangdo tower was one such building and Sangdo one such group: prominent in one district of Seoul but largely unknown as a name-brand corporate group outside of its industry and markets. The tower was constructed in the 2010s in one of the many continuously redeveloping neighborhoods of Seoul where it stood alongside new apartment buildings and shopping centers integrated with the city subway system. The building reflected modern corporate design trends such as sheer glass exteriors and a marbled lobby. The front of the tower showcased Sangdo's own identity: group advertisements, colorful brand banners, and uniformed greeters. Men and women of Sangdo, clad in dark-blue suits and company lanyards, could be seen briskly moving in and out from morning to night.

In the lobby, in front of the elevators, the names of Sangdo's dozen subsidiary companies were etched into the wall in their respective pecking order. At the top of the list was the office of the chairman of the Sangdo Group, followed by the Sangdo holding company. At the bottom of the list, located on lower floors, were the smallest subsidiaries Sangdo Logistics and Sangdo NET, involved in internal servicing for Sangdo's other subsidiaries. In between were the commodity-producing subsidiaries themselves, each involved in different areas of steel and metal production. Spread across many floors, the subsidiaries were largely ordered from the top down by revenue and personnel, with the largest recording annual revenues over a billion US dollars and the smallest in the tens of millions. The two largest, Sangdo South and Sangdo First, occupied multiple floors to accommodate their large sales forces and managerial staff; the smallest offices, such as Sangdo Max and Sangdo One, had to share a floor. (All subsidiary names have been given pseudonyms).

Within the new tower, there were spaces of congregation and interaction for employees. A company café on the fifth floor served as a way-stop for many on the way back from lunch or for meetings with suppliers or customers to order coffee and smoothies. The café offered the image of an effete modern office lifestyle, replete with leather couches for relaxing, postindustrial brick facades, and a carefully constructed wall-length bookshelf filled with vintage Korean and English management books owned by Sangdo's founder. The café was encased on all sides by large bay windows offering views onto the local neighborhood. Adjacent was a permanent museum-like exhibition, detailing the history of Sangdo, its steel products, and key moments in history, along with pictures of the chairman's family. Down the hall was a company gym where employees could go before and after work, donning complimentary Sangdo-branded workout clothes. There were also high-tech conference rooms for meetings or after-work language study. And finally, there was a two-hundred-person stadium-style auditorium where employees gathered for lectures on management from business professors and on culture, such as occasional lectures on classical music.[1]

Traveling up the tower, all Sangdo offices had open floor designs, with desks grouped by teams. Team spaces were enclosed within polygon-like shapes that overtly minimized the hierarchical distinctions among members. Each

individual desk was custom designed based on the Sangdo logo. All employees were provided with designer office chairs that were said to have been handpicked by a member of the ownership. Around the edges of each floor were executive offices with glass windows, offering a partially transparent window
onto the highest members of the office. And adjacent to the executive offices
were both fully transparent meeting rooms for overhead presentations and
floor-to-ceiling white boards for employees to engage in the kind of open-
discussion interactions redolent of Silicon Valley. At the top of the tower, above
the holding company, were tastefully decorated executive conference rooms
with digital sign-in screens and dark wood paneling, surrounded by sculptures
and paintings reminiscent of an art gallery.

To outsiders or visitors, the Sangdo tower, and by extension the Sangdo
Group, evoked different markers of consumer, architectural, and global corporate distinction that combined to distinguish it from the outdated or generic office buildings in its surrounding neighborhood and bring it into reso-
nance with other large prestige corporate towers across the city. The internal
order within offices, visible to employees and authorized visitors, further conveyed elements of these marks of distinction, marking Sangdo and Sangdo-
ites as particular kinds of salaried office workers (*jikjang-in*). In many senses,
employees young and old partook equally in the access to such facilities as the
café, the gym, and the meeting spaces or the basic office artifacts such as office chairs.

However, the tower also encoded new kinds of distinctions, particularly
between organizations. Before moving into the Sangdo tower, each of the subsidiaries had operated with some degree of relative independence in an ownership philosophy that was described to me on various occasions as autonomous management (*jayul gyeong-yeong*). Under this philosophy, subsidiaries
maintained their own office functions, methods of management, and aspects
of production with minimal reporting to the chairman directly from their
CEOs; there were few channels of control that penetrated the subsidiaries
themselves from above. This was partly related to the very different histories
and industries of the subsidiaries, with some locating their own headquarters in historically rivalry-ridden regional areas (Jeolla and Gyeongsang). To
outsiders, what might have appeared as simply a shared steel industry represented to insiders vast differences, whether one sold domestically or interna-
tionally or what kind of steel was being produced. Factory workers at the largest subsidiaries also belonged to different national trade unions that may have

reflected their differences or opposed further integration efforts. In this sense, the move into the Sangdo tower was quite radical and an act of creating a new kind of internal conglomerate order. (I had heard a rumor that CEOs of different subsidiaries were reluctant to fully move into the tower and some maintained their offices at their regional factories as a subtle act of protest at the centralization efforts.)

Like the business towers that simultaneously project themselves to other entities or society at large, corporate groups can appear most coherent from the outside or from afar, such as in consumer exchanges, in public relations language, or in management handbooks and case studies. Anthropologist Marina Welker has described these kinds of encounters as sites where corporations are "enacted." By this, she refers to the concept of the idea of the corporation cohering as a single actor within particular exchanges, despite the fact that corporations are "inherently unstable and indeterminate, multiply authored, always in flux, and comprising both material and immaterial parts."[2] In her ethnography of the American Newmont Mining Corporation and its activities in Indonesia, Welker reveals how different faces of the company emerge across different encounters and exchanges, some that might evoke an image of humanitarianism and others that evoke an image of the company as an agent of environmental destruction. As corporations keep moving out into the world, their images or identities do not travel cleanly with them: even where they exert pressure or corporate might, they are also remade by those they encounter.

What of the internal "enactment" of the corporation or corporate groups where organizational actors interact and recognize those who are not, on the surface, others? It was commonplace during my time in South Korea to think about this question by thinking about corporate groups as having different personalities shaped by a mix of their industry, history, ownership, or size. (A well-traveled joke in the South Korean corporate world purported that the personality of different groups could be known based on how employees react upon seeing a snake in the office: in one version, the Hyundai employee is said to knock the snake out first, and then figure out what to do, while the Samsung employee would give it a payoff to go away; the Hanwha employee goes and asks his chairman what he should do about the snake.) The internal order of corporate groups in South Korea belies much more complex realities where numerous forms of stratification intersect and crisscross. This chapter looks at the elaboration of an internal order at the Sangdo Group not as a representative South Korean conglomerate that was already made with a clear internal order or managerial hierarchy reflective of the steel industry but as one that was in the process of being made and enacted, often in ways that were not entirely predictable. During my research at Sangdo, a new Sangdo order was being constructed, first through the move into the Sangdo tower and then into new areas of centralized management. The encounters within the tower, as much as they condensed (or trapped) people within a new vertical space, also engendered different ways of rendering organizational relationships. The Sangdo holding company that was ambiguously positioned at the top of the tower was the source of new visions for what the conglomerate would be and how members would relate to each other. Certain areas of this elaboration appeared to dovetail with a general rise in corporate prestige of the group that affected all members and signaled more general progress in South Korean corporate social life—the group itself was becoming more distinct in the imagined (and sometimes real) rankings of corporate groups in South Korea. Other areas appeared to impose new distinctions and ways of reconceptualizing how differences between employees or between organizations should be rendered, drawing out new contrasts where none had been before.

Scholars have tended to critique post-hierarchical corporate ideals by contrasting images of happy coparticipation against other kinds of hierarchical imposition that might be invisible to employees. Not surprisingly, participatory ideals are usually in the service of sneaking in new hierarchical impositions. In 1990s South Korea, for instance, sociologist Hagen Koo described how companies began to invest in the "corporate culture movement" by creating "educational programs, recreational clubs and other small group activities, festivals, song contests, retreats and overseas trips for union leaders." The real goal of these programs was, according to Koo, an indirect method of labor placation: "all these company cultures used paternalistic language and symbols to recreate the pseudo-family sharing a common economic fate among the members of the company."[3] This chapter goes beyond this familiar critique of corporate dynamics by attempting to describe how ideas of post-hierarchy in twenty-first-century South Korea converge in ways that point to contradictions, even within high-level corporate spaces, in how participation and distinction should be manifested in office life.

Building on the concept of the supercorporate ideal discussed in the Introduction, I suggest that ideas of distinction and participation are not inherently opposed but become complexly manifest in different areas of management and organizational life. Areas of management, in the abstract, take certain domains of economic life—commodities, people, strategy, money, risks, and so on—as objects of concern that people interact with and attempt to govern or order in some fashion. However, considering the inner world of organizational life, where management moves from an abstract concept to manifestation in things or events, such as documentation, meetings, reporting relationships, or software, imagined forms of distinction or participation do not always predict or correlate with life on the ground. In other words, what might appear to be a clear high-level management strategy to outsiders via a new corporate vision or encased in corporate architecture must also be complexly translated into a variety of domains. The creation of new forms and modes of distinction and participation for others—particularly by experts from on high in the holding company—can also risk something else: echoing the negative associations of hierarchy (and power) in their very creation. After discussing the rise of the holding company at Sangdo, I consider how for a new crop of experts in the Sangdo holding company, translating high level ideas of distinction and participation was itself not always clear in practice. In some cases, they themselves became sites of experiment or found themselves imposing new hierarchies that they did not necessarily intend.

A New Generation of Ownership and a Corporate Stepmother

Sangdo's decades of history have coincided with twists and turns in South Korea's own history, that is, a company rebuilt from scratch. During the journey over the past decades, Sangdo has shared victories, frustrations, joy, and anguish with the growing nation. For both South Korea and Sangdo, it has been an era of dynamism, passion and sweat. Now putting behind all the ups and downs during the course of the last century, the company stands ready to face head-on another historic milestone.

From Sangdo's official book of corporate history (modified for anonymity)

Descriptions such as this one, written in Sangdo's official history book, paint a unitary picture of a single organizational entity bearing the vicissitudes of the twentieth and twenty-first centuries, much like the nation itself. When I arrived in 2014, the group's move into the Sangdo tower was framed as the latest chapter in the group's official narrative in their next leap toward being a global company of innovation. Prior to the tower's construction, however, the group was largely a disparate collection of subsidiaries that shared an industry and a name. However, their teams of salespeople, accountants, procurement managers, and others maintained separate buildings in different areas of Seoul with ties to separate regional factories that were independently run. These subsidiaries, with some exceptions, were each majority owned by a holding company that in turn was owned by an owning family, comprised of the chairman and a few other owner-executives. The holding company at the time only occupied a small office staffed by a handful of employees attached to the headquarters of one of the subsidiaries. Employees who had worked at that holding company office described it as a close-knit office that had minimal managerial oversight within the group, largely carrying out high-level affairs and select cross-group activities that might not interfere with the operations of any subsidiary, such as financial reporting, group marketing, executive promotions, auditing, and matters related to the owning family such as philanthropy.

With the move to the tower and a position right below the chairman's floor, the holding company looked less like a vessel of corporate governance and more like a central planning office at the helm of a large conglomerate. When I first began working at the holding company, it had grown to almost fifty workers spread across nine teams. There are three factors, described below, that contributed to the holding company's rise at the Sangdo Group beginning in the 2010s.

First, government policy following the Asian Financial Crisis of 1997 focused on greater corporate governance reform. Holding companies were seen as vehicles of internal financial transparency and good governance. Ironically, the holding company structure (*jijuhoesa*) had previously been banned as a legal form in the 1980s as it was thought to lead to too much economic concentration by conglomerate owners.[4] By the late 1990s, the ban on holding companies was lifted. Beginning in 2000, holding companies were promoted as a vehicle for proper corporate governance and fiscal transparency, with the government encouraging all conglomerates to straighten out their internal shareholding relationships. The idea was to unwind the complicated circular shareholding ties (*sunhwanchulja*) in which subsidiaries maintained large crossholding relationships with each other, making it difficult to know how much financial capital any entity had or what entity was ultimately in charge. The renewed advent of the holding company signaled a way to make conglomerates more transparent to the government, shareholders, and financial markets; in theory, it would also make it easier to sever or spin off underperforming subsidiaries from a conglomerate instead of spreading their risk to the rest of a group. Under a holding company model, subsidiaries are prohibited from owning shares in each other and could not have more than one layer of subsidiaries themselves. The result looks much like a pyramid structure.[5] (LG Group was one of the first to convert to a holding company; Sangdo also converted along with a large swath of other groups in the first decade of the 2000s.) The Sangdo holding company was itself created by splitting one subsidiary and gradually taking majority ownership in all the subsidiaries, including major new acquisitions.[6]

The second factor leading to the rise of Sangdo was the generational shift of ownership from one chairman to a future one. Though I cannot share details about the family structure due to the uniqueness of owners' families in South Korea, the Sangdo Group was (like many other corporate groups) amid a long-term transition from one generation of family leadership to another. The chairmanship (*hoejang*) is both the highest executive position in a conglomerate and an elevated figurehead of a conglomerate around which the politics, successes and failures, and company culture appear to revolve—even though, as many reports and studies have shown, individual chairmen often own only 1 percent of shares in their conglomerates and they share much of the leadership with professional (non-family) executives. Chairmen also balance ownership responsibilities under the watch of institutional investors, financial institutions, and regulatory entities. Nevertheless, the chairmanship is an important role as the apex of distinction that is partly earned by hereditary right (usually as a direct descendant of a founder) and by business aptitude, personality, industrial knowledge, and class distinctions. Chairmen usually hold the greatest amount of distinction in terms of treatment from others, including having a personal driver, personal assistants, and dedicated teams that may ensure that a chairman's schedule outside of a company tower is minutely planned to ensure smooth treatment. While chairmanships within the traditional family-owned conglomerates (chaebol) have often been transferred to direct heirs (or in some cases, spouses of heirs), they are rarely handed over as a right of heredity alone. As positions, they are demonstrably earned by sons and daughters who must cultivate elaborate experiences in overseas education and prestige degrees; extensive management and strategy experience, sometimes in consulting or finance; and leadership of a division or subsidiary as a test of their potential. (Chairmanship roles, like any other director position, must also be ratified at shareholder meetings.) The politics of succession is a keenly followed topic in domestic news and within companies where potential leaders may be cutting their teeth (not always with success).

At Sangdo, it was not clear when or how such a transition to the next chairman might take place, but the latest members of the owning family were progressing through ranks within different parts of the group. One of them had taken an executive position in the holding company, the growth of which corresponded with the rise of this particular owner. This owner-executive took a hand in recruiting new team managers and executives and growing new areas of managerial expertise under the aegis of the more senior chairman who occupied a rarefied position at the top of the conglomerate, outside of daily managerial affairs. Though it was difficult to locate any explicit policy, it was clear to everyone I met at the holding company that many areas of management (with a few exceptions such as accounting or legal affairs) operated as an extension of that owner-executive's will to turn the holding company into an expert hub. The owner-executive was often the unofficial addressee on project reports and the source of new project ideas. In this sense, the holding company was not just a managerial entity but was being turned into a future strategy office (*miraejeollyaksil*) or planning office (*gihweksil*). At the time, strategy and planning offices were popular at different conglomerates as hubs for collocating the presumed elite experts. They often brought in large numbers of experts from within and outside the company, sometimes numbering hundreds of people, who would act as extensions or delegates of ownership to various sides of conglomerate management.[7]

The third factor that contributed to the rise of the holding company was the state of the global steel industry at the time and Sangdo's seemingly tenuous position within it. As described by assistant manager Baik in the Introduction, Sangdo was on considerably shaky ground in both the global and domestic steel markets. On the domestic front, what was once seen as a stable division of product markets and key supplier relationships in South Korea was suddenly shifting as certain suppliers began to invest in their own steel production. This had led to some notable bankruptcies among other steel company groups. At the same time, Chinese state-supported steel production was flooding the market and dampening prices worldwide, a glut that many thought would take years to resolve. On the other side, the US was seeking to protect (or resurrect) its own steel markets by levying tariffs on many South Korean firms because of what was perceived to be "dumping" (the artificial lowering of commodity prices to gain leverage within a market).

These circumstances led to an environment of crisis management (*wigi gyeong-yeong*) in which subsidiaries were originally supposed to try to cut costs where possible or adopt efficiencies in their businesses.[8] However, many of the issues in Sangdo's steel markets appeared as much more drastic in their consequences: losing the US as a market due to import tariffs, being cut off by one of the largest domestic customers, and facing complicated decisions on what product lines from which subsidiaries might be merged or consolidated. New teams in the holding company, such as the performance management team and the future strategy team, were tasked with identifying opportunities within the group and finding new areas for expansion.

In practice, the role of the holding company was not always clear—even among its members. Some executives saw themselves as setting forth new strategies or plans that subsidiaries would or should adopt. When I first met executive Cho of the HR team, he stated clearly that the HR team only guided (*annaehaechuda*) the rest of the group but did not meddle in their affairs. The holding company's HR team, he attested, stuck to their limited remit, which included evaluating executives and promotion policies, and did not become involved in HR disputes or policies or more complex activities such as union negotiations. When I spoke with team manager Chu about the performance management team, he noted that the holding company formerly only passed along information to the chairman, but now it was attempting to gather more information that might let the chairman know about the specifics of each subsidiary, such as how much their sales were changing every month and whether they were gaining or losing employees. I overheard one executive asking another what services the holding company was providing and whether they needed to be charging subsidiaries or not. For one executive Byun, whom I discuss later in the chapter, he considered his job more about controlling (*gwalli*) subsidiaries than about simply contributing (*giyeo*) to them.

Early in my time at Sangdo, I spoke to a manager on the auditing team of the holding company, as I was trying to get a sense of the internal diversity of Sangdo. Team manager Kim had been with one subsidiary, Sangdo South, his entire career and had moved up to the holding company—first as a team manager and later promoted to executive. His team carried out audits of the entire Sangdo Group, primarily through remote monitoring, document audits, and on-site visits. Kim had been to Sangdo offices in China, Latin America, and Southeast Asia and had seen every factory and office within South Korea. As the auditing director, he had a more intimate grasp of the finances and accounting of every single office than anyone else in the group, as well as the internal differences among them. When I asked to him one day about the seemingly profound differences across the group, particularly the different cultures of its subsidiaries, he said that he "loved Sangdo" (which he expressed in English), referring to Sangdo as a singular entity, a way of deferring on identifying any strong differences among the subsidiaries.

This sentiment elided the fact that his own original employer, Sangdo South, had been part of another conglomerate, and then yet another that had gone bankrupt in the 1990s before being acquired by Sangdo in the early years of the 2000s.[9] Sangdo South's own history had begun even before the founding of the original Sangdo Group. However, it was another subsidiary's starting date that marked the official group founding date in the group history book.

Where team manager Kim might have been trying to avoid revealing any fissures in the group to me as a relative junior, outsider, and foreigner, team manager Jang of the HR department, with whom I came to work with more closely, put it much differently. Jang himself was an outsider to the Sangdo Group, starting only a few years prior to me after more than a decade in HR at a larger multinational conglomerate. He was not a lifelong Sangdo employee and was keenly aware of the holding company's stranger-status within the group. Despite the company's power of financial control over the subsidiaries, he explained that employees at the subsidiaries saw the holding company as their stepmother. That is, legally entitled to occupy a high position, but not having fully established themselves as the rightful *mohoesa* (mother company) just yet.[10]

A New Brand Cosmology

Chon-seureopji?—"Rustic, isn't it?"—commented assistant manager Hong after watching a promotional video on the Sangdo tower elevator's video monitor as he and I rode the elevator after a chat in the company café. The video, which played on loop along with a few other videos, began with a young girl playing a violin and then panned to a shot of businessmen in suits chatting in a conference room before finally turning to a shot of a steel factory interlacing scenes of forging flames and men monitoring machines. The shot returns to the same girl playing the violin as the camera zooms out to the Sangdo tower in the background. The screen fades out and the Sangdo corporate logo appears on a white background. Hong seemed particularly put off by what he considered some of the staged shots of office work—some of which involved his coworkers recruited to stage "meeting" interactions. In South Korea, comments about rusticity can mark a distinction between the rural countryside and the modern metropolis. Such comments also position a speaker as a person not only of taste but also as a person of discernment. In the corporate world, an outdated logo, an in-house advertisement, or a poorly translated English brochure could be a sign of the past and an object for derogation, if not reform. Hong was embarrassed by the fact that his team had produced the video a few years earlier and it was still on replay in the company elevator. Now with a slightly higher position, he was in charge of developing new televisual content for Sangdo. His team's new videos, which featured more dramatic images of the actual steelmaking process by echoing the romance of blue-collar work, were produced with the help of an advertising agency. The videos had been developed for trade shows and uploaded to the Sangdo website, but they had not yet found their way into the elevator's miniature screen.

Hong was one of the managers on a small public relations (PR) team that was tasked with managing the many artifacts of the Sangdo brand across all of its conglomerates. His personal comments to me might have been premised on a binary distinction between a Sangdo of today and a Sangdo of yesterday; however, his team was doing much more than simply revamping the look of Sangdo. They were changing how the Sangdo Group was represented internally to its members. Just as the office tower unified Sangdo as a group by marking it from other corporate groups, the PR team was also creating a unified image of Sangdo that would be found on every floor, every computer screen, and every public encounter for Sangdo's multiple organizational bodies, from the tower down to its factories. This unified image aimed to encompass the subsidiaries within the Sangdo Group in more than just name; they would also be considered part of the same corporate order. In official publications, each of the subsidiaries was simply a member of the broader Sangdo Group rather than an independent entity. What existed, in other words, as discrete entities with their own histories and products was now being advertised as an imagined corporate community.

The effort to promulgate the identity of the Sangdo Group as an abstract organizational container in which diverse interests could claim membership also extended to unified visual and design artifacts. The PR team developed a host of branded tchotchkes adorned with the Sangdo symbol and company colors. These included company notebooks distributed to every employee, company jackets, lapel pins, business cards, PowerPoint templates, branded USB keys, and desktop items such as pens, rulers, and paperweights. The designs were subtle enough that they could even be displayed as fashionable items outside the office. This is, in part, because they were designed neither as company advertisements nor as functional workwear but as prestige items that workers could adorn, akin to other design-minded products that those in Seoul, in particular, were more mindful of as white-collar workers. (Company notebooks were all black and had a unique texture redolent of the Moleskine brand. Even the coffee sleeves at the company café were stamped with the Sangdo brand symbol.) Employees who won awards were also given specialty items such as leather briefcases that subtly encoded the Sangdo logo in one corner. The items were handpicked by or selected with input from the owner-executive who had a personal stake in good corporate design. Together, these created an embellished register of branded qualities inclusive of membership in all companies while being descriptive of none.

Though these products came from the holding company, they were otherwise generically ascribed as Sangdo items, creating the image of a unified brand from nowhere. The holding company PR team also distributed the tchotchkes and other branded goods to those in the tower largely for free (though extras had to be bought at cost). While employees might have thought of themselves as working for Sangdo First or Sangdo South, Sangdo NET or Sangdo FX, the branded elements from "Sangdo" simply echoed the more abstract and singular Sangdo Group that was not necessarily figuratively above them but was a new encompassing, and singular, form of identity.[11]

One of the places where this new cosmology of the Sangdo Group was made visible was within the corporate magazine (sabo). Sangdo Group's employee magazine, Our Sangdo, was produced by the PR team in the holding company three to four times a year and distributed to every Korean-speaking member of the group. Our Sangdo was a professionally produced magazine and contained inspirational messages from the chairman, news updates from around the Sangdo world, thematic management topics for instruction, case studies of successful global companies, profiles of different moments in Sangdo's history, team profiles from sales offices and factory sites, and even wedding, birth, and obituary announcements from local offices. On the back page of each magazine was a tear-off postcard that employees could send back to the PR team with a company history quiz, raffle prize, and space to leave a message for the magazine's editors.

Our Sangdo had been around for decades and existed in different visual and editorial iterations over the years. The latest version of the magazine was rebooted in the early 2010s with a boost from the owner-executive and outsourced help from professional writers, photographers, and graphic designers who refashioned the magazine from glossy pro-corporate productions to a refined aesthetic with more florid language and subtle refinements such as heavy card stock and embossed texts. The magazine situated Sangdo as more global in its outlook, with profiles of American or European companies and professors that offered business lessons and motivations. There were also country profiles of places where Sangdo had overseas offices, reflecting Sangdo's history of doing business multinationally, even if most domestic employees would rarely travel to such locales.

Subsidiaries also published their own employee magazines. In some cases, specific factories and company labor unions issued magazines, highlighting their own membership as separate from the broader Sangdo Group or even their subsidiary corporation. For instance, where a January issue of *Our Sangdo* promoted the chairman's annual New Year's proclamation urging all members of the Sangdo family to work with "renewed hearts and spirits," one factory magazine shared images of a ceremony featuring a roasted pig offering, calling for an "accident-free year" at the factory. The group magazine featured full bleed, color-printed, heavy paper stock with professional photography, depicting clean-cut employees in blue suits and white shirts. The factory magazine, in contrast, featured photos taken with a low-resolution camera and posted as a PDF on the company's intranet bulletin board. In this sense, efforts to create a shared group identity from the holding company were in subtle competition with other ways of imagining the corporate community.

One prominent feature of *Our Sangdo* was the team profile in each issue. The magazine regularly profiled a team from a subsidiary, focusing on the working context and working relationships among team members. The profiles featured professional pictures on the job with team members at their worksites, using equipment or in meetings, and posing heroically or joking around. The

profiles reflected the diversity of roles—sales and exporting in one issue, research and development in factories in another—but the themes underlined
in the profiles were consistent: a central work challenge brought on by issues
in the market faced by a team who needed to overcome such challenges, often through grit, determination, or insight and often abandoning set ways of
thinking about how to solve something. The team managers in the profiles,
usually men in their forties and fifties, were sources of kitschy words of managerial wisdom ("In changing times, you have to live through change," read one;
"You can't manage through feeling, you must have evidence," read another).
One profile of a quality control team at a regional factory described how the
company faced price competition from other South Korean firms. To overcome the challenge, they "abandoned their attitudes and biases to find a new
solution" to achieve a new international certification and gain recognition in
overseas markets. The team profiles did not shy away from representing teams
as differentiated ranks among employees; they emphasized the different roles
that members played on the team and how they contributed to solving each
challenge. This was often in the form of describing different kinds of social personalities. For instance, the quality control team in a regional factory was described in the following way:

> Under the leadership of their team leader Kim, [the quality control team con-
> sisted of] assistant manager Cha who leads the younger members [*hubae*] while
> junior assistant manager Moon is capable and passionate. The technician Ahn
> is hands-on and friendly while the technician Bong is good at his work and is a
> romantic. Last are the junior members, Gil-jun, who is the social spark [*bunuigi
> meikeo*] and Han-gyeol who is so sincere they say he resembles a scholar.

Members of a combined export–sales team at the subsidiary Sangdo FX, which
uniquely had two team managers, featured a mock interview with both, in the
following:

> Magazine: You've both developed teams that communicate well. What's your secret?
> Team manager Lee: When times are tough, we stick together even more, so that's
> how we've grown. Sangdo FX is a latecomer to the Sangdo Group and we
> went through very difficult periods, so we try to have pride [*jabusim*] in
> having overcome those difficulties. No matter how difficult things are, you
> have to have pride to believe you can overcome. I try to get even our new
> junior members to understand this aspect, so we can go forward together.

Team manager Chae: More than criticism, I try really hard to offer compliments. If I
    talk [to an employee] about a mistake for one minute, I speak for five min-
    utes about the things they are doing well, so they will develop some confi-
    dence [*jasin-gam*] and approach things first. Moreover, I work hard to take
    into account each person's family circumstances. Because this is people
    doing this work after all.

Magazine profiles of different teams drew on a friendly frame for talking
about internal differences. Rather than denying intrateam ranks all together,
the magazine framed them as matters of care and leadership. The focus on
individual skill differences and experiences within teams reflected the fact
that employees were ultimately distinct in their abilities at different stages of
their careers and personal lives but nevertheless needed leadership in the face
of adverse conditions. This reflects one aspirational idea around notions of
participatory teamwork in South Korea. Team leaders are not bosses or military leaders but are guides or motivational leaders who help employees to
achieve their individual goals.[12] Team leaders, as represented in the magazine,
did not just exist as higher gradated persons than their team members but as
particular kinds of mentors, seniors (*seonbae*), or persons with philosophies
(*cheolhak*) who were in charge of helping others overcome challenges together.

This focus on team-level diversity nevertheless underscored a new idea:
Sangdo Group's basic parts were composed of unique teams with particular
histories, personalities, and differences across different business units. Beyond the perhaps starry-eyed notions of how these teams worked together,
the magazine also elided other intermediary forms of belonging such as factory culture, subsidiary identity, or even labor unions. In other words, within
the new brand cosmology, teams became a basic object for narrating natural
distinctions (as a form of age and experience differences) coexistent with positive forms of participation (via earnest problem solving). The magazine did
not need to mention the other kinds of organizational distinctions (or negative hierarchical aspects) that might lie within such teams or elsewhere in the
Sangdo Group.

Sociotechnical Distinctions

If PR was primarily invested in ideas of a generic Sangdo brand brought into a
relationship of distinction with branded products and images of harmonious
participation at the team level, the HR department in the holding company

was more invested in the machinery of how interpersonal distinctions were measured and administered. They were partially limited in how far they could reach into the infrastructure of other subsidiaries' individual workplaces. As executive Cho noted when I first met him, the HR team could only attempt to "guide" subsidiaries in new methods. This meant that they had to test new projects on themselves first before other subsidiaries would adopt them. When I joined the HR team in the holding company, they were involved in a number of new projects for their own holding company (that one colleague in another team described as "experimental"). One project was an in-house system for tracking and monitoring work projects called DRIVE. To the creators of the system (executive Cho, team manager Jang, and an assistant manager, Jisoon), DRIVE was meant to solve what they saw as a major managerial problem not just at Sangdo but in South Korea more generally: how workers were evaluated to generate a rational basis for interpersonal distinctions.

Evaluations (*pyeong-ga*) are instrumental in deciding promotions and bonuses in South Korea. Since the early years of the 2000s, it had been common for South Korean employees to set annual goals that would be tied to key performance indicators (KPIs) as the basis of measuring their performance. KPIs, which set specific numerical targets for specific kinds of work, help resolve a basic problem of how to measure different work types and levels across different fields. Instead of uniform goals, each worker or each job may have its own categories and metrics of KPIs that they set for themselves. As expert practitioners, the HR managers at the holding company, however, came to dislike KPI systems: KPIs could be manipulated to make them easy to attain, were not necessarily reflective of the actual work that employees did, and were time consuming to develop and track. Furthermore, because KPIs provided only a set of arbitrary numbers (such as "numbers of customers satisfied"), employees might focus on the numbers and not on the work itself.

The HR managers had been preparing DRIVE, which was intended to connect evaluations more closely with actual work by creating an ongoing record of employees' individual performances on projects. (The original idea for DRIVE had come from one manager reading a case about performance evaluations at British Airways, where flight crew provided evaluations immediately after every flight.) DRIVE existed as a fixed application within the company's Enterprise Resource Planning (ERP) system. (ERP is a conventional name for business software that is commonly used in supply chain management and accounting. ERP at Sangdo was mostly used for accounting but it could in theory be used for any kind of business process.) The core idea behind the DRIVE program was to link any given work project to a form of evaluation, so that annual evaluation was not an end-of-year tally of numbers that had no temporal record of progress or reflection but one based on a clear record that could be referred to. Instead of having separate KPIs that stood outside of work, DRIVE would measure projects as they were beginning and ending. In doing so, DRIVE subtly intervened in the social relation between team manager and team member. In theory, a team manager could more closely oversee projects of those under them and employees would have clear ideas about what the goals, output, and expectations were for a given project.

Like a map that that attempts to replicate territory perfectly, purifying the manager-employee relationship meant re-creating work on a digital platform. Assistant manager Ji-soon worked closely with an information technology (IT) worker to program a new software that would incorporate all the elements in an interface that employees could use. This involved creating the elements of the interface from scratch, including basic descriptors such as what a manager was, what a team member was, project names, start and end dates, and various sub-categories of projects. The system had text boxes that would allow employees to fill in information about their projects, their goals, the expected outcome of the projects, and what was expected of the employee. Such basic elements for describing work were simple but quite radical: the DRIVE application had the effect of casting work as sequences of ongoing projects that had very specific kinds of goals, tasks, outputs, starts, and finishes. Moreover, it assumed all work was completed by one employee and overseen by one manager, with grades for each element given to one employee only.

DRIVE created new decisions and modes of evaluations for managers. Prior to the start of a project, an employee had to fill out the text boxes and work information, which then had to be approved by his or her team manager. At the end of a given project, the team manager had to log back in and fill out grades for the project in four areas: timeliness, quality, importance, and collaboration. These grades were based on an A, B, C, D grading format. Together with a weight attached to each project, the separate grades of each project would tally up at the end of the year to provide an overall grade for employee performance on their work, one of two measures used in determining annual performance evaluations. (The other measure was an employee's reflection of company values, as determined by his or her team manager.) To the HR managers, this was an improvement over KPIs in which acts of evaluation by a manager might only happen at one time (at the end of the year). With DRIVE, a manager's role as evaluator was divvied up over the course of a year. This was meant to prevent the cognitive tendency of team managers to evaluate an employee based on their latest impression, KPI targets, or even their rank or position in the company. It was also meant to prevent any kind of social favoritism or equity challenges that might emerge at the end of the year, such as a case where a team manager might try to balance out grades among employees.

One of the unique features of DRIVE was that it had a built-in measure for employees and HR managers to oversee each other's proper participation. Once a manager had submitted the grades for a given project, there was a box that only the employee could check: whether the manager had met with the employee to discuss the project and the grades. In order to submit the grades as an official record, the manager had to defer to the employee to acknowledge a face-to-face meeting took place in which he or she and the manager discussed the evaluation. The meeting was meant to cover the positive outcomes of the project improvement points. Also privy to seeing this were the managers from the HR team who had access to the ERP master view and could see who was submitting DRIVE projects and who was not. They could see, for instance, that many team members had input their projects but not completed them and that certain team managers had not done their evaluations. Ji-soon was developing a visual dashboard for executives so they could monitor their team managers' managerial abilities in a kind of double-layered form of surveillance around proper participation.

As DRIVE was launched in the second half of 2014, Ji-soon kept active track of how the project was going. She periodically emailed updates to members of the holding company to show them how many total projects were being input to DRIVE in a given month or quarter while offering tips on how to fill in their subprojects better. At one point, it was decided to create an award called "Best DRIVEr" to highlight which employee had successfully completed the most DRIVE projects (regardless of grades). Privately, however, Ji-soon discussed with Jang the state of different teams or problematic team managers, figuring out ways to convince them to participate in what was supposed to be a more rational system for work tracking.

One of the larger goals of the project was to eventually create an HR system that the subsidiaries could also implement within their own organizations. Team manager Jang began to share details of the program with two of the major subsidiaries, Sangdo First and Sangdo South. In one presentation, which I was permitted to attend, Jang shared details about the new program with an executive. Jang adopted an obsequiously respectful and cheerful demeanor as he spoke glowingly of the new program's features, careful not to insult Sangdo First's existing KPI program. The executive, who had not worked in HR and did not seem to care much for it, gave it a lukewarm reception. Later Jang told me that the purpose was not to try to sell him on it immediately but to get them to implement it over time, perhaps after other subsidiaries. Sangdo South, on the other hand, was more receptive to the program and began to implement their own version of the program. It was not a direct copy but was adapted to their organization and managed by their own IT people. In this way, they were running a parallel system that was not a direct copy of DRIVE. Team manager Jang acknowledged to me that by letting them adapt it on their own, it would not be the same as the holding company forcing it on them directly. Sangdo South even made improvements in the software that they shared with the holding company.

DRIVE depicted the problem of distinction and participation as closely calibrated issues that needed to be technically coordinated, to create an accurate picture of work, its modes of completion, and instances of evaluation. Through minute technical details, it also implicitly sought to model idealized team relations, in part by forcing managers to write out their evaluations and justify them in face-to-face meetings with employees. DRIVE was thus a mechanism for creating idealized forms of participation through face-to-face contact around matters of distinction themselves (that is, what an employee did well and what could be improved). As I discuss in Chapter 3, it was also a model that implicitly targeted team managers as the source of bias and favoritism. (Not all team managers in the holding company were proponents of the new process. One manager I spoke with said he delayed completing the DRIVE forms until the last minute and clicked through the boxes confirming that he had met with the employees; I gather he also asked his employees to collude.) The kind of experimental program that DRIVE represented was nevertheless framed as a model or pilot program of contemporary HR management that could eventually be spread to the whole Sangdo Group over time and with technical refinement.

In modeling new relations among team members and their managers, DRIVE imposed an imagined interactional relationship between team managers and team members that might aid but ultimately supersede managers' own styles. The manager who didn't like the DRIVE program was himself well-liked by his team members and saw no need for a new managing model. The creation of DRIVE also put HR itself into the dual roles of architects and witnesses to the projects, tasks, and progress of every other team, not to mention adopters themselves. Interactionally, this was a peculiar role to take on vis-à-vis their coworkers who stood equal to them in organizational status but whose work they were now managing, albeit indirectly. Where we might expect HR to be nominally involved in viewing the corporation as a collection of people with different tasks and responsibilities that needed to be evaluated better, HR attempted to redefine the nature of work itself, both in its participatory dimensions and its role as a basic site for distinction making. In the process, the HR team also became entangled with the nature of manager-employee relations and subsidiaries who had invested in their own styles and habits of tracking distinctions.

The gap between a small ERP program and the world of the conglomerate was wide, but it nevertheless reflected one notion of the holding company: as a site of experimentation and piloting of new programs that one day might trickle down to the other subsidiaries. Where the HR team saw the need to burnish their expertise within the group, it also entailed convincing their own coworkers of the need for the project first, a difficult task among experts who did not always consider themselves as generic steel company managers. Such radical impositions of new categories and ways of grading was also something that would affect their own salaries, bonuses, and promotion futures. Even as the HR team developed a bona fide system that radically reshaped what they saw as central problems in South Korean personnel systems, they did not deem it a successful project until it was adopted by the rest of the group and their own brand of expertise could be properly recognized.

The Heel of the Holding Company

In sociologist Arlie Hochschild's classic book on corporate management, *The Managed Heart*, she developed the well-known concept of emotional labor that describes jobs that require employees or workers to manage the emotional states of the public. The account is well remembered for the work of flight attendants who must manufacture feelings of gratitude in clients. However, she also studied the flipside of corporate emotion among bill collectors, whom she describes as the "heel" of the corporate world for the ways they must trick or malign customers into paying their debts: "at the heel . . . money is owing, and it must be extracted even if the customer must be wrung dry of self-respect."[13] At the Sangdo holding company, three teams were interested in the productive performance of subsidiaries: strategy, performance management, and auditing. While strategy was concerned with future markets and new directions, auditing and performance management teams' responsibilities were very much Sangdo's "heels" in that they searched for potentially unethical and underperforming sites in the group, respectively. The performance management team, in particular, had the role of collecting and summarizing subsidiary sales reports every month, creating a new channel of reporting within the Sangdo tower.

A newly hired executive in the performance management team, Byun, had been brought in to shake things up within the team and the subsidiaries. He had spent his entire career at one of South Korea's top conglomerates where he had risen through the ranks before making a late-stage switch to Sangdo. He had a demonstrably different style than the previous executive who himself was a lifelong Sangdo employee and worked within one subsidiary his entire career. On his first day, Byun made a warm gesture by buying everyone on the floor smoothies from the company café, but otherwise he was overheard speaking loudly during hours-long meetings from inside his office with the assistant managers on his team. When I interviewed Byun one-on-one, he remarked how different Sangdo was from other big companies. In his view, the conglomerate was inexperienced: certain teams, he remarked, even in the holding company, knew little about their own areas of expertise. And he was surprised to see that subsidiaries did not listen to the chairman at all while certain owning family members could simply interrupt work whenever they wished. For him, the Sangdo tower was not particularly prestigious; rather, it was comparatively lower to his former employer, which operated like a pyramid where everyone acted under the philosophy of moving in perfect order (*ilssabullan*). Reflecting this view, he believed the holding company needed to take a stronger role in gathering information and reporting to the chairman.

When I spent a few days on loan from HR with the performance management team, the three assistant managers, a team manager, and the new executive were in the midst of revamping a monthly reporting process for subsidiaries. Each subsidiary had to send updated results on sales figures for each branch every month for the chairman's review. The team was debating a new format for submitting the monthly reports. What was initially a logistical issue also turned into an ethical one. Of concern for the all-male team was how to re-form a report that could only be produced within a very narrow time span and textual space. Getting this information in the days following the end of every month, the team had little time to compile the information into PowerPoint and report it to the chairman and other owners for their reading. These reports, despite continuing important financial and sales information, had very short shelf lives: there was pressure on the performance management team to sub-mit them at the end of the month to the chairman in time for him to make any decisions or evaluations that could, in theory, be passed back down; after this brief window, they would lose their value as indicators of a current economic state and utility for making decisions. The information, if not reported on time, for example, could be considered trash (*sseuregi*), in the words of one manager.

One junior manager, Dong-ho, relayed to me that the team was in the dif-ficult position of trying to relay "data" while producing "information." Data to him was simply what subsidiaries reported; information was the value-added insight that his team could or should offer as experts. In a pair of meetings called by Byun to discuss the monthly reports, employees discussed differ-ent options for what they believed the ownership would want. Unlike the PR team, they were not translating an owner's wish into material prestige objects that would go out to everyone; and unlike the HR team, they were not tweak-ing the mechanisms of distinction-making itself via a new sociotechnical sys-tem. Rather, they were reconciling their own position as a node between the chairman and the subsidiaries. At issue was how much the team should mark their own contribution versus simply giving the chairman raw data.

They debated, for instance, whether they should mix the content of the report between "60:40" quantitative and qualitative information, "80:20," or even "40:60." Quantitative information such as sales figures was useful, but it would not provide any interpretation of what the data meant, a gap that the qualitative information could provide. Qualitative information, such as anal-yses of market trends or rationalizations from subsidiaries about increases or decreases in sales, would be more beneficial to interpreting the data. Doing so, however, would require subjective interpretation on their part, more informa-tion gathering, and a longer production time to analyze data and make consis-tently useful insights. Dong-ho pondered in the meeting about the risk of run-ning out of insightful things to say after a few months. In this sense, they were not only concerned about the relation between the source information and its visual layout; they were also concerned with how their own labor and expertise would be seen by others.

A more value-added approach (with more qualitative data to allow interpretation of the quantitative data) would take longer, they reasoned. This meant that, if they added in time for weekends, the chairman and other owners might not see the reports until the twelfth day of a given month instead of the eighth. Executive Byun believed this would make the reports useless since it was already too late to get use out of the reports to make changes on a month-to-month basis. Asking subsidiaries to submit the information in a shorter period by a fixed date (such as the thirtieth day of the month) would mean that subsidiary representatives would have to work on weekends or holidays. The managers happened to be discussing this in May, a month with a number of national holidays (Kid's Day, Father's Day, Worker's Day, Teacher's Day, and Couple's Day). This fact seemed particularly salient to the younger assistant managers. They deemed it unfair to make subsidiary employees work over the holidays. Executive Byun, who had come from a conglomerate where workers took little vacation and had less sympathy, unless they could find another way to reduce the time to deliver the reports. He also considered excuses for being late, such as holidays, to be suspicious. He harbored some skepticism toward the subsidiaries (whom he referred to on occasions diminutively as *ae-deul*, or children) and their motivations. He even described those who were late as rotten excuse-makers (*birinnaemsena-neun bbenjjiri*), meaning they were only late because they were trying to hide poor results from the holding company. To the assistant managers such as Dong-ho, it was clear that Byun was attempting to institute a new kind of managerial hierarchy through the way the team managed reports; rather than doing it as a free gift (like the PR team's tchotchkes or the HR team's application), which overtly concealed any notion of imposition from above, the performance management team was precisely marking a new hierarchy where there was meant to be one, at least in Byun's eyes. However, it was Dong-ho and his coworkers who would be the ones to enact this hierarchical relationship by calling the representatives from other subsidiaries individually and demanding they send in the information.

In the meeting, Byun gave a long explanation about the importance of the physical act of delivering the report to the chairman. If Byun were to deliver the numbers with no analysis but on time, then there would be no value for their team. They would be merely conduits of numbers. As members of the chairman's staff, however, they should come up with some analysis to include in the report, or else the executive would look ineffectual in front of the chairman with nothing to say. As they debated what kinds of qualitative information to include, one joked that too much information would resemble a school textbook. Thick reports, however, were the preferences of the new owner-executive, another manager chimed in. Even if it looked like too much to the chairman who preferred shorter reports, the other owner-executive might find it useful and could be covertly tailored to this style, even though he wasn't the official audience. Byun was ultimately adamant that the team's contribution on the reports be visible; otherwise, they would be (seen as) passively submitting numbers—and not experts of distinction at all.

Distinctions Made and Hierarchies Hidden

This chapter has focused on the diversity of managerial relationships that were marked by new ideas of distinction and participation that emerged in the move to the Sangdo tower and the rise of the holding company. Holding companies are useful to think with because as minimal types of corporate form, they do not inherently engender any relationship to governance, hierarchy, or control—they are entities both owned and owning, and they can be figuratively empty of people or full of power. As such, the floor of the holding company was a site of complex ideas about what it meant to sit atop others, either as a guide or as a controller. Each of the other teams that I have not focused on, such as legal affairs, general affairs, auditing, and finance, shaped their own relationship to the rest of the conglomerate in unique ways. This reflects the fact that orders in one domain, such as architecture, do not cleanly translate into other domains, such as HR. Likewise, ideas of national development and how a place like Sangdo might fit into a national imaginary must also be complexly translated within the time frames of everyday managerial work. It is at such zones of translation, so to speak, that managers and others must learn to reconcile broad participatory ideals alongside the realities of actual participation. It was at those zones, in other words, where new understandings of Sangdo were being enacted. Managers at the Sangdo holding company saw such heterogeneity as a sign that the company would not be a good case study for academic research in the first place (with the recommendation that I should be studying firms with clear-cut internal orders such as

Samsung). This chapter would suggest, however, that ideas around corporate types are less useful than understanding how heterogeneous corporations operate in practice and the ways they become enacted in different encounters, even internally. It is within these encounters that the specter of negative forms of interpersonal and interorganizational hierarchy loomed large for many managers, navigating the fine line between distinction as a form of positive difference and hierarchy as a negative difference. For some managers, such as those in performance management, distinction ultimately and uncomfortably appeared to depend on imposing a new hierarchy.

Returning to the tower itself, it is also worth pointing out where certain distinctions were concealed. For the Sangdo tower to function as a unified order of distinction, it depended on corporate others to help it function. Nearly half of the tower was rented out to other companies in industries such as life insurance, finance, and IT. These workers' companies occupied the middle and lower floors and could be distinguished from the blue suit, white shirt, and dark tie appearance of the mostly young and male Sangdo workforce. However, those who dressed as Sangdo workers were not formally Sangdo people either: the uniformed greeters in branded Sangdo outfits in the lobby were contracted from a large security firm that supplied security to buildings across the city. So, too, were the café workers, gym workers, and custodial staff, each contracted from separate companies. A largely out-of-sight management company ran the operations for the building. Operations personnel worked underground, behind walls, and in spaces not visible to the public and only rarely encountered by office workers themselves. Custodial and security workers had their own rest and lounge areas deep in the underground parking lot below the tower, behind unmarked doors.

The very apex of the tower, in contrast, hid a different kind of organization: right behind the twenty-foot-high logo that could be spotted from a distance was a military helipad, visible only from a single access point. The helipad, mostly off limits, had been outfitted with a munition storage in case of military necessity. Like many other skyscrapers in Seoul, the Sangdo tower could be deputized by the South Korean military in the case of a national emergency from North Korea, which lies only thirty-five miles north of the urban metropolis.

These facts might be unremarkable to corporate workers who are used to understanding that different classes and types of workers converge in and around corporate towers, not all of whom are marked off as those on managerial tracks. But their very hidden-ness or blended-in-ness are worth highlighting, because they reveal that places like the Sangdo tower were meant to foreground certain kinds of distinction, while also concealing completely other kinds of urban hierarchies on which Sangdo depended.

2

Infrastructures of Distinction

ON THE HEELS of the Asian Financial Crisis of 1997, the South Korean government, together with the IMF, banks, corporate leaders, and unions, instituted
a bevy of corporate governance reforms. Many of these policies were implicitly
and explicitly aimed at making vulnerable conglomerates fiscally stable after
seeing extremely high debt-to-equity ratios and excessive industrial expansion in the mid-1990s. Externally, reforms allowed foreign investors to take
higher financial stakes in domestic companies, created more transparency in
financial reporting, and updated governance measures to align with Western
financial market standards. Internally, the corporate sector saw changes to
the election and proportion of outside directors, institutions of corporate ethics guidelines, assurances of minority shareholder rights, and prohibitions on
conglomerate internal dealing. All of these changes were aimed at what was
referred to simply as the "chaebol problem."[1]

As economists Ha-joon Chang and Jang-sup Shin noted, the "reform of
corporate governance was particularly predicated on the perception that the
'dictatorial' management by the 'owner' families was the root cause of their
'reckless' expansion and the consequent national financial crisis."[2] Stories of a
fast repayment of IMF loans and dramatic corporate reorganizations abound,
celebrating the nation's collective effort in moving past the crisis. However,
whether the large conglomerates actually submitted to these new international market forces, covertly retained and revested their power in new forms,
or offloaded economic and financial risks onto unions and other firms is still a

matter of debate two decades later. The crisis nevertheless serves as a key moment of national-organizational sensemaking in the longer narrative of South Korea's political and economic history.

One organizational narrative that also emerged at the time was that South Korean corporate culture was deemed too vertical and in need of delayering, reflecting a broader ideological movement against managerial layers around the world.[3] A host of reforms were pursued across many levels of HR practices with the assumption that even HR reforms were part of the "IMF way."[4] Beginning in the first decade of the new millennium, many large corporate groups, from the mega-giant Samsung to the public corporation KT, began experimenting with flattening their organizational management ranks as a response to criticism from both outsiders and insiders. Corporate groups began to tinker with their ranking systems by experimenting with the appropriate number of ranks, the titles that employees are called, decision-making procedures, conversational styles, and even the definition of rank itself.

In 2014, I interviewed an HR representative from the Minjong Group (a pseudonym), a large blue-chip conglomerate with dozens of subsidiaries and tens of thousands of employees around the world. Minjong had recently implemented what it called a new manager system (*maenijeoje*). On the surface, Minjong's system removed the differentiated titles for ranks that were standard at almost all private and public corporations. Workers between the entry level (*sawon*) and the fifth level (*bujang*) would be relabeled as managers (*maenijeo*), a categorical inclusion that could span ages of those in their twenties to those in their fifties. This appeared as a radical act of organizational flattening (*supyeonghwa*), conducted through the most visible symbol of verticality—ranks and titles. Employees were not just called *maenijeo* but were also meant to address each other as *maenijeo*, attaching the honorific -*nim* situating it within an honorific formula of address. Publicly, the new titles were said to contribute to the efficiency (*hyoyul*) of the office while also democratizing the internal culture for young people. An experiment such as Minjong's had in mind internal efficiency by reducing the number of approvals needed on internal decision-making in which signatures and approvals were required at each rank. All "managers" would directly report to "team managers" instead of needing to gain a signature at each rank. The experiment was intended to promote more equitable working relations between employees, relations that were based on skill and merit rather than on rank. If everyone is a manager, in theory, it lightens the burden for newer or younger members since they are

Table 2.1 Corporate flat-title policies between 2000 and 2017

Ajou Group	Every employee is called manager except for designated managers or executives
Amore Pacific	Every employee is called [first name + *nim*] except for designated managers or executives (in 2011 changed to every employee)
Cheil	Every employee is addressed as *pro* (short for professional)
CJ	Every employee is called by [first name + *nim*]
Hanwha Chemical	Entry-level (*sawon*) employees are called [first name + *ssi*]; second to fourth rank (*daeri* to *gwajang*) are called manager
Kakao	Employees address each other in Korean using English names or nicknames without honorifics
Naver	No titles; team leaders are called leader
POSCO	Entry-level (*sawon*) employees are called associate; second to fourth rank (*daeri* to *gwajang*) are called manager
Samsung Electronics	Employees can address each other as *nim*, *pro*, *seonhubaenim/ hubaenim* (senior/junior), or English name, including company presidents
Sangdo holding company (pseudonym)	Managers above third rank can be addressed as *suseok* (chief)
SK Hynix	Employees can decide between addressing others as *nim* or manager
SK Telecom	Every employee is called manager except for designated managers
Yuhan Kimberly	Every employee is called [first name + *nim*]

Note: This table captures different experiments with flat titles (*supyeong jikching*), particularly around how employees should address each other interactionally. Many of the titles are sourced from American English managerial terminology, but there is a marked difference between those that reflect terms of respect (or raising, such as use of "manager") and those that reflect terms of casualness (or lowering, such as use of English nicknames).
Source: Data collected from news sources and interviews and translated by the author.

equal to others, at least in terms of title. Title raising, like the manager system of Minjong, lifts the respect of all employees in the company without directly lowering anyone, at least linguistically. Flattening such ranks would be one way to level the playing field and allow only those with good performance to advance on their own merits. This brought to fruition one particular ideology around the proper way to promote people to managers—through merit instead of deservedness based on tenure. This was nevertheless a means of purifying one set of distinctions (managerial ranks) by removing ranks as a mediating factor to allow another set of putative distinctions to emerge in their place.

Flat-title policies rely on a series of assumptions about the relationship between language change and organizational structure.[5] Primarily, they assume that roles or a division of labor can be reduced to the basic titles that conventionally distinguish people, and that changing the names or titles will in turn effect the wider set of distinctions between people or the organization overall. Moreover, one of the ways this process is imagined to work is that by virtue of people speaking to each other on equal footing (such as addressing each other as "manager"), this will putatively create the conditions on which other distinctions might be eradicated. To move from one form of language to its broader effect on business culture, however, a number of other factors must be kept at bay, such as how language creates asymmetries, how people experience distinctions in work, and other ways of marking distinctions. The idea of flat-title policies is also itself embedded in a larger set of distinctions that invisibly shape their uptake: a global distinction between East-as-vertical and West-as-flat. At the time of my research, it was widely assumed in South Korea that the office cultures of American companies, such as Apple and Google, were successful in part because those companies were imagined to be flat or hierarchy-less office cultures where employees and bosses called each other by their first names.[6]

For Minjong and some other companies such as KT, the new manager system experiments were abandoned after a few years due to problems of employee resistance, customer confusion, and continued use of the terms from the previous system. KT, after having instituted their version of a manager system in 2006, reverted back with a newspaper headline at the time reading, "Longing for vertical culture . . . KT dumps manager system, back to rank system."[7] The reversion to the five-tier ladder of traditional rankings was seen as a way to boost employee spirit (sagi jinjak), (even though the initial promise of flattening was to increase worker cooperation [eommu gongjo]). A news article reporting on Minjong noted that because of the manager system, the conglomerate had fallen far from everyday work and that employees wanted to return to their old system and old titles. Minjong's unions, too, wanted to return to the policies of a seniority system (hobong) in which ranks were fixed and promotions based largely on time served rather than on annual performance scores.[8] Indeed, when I spoke to manager Choi at Minjong in 2014 during their experiment with a flat system, it seemed that not much had changed from his perspective. He noted that from an HR perspective, there was still a need for differentiating employees: "To differentiate [employees], we have G1, G2, up to G9, in grades. These are written out elsewhere (ddaro)." By the grades, he was referring to internal ranks that HR maintained in its system.

The use of ordinal number ranks without any linguistic embellishment suggested that they were a less visible form of technocratic management that lay
behind the new manager system. Thus, even as the manager system aimed
to project a flat, posthierarchical image onto the Minjong Group and create
a level playing field from which to properly evaluate employees, for HR, and
perhaps for top executives at the group, there was still a need to maintain differentiated grades to keep track of and sort employees.

Many large South Korean groups such as SK Telecom and the media and
fashion company Cheil have, in fact, kept flat reforms among their workforces. Internet and tech companies such as Kakao and Naver have gone even
further with how employees address each other and how employee relations
are structured by organizing teams into larger units called cells (*sel*). In this
sense, there is no paradigmatic company that might reflect ingrained assumptions about South Korean socioeconomic development as marked by either an
inability to adapt to Western standards or a radical imposition of them. What
is more interesting, this chapter suggests, is the relationship between what
one might think of as the surface forms of distinction (such as titles) and the
internal plumbing of distinctions, managed by HR professionals and others.
As I describe in this chapter, HR professionals do not just navigate systems of
personnel management such as performance or promotion; they also navigate
the zone between knowledge about distinctions, what employees learn about
such distinctions, and how employees respond to such distinctions. The chapter shows that the gap between what is made visible to employees (or the public) and what is kept internally is not necessarily one of management obfuscation; it also reflects the complicated nature of managing what I describe as
infrastructures of distinction that lie at the heart of many modern corporate
organizations.

Like physical infrastructures, infrastructures of distinction are not necessarily invisible but are encountered at certain times and places. For the average employee, infrastructures come into focus more at key moments like annual evaluations where their differences vis-à-vis other employees come into
focus. Certain markers like titles might be a matter of everyday identity and
interaction with others, but the larger substratum of distinction-making techniques and processes is not always visible. To HR employees, however, such
infrastructures are fundamentally their "topic" of concern, to borrow a phrase
from science historian Susan Leigh Star.[9] If titles or ranks represent one kind of
surface structure of distinction, other kinds of practices and systems comprise

the infrastructure that keeps track of the elements that make distinctions legible, stable, and legitimate. These include the materiality of HR and IT professionals that tracks people on paper through things such as personnel cards, work histories, and educational credentials and in digital systems such as performance records, salary information, vacation and leave requests, disputes, and education and training history. This infrastructure also includes the systems that keep track of various pieces of activity and evaluation such as entrance exams, promotional exams, feedback systems, and evaluation systems. These various systems reflect a basic function of HR management in South Korea: to facilitate the conversion of people from one type of role to another—from outsiders to insiders and from lower ranks to higher ranks. Conversion techniques require detailed charts and tables that allow qualitative skills to be fairly or evenly evaluated based on specific kinds of work. Helping to keep such infrastructures coherent and intelligible are handbooks, textbooks, and guidelines for HR professionals, as well as private educational training centers or certificate university management programs where mid-level managers or executives go to learn new managerial qualities around problem solving, economic analysis, and management to allow them to remain legible within such infrastructures.

In this chapter, I focus on how HR managers at the Sangdo holding company moved between the management of various aspects of the infrastructures of distinction and how other employees encountered such distinctions. Managers at Sangdo did not undertake any dramatic flattening or even delayering projects during my time there. This does not mean that they were not tinkering with core elements of their own infrastructures of distinction, such as changes to how executives and team managers were evaluated, how work assignments were handed out (as discussed in the previous chapter), how bonuses were distributed, and even how business cards were designed. While much of this work happened in the humdrum everyday of office life, HR managers were keenly aware of how subtle changes in areas of distinction could have an impact on employees who were perceptive regarding changes that might affect their promotions, social standing, and interpersonal relations. The managers were also aware of how attending to different topics brought their own status vis-à-vis subsidiaries and other corporate groups into comparison. Observing the work of HR managers at places such as Sangdo reveals that much of what managers must do is attend to their own infrastructures; they do so, in part, by making sure that problems of distinction do not arise to the surface. This chapter argues that much of what HR managers do is to manage the complex substratum of interpersonal distinctions, particularly the ways that different signs of distinction can come into radical alignment, sometimes unexpectedly, in ways that could undermine the outward stability of such HR systems on which many employees' professional identities seem to hinge. This meant that HR managers are engaged in acts of concealment as much as those of revelation.

Secrecy and the Risks of Hyperdistinction

One day in March 2014, the junior member of the HR team, Ki-ho, who sat adjacent to me printed out a large A3-sized spreadsheet and laid it across his desk. He was reviewing it with team manager Jang. Down the side of the spreadsheet were the names of each of the dozen subsidiaries of the Sangdo Group. Across the top of the spreadsheet were different categories: title system, promotion length time, average salary, annual bonus range, average vacation time, amount given for weddings and funerals, and a few others. In each cell on the spreadsheet, Ki-ho had collected and filled in short details of the respective policy for each company. This document granted the team a partially synoptic view of the basic employment policies of every subsidiary in the group on a comparative basis. They could see that Sangdo First paid more in overtime than Sangdo South and that Sangdo NET did not have a clear vacation policy or holiday bonus plan for its workers. The document operated as a blueprint for understanding each company; it was one of the basic elements of the infrastructure of distinction that the HR team was building from afar. The fact that they were doing so on Excel spreadsheets collected through simple requests to the subsidiaries partly reflected that the holding company had almost no infrastructure to its name before then.

Physical infrastructures, such as water, trash, or roads, are managed by specialized workers whose work remains largely unseen by everyday citizens. The same is true for jobs in large organizations: HR teams are in charge of managing the basic elements of employment in the company. And like other kinds of infrastructure workers, the basics of this work remain largely invisible to outsiders. Ki-ho was not allowed to share that document outside of the HR team; only the team's executive and company owners were allowed to see it. If other workers in the Sangdo holding company came to Ki-ho's desk, he covered it up or placed it out of sight. Even I was only allowed a passing glance at it, briefly over Ki-ho's shoulder. Its leak, even if inadvertent, could have wreaked havoc over the entire workforce of Sangdo. It was the only document of its kind that compared the discrepancies around personnel policies between subsidiaries. Distinctions between subsidiaries could be largely suspected or shared among employees, but an actual elaboration of the policies themselves was largely unknown. Revealing the document could throw off union negotiations, create competitions between subsidiaries, or lead to alienation if certain subsidiaries realized they were getting a different deal from others. For Ki-ho and team manager Jang, the goal was not to influence policies or negotiations across the group directly; rather, it was to begin the first steps toward understanding the wider policies across the Sangdo Group while building out their own infrastructure from the holding company to the wider group.

Much information like this within HR remained secret during my time there: employee information cards, annual evaluations, promotion decisions, salaries and bonuses, and personnel information. This information was stored in paper files, inside locked cabinets, on computer files, and within digital records systems (known as Human Resources Information Systems [HRIS]) and on intranets. The HR team was in charge of managing this information in ways that other employees—including low-level employees in HR themselves—were not allowed to see. Employees could only see their own information and not the information of others, certainly not the broader system or mechanisms by how such things were decided.

Why are the basic materials of such an infrastructure kept secret? Part of the answer is that as many public institutions increasingly come under the logic of a transparency in South Korea and around the world, identity-linked information and data in turn have become highly protected categories.[10] According to South Korea's Personal Information Protection Act, heavy fines can be levied on companies if they share, copy, or move personal information of individual employees to places where it should not be—including in other companies even within a group. The South Korean government regularly provides information and policy advice to employers about how to protect personal information and has strict guidelines about the collection of information, surveillance of employees, storage of data, and destruction of records. The government has also given out fines to companies that do not properly manage the personal information of their employees. Hacking and corporate leaks around personal information are persistent threats.

Part of the answer to the question of secrecy, however, is that such infrastructures are powerful social forces of potential hyperdistinction. By hyperdistinction, I refer to ways of rendering relations through multiple categories
or scales of distinction that appear to overwhelm social relations altogether.
In the nineteenth century, sociologist Georg Simmel first worried about this
problem through the lens of money and its capacity to render all qualitative
aspects of social relations in quantitative terms. Contemporary organizations represent sites not just of monetization or quantification but of an over-
loading of multiple categories of distinction.[11] Organizations of all stripes
amass points of distinction about individuals that, if handled improperly or
released, could create conditions in which individuals are qualitatively and
quantitatively compared across too many points of distinction. In South Korea, the risks of hyperdistinction often occur during a period of annual reviews (*insacheol*) when employees might receive performance evaluations and
certain employees may be promoted. Employees are given grades on their performances (S, A, B, C, or D, with S being the top grade), and depending on
the company or the boss, there might be a forced distribution for each grade.
These grades might also align with year-end bonuses. One popular newspaper
column termed this period at the end of the year as *sinsungsaengsung* (feeling
restless) at the thought of the evaluations.[12] This is partly why the HR department at the Sangdo holding company engaged in strategies of concealment to
minimize potential moral and social hazards if employees became hyperdis-
tinguished from each other in public. These strategies included things such
as releasing the list of annual promotions over email at an unexpected date
and time; the sharing of one's annual performance evaluation in a one-on-
one meeting with an HR manager, in which the manager read the evaluation
to the employee; the use of anonymized league tables between companies to
show workplace satisfaction; and tight control within the HR team of access
to personnel information through IT access controls and things as simple as
keeping information under lock and key.

Attending to Gaps

The space of private team meetings can be one place where the reimagining of
inter-employee distinctions can be entertained and discussed while their wider
social threat can be held at bay. When team manager Jang, assistant manager
Min-sup, and assistant manager Ji-soon, along with me, gathered to discuss the

base wage increases and bonuses for the fifty or so Sangdo holding company employees, the team was dealing with one significant area of responsibility. Until that year, it had been standard to increase wages and bonuses incrementally, always in proportion to rank and seniority. The Sangdo holding company had followed a conventional approach to bonus distribution: proportional in amount by rank and not determined by annual performance grade. That year, however, one of the Sangdo owner-executives had asked the HR managers to develop a new method of bonus distribution based on individual performance grades as a way to motivate younger employees. The directive to the HR team was clear but underdefined. The three members had to figure out how to make bonuses commensurate with individual performances. Their meeting was the first attempt to brainstorm what such a system should look like. They were not only evaluating the technical possibilities for a rational distribution that would meet the executive's wishes; they were also creating a new system of performance pay metrics that would redefine relations among employees and bring their own relationship to subsidiaries into focus.

Team manager Jang began the meeting in a somewhat humorous way by taking a survey of those in attendance: "Should we earn more than our subsidiaries or should we earn less than our subsidiaries compared to their rank-based system? Be honest." He was asking for a vote, and both Min-sup and Ji-soon raised their hands in the affirmative "yes"—the holding company employees should earn more. The specter of democracy was of course satire due to the awkward fact of having to decide their own fates as employees in such a decision. For HR managers, monetary choices can be inherently dangerous as they are a form of commensuration not only between individuals and groups within an organization but between organizations bringing a much wider field of distinction into play. If too much information circulates on salary or bonuses, a company or group itself might become implicitly ranked on the labor market; such information might also throw off union or salary negotiations if it were found out that managers in the holding company received a large pay raise. But it is important to remember that HR managers such as the three at the meeting were not concerned about the fact of receiving money at work per se but were concerned with the proper relationship between work, money, and motivation along with the potential pitfalls that any new combination of those might create.

Maintaining proper gaps between employees has become more complicated in what is known as the performance era (*seong-gwa sidae*) in the South

Korean workplace. This era reflects a time beginning in the first decade of the 2000s when performance grades and performance bonuses (*seong-gwageup*) became new icons of flexibilization and mobility within organizational labor markets. Because bonuses are a variable form of pay associated with both a company's annual performance and an individual's work performance, they have commanded a greater role in corporate employees' basic salary composition, replacing fixed bonuses. (Performance or merit bonuses did exist in the 1990s, but they were smaller in proportion to fixed or shared bonuses.) Many junior employees saw individual performance-based bonuses as a fair recognition for what was otherwise a senior-dominated form of distribution (as they reported on the satisfaction survey described in Chapter 4).

The HR managers knew that scientifically calculating performance pay across different professional categories was not technically possible; it was at best an estimation across many different types of work and a human-based evaluation system (where team managers track and grade their team members). The concern of the HR managers was an ethical one based on proportionality, instead. Team manager Jang initially proposed the idea that the holding company managers should get a proportionally higher bonus (1.5 or 2 times the subsidiary rates) because the work they did at the top of the conglomerate and the qualifications of the managers justified a higher reward. Such a bonus might also mark out the distinctiveness as a more progressive workplace where employees were rewarded, with the possibility that other subsidiaries might follow suit if they saw how motivated holding company employees were. There were other complications, however: they were also concerned with announcing the matter in a politically acceptable way that would lead employees to accept the new terms without harming their own reputation or the dynamics within teams. Abandoning their mock vote, they decided the most sensible thing to do would be to base any raises on the average of what subsidiaries gave so that they would not receive more or less than others in the group. At the end of the brainstorming meeting, the HR managers joked that they should hire a famous comedian, No Heung-cheol, to help announce the decisions to their coworkers. They were already anticipating a difficult reaction to any changes in the bonus scheme, in part because other employees might not see the complexity of the interorganizational calculations they had to consider.

When they did announce the new program later that year, assistant manager Min-sup told me it was supposed to be an "informative" and not a "persuading" meeting. Min-sup began the meeting with a PowerPoint presentation, one that contained only two slides. The first slide announced the change: instead of a shared bonus for everyone in the company, team- and individual-based bonuses would now comprise half of their bonuses. That is, their total bonuses would be based on three kinds of evaluation: one decided by the chairman that applied to everyone equally, another based on ranked grades of teams, and another based on ranked grades of individuals. Min-sup then went on to the next slide, which demonstrated how these changes would affect individual bonuses, using an example of employee "Kim" who got an S grade (the highest) and employee "Lee" who got a B grade. The point of the demonstration was to show that no employee was losing money under the new system, but teams or employees who performed better would be relatively more compensated than the average. His explanation used a comparison between two imaginary employees to specify possible bonuses without revealing real ones.

Despite the HR team's attempt to present the content in a reduced format, the other coworkers in attendance started to badger the team members with questions, pushing the meeting to over an hour in length. One of the major concerns, coming from an older experienced manager, was the gap (*gyeokja*) between grades: "Why was the gap so wide between the S, A, B, C, and D scores?" he asked. He was not opposed to individual bonuses but he was put off by the fact that "S" ranking employees would get twice as high a bonus as those who were "B" ranking.[13] Using that as a platform, members of one whole team began to argue that the HR team had not received enough feedback from the employees about this system before implementing it. The strategy team members said that the timing of performance grades and performance bonuses would not align with the fixed bonus. By the time the meeting ended, one older manager was still complaining to team manager Jang about the division of grades. The manager was suggesting that the gaps between grades (such as S and C) were too wide and would cause disruption and competition among the employees, affecting the team environment.

Team manager Jang and the other HR managers were not happy with how the meeting ended. The other employees were not aware of the complicated mathematics and political calculations about subsidiary bonuses that went into their methodology, which the HR team had been working on for six months. The plan had also been already approved by the chairman and other owner-executives. The employees were mostly focused on potential interpersonal differences related to gaps between employees and the impact on team inter-actions. Even as the HR managers tried to manage the meeting and the release of the information—a system that in theory would not negatively affect any employee—they had to disclose more information about the decision-making process. In defending the work at the meeting, team manager Jang repeatedly emphasized that these were the decisions of the chairman and that the system was benchmarked to industry standards. He also repeatedly depicted himself as an employee like them and not an HR manager, referring to himself as one of the affected employees.

Despite the complaints, the new performance bonus system went into ef-fect the year after I left. Because evaluation grades and bonuses are confiden-tial (and were not given to interns), it was difficult to know what effect they had on employee dynamics, if any. Financial considerations around money were not about the abstract value of money but rather about its relative distribution among coworkers. Even though no employee was losing money, employees fo-cused on gaps with other employees as a site of social risk. The HR managers felt that their technical expertise was being challenged by employees who did not understand the complicated decisions in maintaining an infrastructure of distinction that might benefit them, at least as individuals.

Translating Distinctions

I was asked near the end of my time at Sangdo to help update the translation of job titles into English for the entire Sangdo Group. At Sangdo, different subsidiary companies had developed their own translations for standard job titles. For example, at Sangdo South, *bujang* was translated as "senior man-ager" whereas at Sangdo First it was translated as "general manager." These translations did not reflect what kinds of jobs Sangdo employees were actually doing; they were generalized managerial ranks. The owner-executive asked the HR team to create a more unified system that could indicate what ac-tual functions employees held and to align them with global standards. To the owner-executive, having separate systems was a sign that the Sangdo Group was not unified as a corporate group. The Sangdo holding company HR team was tasked with developing the new system. English translations of job titles existed but were mainly used on business cards. (Even small-time business owners whose business was entirely domestic almost always had an English translation on the back of their business cards.) Compared to other aspects of business, bilingual business cards themselves are functionally rather meaningless. Most employees will neither encounter foreign workers nor use English in their work. Even if they do, most foreigners will have little understanding of what Korean titles mean. However, as small windows of distinction, they carry significant weight in how certain employees or executives come to see their own place—especially vis-à-vis others. They are one of the few points that confirm one's identity in public in a prestige language while indexing that one might speak English or conduct international business.

Updating the translations nevertheless turned out to be a complicated social process. Translating in this sense was never about a pure "linguistic" translation between codes to find the most accurate translation; in the case of English ranks and titles, it was about confirming one set of implicit distinctions embedded in the titles across languages. There were two immediate problems: first, the Korean job title system itself reflects an older system of titles that no longer has reference to actual Korean jobs. For instance, a *bujang* is someone who technically manages a *bu* (a department unit). In the mid-1990s, *bu* went out of fashion with the advent of teams (*tim*), and the department leader was replaced by team leader (*timjang*). According to business scholar Park Won-woo, the shift to teams in South Korea was not just a change in terminology but reflected a new era in business—the metrics and information era—in which top-down control was no longer useful. Instead, organizational ranks should exist to facilitate what is necessary for a business rather than being concerned with promotion alone. The concept of teams, led by team leaders, was first introduced as an effort to combine the motivation necessary to encourage work units to work together and to be a source of team metrics like sales or production.[14] Team managers were simply there to facilitate the work carried out by individual team members. This was implicitly an early form of delayering, as it was one of the first instances in South Korea where seniority was decoupled from responsibility—team leaders were now elected or chosen separately from managerial ranks. Second, American and other global firms had entirely different employment systems and structures. Many Sangdo managers I talked with about the issue were surprised to discover that American companies did not have basic ranks for employees like *sawon*, *daeri*, and *gwajang* that followed a managerial track or progression as in South Korea. The South Korean formal register for job titles is much more elaborate (if complex) than that of the English-speaking countries they thought they might be trying to benchmark against.

After researching different naming standards in the global steel industry, I made two recommendations to team manager Jang. First, I attempted to unify the diverse practices across Sangdo's subsidiaries. Looking across the organizational charts of all the subsidiary companies, I noticed that the person who occupied the CEO role (the highest rank of each company) was called differently in Korean: *sajang, buhoejang, daepyo-isa*, or even *busajang*. These each had their own English translations such as President, CEO/President, Executive Vice President, and Senior Executive Vice President. I recommended that these all be translated as "CEO" in English so that outsiders could understand who the top decision-maker was at each subsidiary. Team manager Jang immediately crossed out my proposed change on his review. He told me that even after a year of working at Sangdo, I had learned nothing about the Korean office. As he explained it to me, titles for executives were very personal and were not simply generic titles. Each executive had a specific title based on his or her career and political decisions. Some CEOs, for example, were called *buhoejang* (literally, vice chairman) because they saw themselves as having an important role—the title itself meant nothing in terms of its literal reference to a place in the organizational structure.

Second, I recommended to change titles for everyone who was currently called a "manager" to "associate." The only real managers (in functional terms) were *timjang* (or "team managers"), not *bujang* or *chajang*. I recommended a new gradation between "associate," "junior associate," and "senior associate." This was similar to how international English-speaking companies labeled their own ranks. Team manager Jang again came back to me and said that if we actually proposed this, all the employees would have negative feelings toward the holding company and would want to "kill us," figuratively speaking. Even if the new term "associate" was more denotationally accurate, the act of changing the translation itself from manager to associate would appear as a demotion, especially for *bujang* and *chajang* (typically the fourth and fifth ranks) who had been in relatively high positions and had been at Sangdo for likely more than a decade. Such a term would be a symbolic demotion in linguistic terms and appear as a further act of subordination if the change came straight from the holding company.

At this point, team manager Jang gave me a lesson in how the infrastructure of titles at Sangdo, and in South Korea more generally, was managed. While I had understood it as an abstract system made up of different albeit imperfect signs, he instructed me that each company had its own kind of formation. Unlike American companies where people fill existing roles, in South Korea, he noted organizations create roles for people, especially as they stay longer in an organization. As individuals become promoted beyond the five basic ranks to upper management and then executive positions, certain positions are created for them to reflect their status. When South Korean companies often carry out rather dramatic structural reorganizations (*gujojo-jeong*) every few years, rearranging how units are grouped and what divisions are called, these are not attempts to realign the business structure to make it more efficient. Rather, they are to realign the organization as new people moved into new positions and distinctions among executives have to be recalibrated. This is why the roles of each Sangdo subsidiary looked so different despite the fact that they were in the same industry and even worked in the same building. Somewhat rare titles such as *damdang* (person responsible), *bubon-bujang* (vice division head), and *bumunjang* (division head), for instance, were conventional terms but they existed as singular labels with specific purposes for each individual organization. This point reflects less the power of vertical authority and more the continued need for what sociologist Erving Goffman called "presentational rituals."[15] Such rituals are ways of signaling one's respect or appreciation to another in a ceremonial fashion. As employees continue to work in an organization, departments such as HR provide them with symbolic gifts by bestowing on them semantically enhanced or simply additional titles. Thus, a successful employee or executive in the South Korean corporate world can end up with three different titles such as *bujang* (a rank of general manager), *yeong-eop damdang* (a function of sales lead), and *timjang* (a managerial function as team leader) all at the same time.[16]

Team manager Jang himself had a formal rank and a title of *suseok* (chief), a title of address extended to all managers above the second level, so he understood these dynamics better than I did. He eventually took over to develop a system of English titles that could be both unified across companies and flexible to the ways executives might read into the change from one to another. He created a new nomenclature that could be flexible, particularly for the highest members of organizations but simplified for the lower levels. This nomenclature resembled a new morphology that could properly convey titles in English yet still be understandable in translation from their Korean counterpart.

Their new job-naming system illustrates the use of common international English titles while also properly translating the gradations among Korean job titles recognizable to every Korean employee. There is even a slight

Table 2.2 Description of new translations for high and low positions at Sangdo

1. English translations for nonexecutives
   buseowon
   Associate

sawon	*daeri*	*gwajang*	*cha/bujang*
Junior Associate	Associate	Senior Associate	General Manager

2. English translations for senior executives
   daepyo-isa   President and CEO
   Exceptions: (bu)hoejang (Vice) Chairman and CEO, for presidents and higher

Note: Some other positions have not been included to preserve confidentiality.

contradiction in the system: even though all nonexecutives (*buseowon*) are described as associates, *chajang* and *bujang* ranks are still labeled as general managers, preserving their differences from lower-level employees. Furthermore, high level positions such as the *daepyo isa* (CEO level) receive more specialized rules and customizations, even though they only represent a few dozen people in contrast to the thousands at lower ranks. The new names were meant to be a "new start to improve communication without the burden of domestic conventions," according to the explanatory slide that accompanied them. Yet, in many ways they reflect the peculiarities of organizational dynamics where HR managers must also give more of their attention to the distinctions of the few: the new translations were accompanied by special rules and exceptions for each high-ranking executive. Thus, the HR managers successfully translated one small piece of distinction (ranks and titles) into English to nominally align with international standards while also reflecting the need to preserve proper ceremonialism in the office. In this sense, managing this infrastructure of distinction was not only about generic organizational categories but about specific ones that were embedded within generic titles, a fact that HR managers made no mention of in their final report.

From Surface to Infrastructure

A 2018 article from an online political magazine of the People's Participation for Social Solidarity (*chamyeo yeondae*) asked, "If they get rid of titles, will organizational culture change?"[17] The author of the article noted that just changing the titles of corporations would not be enough to change vertical Korean organizational cultures into flat American companies. According to the author, this kind of reform merely replicates the "surface" of company culture, particularly that of Silicon Valley start-ups. But it ignores deeper problems. The "fundamental problem," the article said, were other underlying causes such as the "culture of top-down authority, the rigid organizational culture, the fussiness of older men, and the dogmatism of leaders." Such explanations point to deeper kinds of infrastructure that underlie modern organizational problems, such as culture, psychology, and generational differences. It is the psychology of older male managers and leadership, for example, that is often seen as an explanation for deeper problems in fixing infrastructures of distinction.

This chapter has discussed some of the actual management of infrastructures of distinction, recounting the sensitive work around the maintenance of markers such as titles and performance bonuses. I have suggested that this work is more like the maintenance of a physical infrastructure, such as a subway or waterworks, where professionals must manage and maintain important (and at times messy) work from out of sight of others who see such infrastructures as basic sets of surface markers but do not necessarily see the concerns that go into maintaining them. While one might imagine these kinds of activities as the practices of elite experts imposing their own views behind closed doors, there are also ethical concerns at the heart of much of this kind of work, especially where employees might seek proper individual distinction as a desirable outcome. For professionals such as team manager Jang, these everyday sites had to be carefully attended to, whether it be around material things such as the distribution of bonuses or seemingly ceremonial things such as the English language titles. Revelations of too much information about how HR information is gathered or how a new system was made can risk what I've described as hyperdistinction as well as feelings of misalignment in what might be more everyday senses or perceptions of distinctions between team members. Such a view does not mean an end to the idea of flatness or South Korean relations not marked by some concern over the distinctions of those at the top; rather, it points to the ways that distinctions between employees are both a target of reform at the surface and an object of management underneath.

3

Old Spirits of Capitalism

A SPECIAL SECTION in a 2013 issue of the Sangdo Group employee magazine *Our Sangdo* carried the headline "Taking Care of Juniors vs. Working with Seniors." The themed section framed company life as marked by a generational divide between employees: young employees (juniors) and managers (seniors) who fundamentally did not understand each other. The article was written as a series of hypothetical workplace problems together with short advice on how to resolve them. It suggested that both parties had different moral obligations to each other: juniors should be polite to older managers and understand their working histories, while seniors should be respectful to their juniors. The article drew on the positive notion of mentoring (*mentoring*) to suggest that juniors and seniors could bridge the generational divide through warmer one-on-one relations redolent of university junior-senior relations and through better communication (*sotong*). The magazine also had a pledge intermixed with the specific points of advice:

> In the new year 2013
> How about we pledge to do more *sotong*?
> Understanding the differences between me and my coworkers
> While thinking about the other's point of view one more time,
> Between one person and another, connecting a bridge to their heart-mind
>   [*maeum*].
> We hope that we can become a Sangdo Family.

Such a framing around juniors and seniors reflected an awareness of a generational divide that permeated Sangdo and broader discussions of South Korean office life at the time of my research. While the employee magazine was diplomatic about this generational gap and framed the issue as one of misunderstanding that could be overcome with greater intersubjective compassion and communication, other outlets were more direct about generational issues. An anonymous comment on the Sangdo employee survey suggested, "We should set up preventative education program for POWER HARASSMENT," with the last phrase written in all caps in English, while another suggested that "the attitude of an oppressive boss: the boss who says unconditionally 'just do it' (*harasik*) psychologically and physically causes employee stress." In a taxi ride across Seoul one day, a Sangdo holding company manager in his late thirties lamented, in the privacy of the taxi, that Sangdo would only be successful if they could remove the layer of older managers who slowed everything down in the group. A newspaper headline put the problem bluntly with the headline "Old men (*gocham*) have got to go!" and attributing blame to their high salaries accrued over many years that were a financial burden on corporations and by extension on the national economy.[1]

This chapter explores the ways that perceptions of a stark generational divide caused problems in the broader machinery of distinction. At a basic level, this generational divide spanned two categories: older male managers (the seniors) on one side, and younger male and female office workers (the juniors) on the other. Seniors could be generally characterized as career office workers in their forties and fifties who were raised in the early days of South Korean industrialization in the 1970s and 1980s, whose experiences have been extensively shaped by military service, a seniority-based promotion system, and hardworking hierarchical office culture. Juniors could be relatively young office workers who grew up in the period of globalization, consumption, and individualization of the 1990s and have different expectations for boss-subordinate relations, merit-based advancement, and office democracy. Such generational talk is quite common in South Korea (known as *sedaeron*) and is a common frame for locating and explaining structural problems in politics, economics, and society.[2] In the context of office work at Sangdo, whether such a generational divide truly exists with mutually exclusive differences and opposing psychological or demographic characteristics is difficult to say. Office work is stratified by people of all ages who have unique biographic constellations and working styles and can be distinguished or lumped together on any number of accounts. Instead, it is helpful to think of the two generations as socially constructed categories, what anthropologist Eitan Wilf has described as "cardinal points of orientation" for basic economic types.[3] This chapter looks at the way these types—and judgments about them—are highly productive for concretizing problems in the fabric of office life, rather than simply being cultural narratives. Positive and negative qualities of these figures themselves become coded into new techniques of distinguishing office work and office workers.

Distinguishing between generations and broader changes in capitalist discourse are not unrelated. In the 1990s, sociologists Luc Boltanski and Eve Chiapello coined the term a "new spirit of capitalism" to showcase how a new capitalist ethos emerged in France, borrowing from Max Weber's notion of the "spirit of capitalism" that described the role of religious motivation as a key driver for early capitalist practice in the West. Boltanski and Chiapello's new spirit marked the emergence of new discourses around positive management and new figures such as the "managerial hero" who served as an aspirational figure to legitimize changes in the organization of capitalism in France. The figure of the "managerial hero" was contrasted with antiheroes of a previous era such as "petty tyrants" or *cadres* of the French office who served as examples of "yesterday's enemies" for their rigid and bureaucratic style of management.[4] The authors' work highlights how new epochs of capitalism generate their own positive language, roles, behaviors, and organizational structures that can justify or motivate a new kind of capitalism. Implicit in their argument is that an old regime must also be disavowed by making it not only the opposite of what is needed in the present (vertical: flat; slow: fast; rigid: flexible) but also identifying it as a problem to the proper functioning of a new capitalism in the present. That is, the new relies on the disavowal of the old from which it emerges as a point of differentiation. Building on these ideas, this chapter explores the qualities of how such an old spirit of capitalism, manifested in the bad behaviors of aging South Korean male managers, provided a moral argument to delegitimate certain imagined occupants in the office landscape and furnished a recognizable register of office-level sociality that could make room for new forms of a positive workplace environment for a younger generation. While the older male manager may be seen as an economically unproductive member of contemporary corporate society, the figure itself is culturally productive for articulating and motivating new reforms to office social life and corporate practices. It also reflects how even infrastructures of distinction, which aim to create neutral, quasi-scientific schemes between people, can also fall back on broader cultural categories of person-types where the differences between people are already known.

Concerns around older male manager figures in South Korea resonate with broader images of the salaryman in East Asia. The figure of the salaryman has populated academic accounts of East Asian capitalism for half a century, emerging first as an aspirational figure in accounts of Japan, where dutiful white-collar men contributed to the peaceful, postwar transformation of Japan into a middle-class society.[5] Today, the salaryman remains a common sociological point of reference and a figure of aspiration, even as the possibilities for living the salaryman lifestyle (including its broader middle-class connotations) are harder to come by—what Robin LeBlanc has called a "ghost" of a global "breadwinner imaginary" now past.[6] Narratives around white-collar office work in South Korea, marked by similar aesthetic and organizational qualities, nevertheless emerged within a very different context, amid what Kyung-Sup Chang has described as "compressed modernity" in which village agricultural life rapidly turned to urban office-based salary work, part of the great upheaval ushered in by Park Chung-hee's industrialization drives in the 1960s and 1970s.[7] Achieving recognized distinctions such as a *hoesawon* (company member) or simply living *jikjang saenghwal* (the office worker's life) are common reference points to indicate that someone occupies a space in such a modernizing world.[8]

Full-time office work may still be a point of aspiration in South Korea, but the figure of the office worker is not singular. South Korean office workers might readily distinguish those of an older style of office work and those who adopt a newer style, differences that seem to cohere in sharp generational divisions. I suggest that the old style has become categorically differentiated from consideration of the new. In this sense, it is not a point of distinction but rather one of differentiation. In the context of this book, distinction specifies an array of talents, sales numbers, tenure, experience, wealth, or even class markers; such distinctions are fundamentally part of recognized and legitimated groups of people who see themselves as part of such processes of distinction. Differentiation, however, suggests categorical differences that are outside of points of distinction altogether. This tension appears frequently around issues with old age and modern capitalist work, where older employees may appear to be outside the normal understanding of what a worker is and become recategorized into a different social type, justifying their out-of-place status in modern work regimes. In Japan, the sociologist Yuko Ogasawara described the figure of the *ojisan* (uncle or mister) stereotype of older office men in Japan with poor style and boorish habits, regularly lampooned by younger female office workers in gossip and magazines.[9] Anthropologist Anne Alison has similarly described the phenomenon of *madogiwazoku* or the type of "salaryman that 'sits by windows'" because they have failed at getting promoted but cannot be fired.[10] The same phenomenon has also been present in American discourses around the staidness of management: in the 1990s, US business discourse promoted explicit ideas of "new management" that sought to transform administration-oriented managers into free agents who could contribute to organizational goals through discrete areas of knowledge, not delegations of power.[11] In contrast, older managers have been castigated, as in anthropologist Karen Ho's description of negative accounts of older Wall Street workers described as "clock-watching, stagnant, fat, lazy, dead wood that needs to be pruned."[12] The aesthetic of a new Silicon Valley management style marked by casual dress code, flat structures, and informal communication takes inspiration directly from its opposition to the vertical, formal, and serious images of office cultures in the past that cohered directly in the figure of the organization man and his (individuality-denying) gray flannel suit captured by William Whyte.[13]

In this regard, old spirits (or figures or types) are not just ushered off stage but play a vital role in how new corporate programs shape the structural and oppositional character of new spirits themselves. In South Korea, a markedly older and gendered office worker has emerged not as a relic of past national success or industrialist nostalgia but as what Erving Goffman would have described as a "figure of alterity." Figures of alterity are reviled or taboo social types who act as models of deviance against which other identities are rendered normal and unmarked.[14] Such figures do not have to exist demographically to be imbued with hidden power. They can also appear as represented figures, enacted in specific types of people and in popular media. Older male managers have become easy to locate as the source or embodiment of a host of social problems related to the negative aspects of unfair distinction and unwanted participation in the South Korean workplace.

A Divided Figure

During the period of my fieldwork in Seoul, discussions of older men and their bad habits abounded. This included discussion of older men's bad habits in public (such as taking up too much space on public transportation) and their bad humor (*ajae* jokes), along with causal attribution of their negative effect on South Korean society.[15] Within this, there were also negative media depictions of older male managers in corporate settings: these images had recognizable visual and linguistic features such as a rough voice quality, outdated office wear, the use of half speech or informal talk to subordinates (*banmal*), emotional volatility, and the depiction of illicit behaviors such as drinking, smoking, or taking bribes. These media characterizations of older male managers were often embedded within interactional routines that involved conflicts with markedly younger (male and female) employees who were staged as innocent victims of an oppressive corporate culture manifest in the older male manager. In contrast, younger male and female office workers were depicted as sincere, progressive, and able to express meta-commentary in contrast to their aloof and unchanging bosses. A common scene might involve an older manager bursting into a fit of anger at the poor quality of a subordinate's work or making coworkers go for an unwanted after-work drink. These scenes frequently took place within scenes of office work itself—the moment of submitting documents, making presentations, walking down the hallway, or leaving work, such that the figure of the older managers appeared to permeate all corners of office life from work to (supposedly) non-work.

In the popular graphic novel turned television drama, *Misaeng* (*An Incomplete Life*), the sympathetic protagonists of Sales Team #2 of the fictional corporation One International face various internal enemies around the office: chief among these is general manager Ma played by the actor Son Jong-hak. In the drama, general manager (*bujang*) Ma represents the old guard who has *ggondaeryeok* (old-man power), not just within One International but within South Korean work life more broadly, for his repeated outbursts of anger and misogynistic comments toward female employees. As a sign of his power, lower-level male managers below him reconfigure their own teams and relations in fear of what reaction they might garner from Ma, creating multiple tiers of stress and groveling. Ma receives his moral (if not organizational) comeuppance when in a large meeting, his hidden history as a sexual harasser comes out and he reveals to a room of subordinates his outdated views on women's place in the South Korean office that even junior men know is publicly indefensible.

The figure of the older male manager derives its distaste precisely from what anthropologist Marshall Sahlins described as acts of "negative reciprocity"—acts that try to get something without giving by abusing someone else's time, labor, or dignity.[16] In this sense, it is not simply one who drinks excessively but one who forces others to drink against their will; not one who shows diligence by working late but one who forces others to work late.[17] And these singular interactional violations are regularly invoked not just as a corporate problem but also as a national problem. In cultural critic Jun-man Kang's terms, South Korean society as a whole is composed of a dynamic around *gap* (alphas) and *eul* (betas). Social elites are often targeted for their negative behavior (*gapjil*, akin to alpha abuse) toward commoners or service workers for whom small mistakes are treated as major affronts. A frequently recurring (but not only) example of the alpha type is the older male manager. This was the case of the *ramyeon sangmu* (ramen executive) in 2013. A male corporate executive berated a female airline attendant for improperly cooking his instant noodles on a flight. In this case, the beta is a low-ranking employee or service worker who endured emotional abuse at an older person's hand.

This kind of dichotomization follows some familiar binaries of contrasting types found elsewhere in South Korea: global-local, old-young, traditional-modern, and rural-urban.[18] These differentiations, such as among workers or within genders, can help demarcate harder boundaries of institutional belonging or presence, going farther than just categories of distinction alone. For instance, anthropologist Hyun Mee Kim described how, in the wake of the Asian Financial Crisis of 1997, blue-collar steel workers, once heralded as the flowers (*ggot*) of the labor force, began to differentiate among themselves in binary terms, as those with skills and those without skills, as new ideas about economic productivity started to trickle down and create a new social division around work. Similarly, anthropologist Jesook Song described how categories of the deserving and undeserving unemployed emerged after the crisis, creating a sharp difference between those who contributed to the national economy, and thus deserved welfare, and those who did not.[19]

Despite the many distinctions, gradations, and organizational relationships that comprise office life, the generational focus of the office has effectively bifurcated office workers: one marked and one unmarked. The marked position of the older male manager stands as a figure of alterity, not only because of qualities that do not fit but as a central causal block in more utopian forms of merit-based office work. This is visualized through a range of (perceived) qualities: his non-productive presence, weight on the economy, harm to social progress, and parasitic presence on others' professional achievements. Because of his inherited high status (as a long-serving employee who cannot be fired), he is seen as not worthy to occupy such privileged spots in an economy premised on individual advancement and merit-based distinction. This resonates with a reliable South Korean frame in which the past is seen as rough, harsh, and undeveloped, qualities that inhere in people and objects, such as the quality of voices, as broader indexes of both class mobility and modern development.[20] Frequently depicting older male managers as not only outdated and old but abusive, inefficient, or self-profiting means that they are not just out of place but are hurting those in the present. It also provides justification for dramatic workplace changes from legitimate figures of organizational authority such as company ownership or HR departments.

Encountering Older Male Managers

For rank-stratified employees in the Korean office, identifying who is an older manager (and who is not) is different from how they might be configured in the media. The distinction between management and labor, top and bottom, is not always clear in an office setting, as many job titles encode manager (-jang) in them, even for lower-level ranks such as assistant manager (gwajang). Furthermore, due to annual cohort hiring and regular promotion intervals every four or five years, offices have large arrays of individuals with gradations of authority in terms of working tenure, work responsibilities, biographical histories, and other social distinctions. Moreover, office environments themselves are complex and are marked by multiple modalities of documentation, interaction, and other forms of literacy that structure local participation (such as meetings) and through which authority relations are mediated. In this sense, it is rare to encounter highly coherent tropes or images of older managers in the office. This makes them no less salient, however, as traces of this figure can appear in almost any kind of office activity or narrativization. For male managers in their thirties and forties with whom I interacted most often at the Sangdo holding company, complaints about older male managers were frequent, reflecting both the younger managers' insider awareness of the social landscape and a pragmatic attempt to distance themselves from being considered as the wrong kind of older manager in turn.

While having lunch with a team of employees from another Sangdo department, the boss, executive Kang, asked me what new projects the HR team was working on. I relayed that HR was developing a new 360-degree feedback

Table 3.1 Examples of qualitative contrasts in executive Kang's impromptu description

A. Emergent contrasts in executive Kang's narrative	
Older Korean manager	Global manager
Retaliating against feedback	Accepting of feedback
Losing composure	Maintaining composure
Working at Korean company	Working at global company
Twenty-year workers	[none]
Control-oriented/nitpicking	Visionary
B. Imagined speech of older male managers	
Korean	*English translation*
geu seggi nugunyago	[asking] "who is that SOB"
nuga sseonyago	[asking] "who wrote this"
jal gochyeora	[saying] "fix it well" [that is, "you know what to write"]

technique for the development of executives and team managers. This kind of feedback, originally popularized in American management theory, is a form of evaluation in which subordinates, peers, and superiors provide anonymous feedback about an individual (usually a manager). Executive Kang, himself having worked for an American consulting firm in Seoul prior to joining Sangdo, was familiar with the technique. He was convinced that the HR team at Sangdo would have a tough time implementing it, because more traditional South Korean managers would not be able to handle the feedback: it conflicted with their common mode of authority—giving, rather than receiving, feedback. These managers, he said, would be shocked and unable to control their anger at gossip about them from below, while American managers were more able to handle blunt feedback. In painting emergent contrasts between different types, noted in table 3.1, executive Kang marked out a division between managers who can adapt to things global and those who cannot, those who can stay calm and those who explode, enfiguring the imaginary South Korean manager as not fit for modern feedback techniques. In doing so, he used different reported speech elements to voice the manager who, upon getting feedback from his subordinates, would retaliate against them with particularly harsh language.[21]

Here, executive Kang used a distinction between American and South Korean managers as a way to make a distinction between South Korean managers.[22] Citing this figure through contrasts and marked voicings grounds his own identity partly in oppositional terms. Kang himself was only in his mid-forties but he was demographically and organizationally indistinguishable from the older-type managers who were of similar rank or age. In fact, his position was higher and his age lower than some of the recognizable old men around the office.

After this exchange, executive Kang went further, enacting a mock 360-degree feedback session right at the lunch table: he asked his team members what style of manager they thought he was. One of his team members, a junior manager, commented that he was a "visionary dictator." Another followed by saying that he was a "visionary facilitator." Both used English loanwords and garnered laughs for the obvious over-the-top flattery. The jokes here were double layered: in one sense, they were telling the executive what he wanted to hear by showering him with phony praise. In another sense, they were also avoiding specifically labeling him one or the other type, instead combining them into oxymoronic combinations (visionary with dictator), which executive Kang and the other team members found quite clever. Even though Kang took advantage of his situational authority to put his team members on the spot, he nevertheless proved his own point: he could handle direct teasing from his own subordinates without exploding. In this setting, then, the figure of the older manager provided inspiration for working out what kind of subjects the executive and managers thought themselves to be. The imagined figure has a narrative utility for amusement or humor, even in the absence of any real such manager present.

More than just characterological distinctions, having a reflexive stance to the office and its characters can mark one as an experienced lay ethnographer of the office itself, especially via complaint.[23] That is, the act of hunting for signs marks one not just as the opposite in a pair of manager types but as one who demonstrates better analytical qualities. Team manager Jang in HR frequently exhibited savvy at finding signs of older manager presence around the office. As we daily rode the elevator or talked in the hallway, he frequently alerted my attention to the invisible aspects of the older manager on our floor or in the tower in general. The targets of his rebukes were *oldeuboi* (old boys), a term that refers narrowly to tight-knit male cliques from middle or high school.[24] The term can also refer to those who have worked at one company or conglomerate their entire careers, are trained in diverse managerial fields, and maintain strong company loyalty.[25] At the Sangdo holding company, *oldeuboi* referred to men who had started their careers at a Sangdo subsidiary and for various reasons had been transferred up to the holding company later in the careers. These kinds of managers were on teams such as auditing, performance management, and accounting that required thorough knowledge of and experience with the conglomerate's various businesses; other teams such as PR, HR, strategy, or the legal team were composed of more general experts brought in from outside. Team manager Jang, himself a transplant from another conglomerate, had an aversion to the old boy-style of managers precisely because they appeared to be rank loyalists—eager to appear as yes-men for higher up executives or owners—but were not necessarily committed to the company's future in a more abstract sense. (Some managers, even across HR, differed in the degree to which they thought management training was an effective use of resources; Jang was affirmatively on the side that older managers could not be retrained or reeducated to be better managers and that promotion of competent team managers would be better.)

During my research at Sangdo, I received a majority of my background information on the group from team manager Jang, in part because he was effectively my boss during my work at Sangdo. During smoking breaks outside, we would have a chance to chat one-on-one. At those times, he would often help me interpret different acts or events around the office, including after I had spoken with other managers. For instance, when I had a chat with another team manager who used a peculiar phrase to describe office life (*ageuro ggangeuro*), team manager Jang told me that it was an old phrase used in the military (similar to "no guts, no glory"). When I interviewed the outgoing CEO before his retirement, he spoke of Sangdo and Sangdo people as *uryanga* (hearty kids). When I mentioned this phrase to team manager Jang, he laughed a bit, noting that it was a phrase used in the 1970s—and a sign that the CEO was truly from the generation that believed hard work was the main ingredient for success. Such a sentiment might have been true in the heyday when much of the South Korean economy was premised on the volume of production and assembly of commodities, but it would not suffice in today's more complex and competitive steel market in which South Korea was a leading player but where state-run Chinese steel firms were outproducing everyone else, to the detriment of the market. Jang also expressed some moral concerns: on one occasion, he expressed concern about how a new male junior employee was taken out drinking with older managers who made the junior employee pay for his own food and drinks. His concern was that it was irresponsible for managers to make a junior team member, especially a new one, pay for his own meal.

By marking off features of these other men's behavior, team manager Jang framed himself as a friendly, progressive manager. He expressed this in ways that contrasted the familiar tropes of older managers, such as telling his own employees to go home on time, speaking to them in polite or neutral speech, and pointedly asking for their honest opinions in meetings. In many ways, these were emergent across different activities: whereas other team managers had formalized team meetings in the conference room, Jang would hold them in cozy coffee shops outside the building; whereas other team managers took their employees to go drinking after work, Jang encouraged playing games, going to fun restaurants, or singing karaoke (*noraebang*) together. (As I discuss in Chapter 6, however, even these categories of fun embedded their own elements of coercion.) It is worth noting that the age differences between team manager Jang and other managers around the office was slight—all were between their late thirties and early fifties. However, for him, they seemed of an entirely different generation, qualities that more likely reflected different class backgrounds, education, and work experience. Jang, for instance, had gone to a top university in Seoul, lived in three different countries, and spoke four languages as part of his work as an international HR manager. The lifelong managers at Sangdo more commonly had graduated from regional Korean universities, gotten their starts at a local Sangdo subsidiary, moved up to Seoul at various points in their careers, and had to attend English-language classes for continual promotion. Nevertheless, having the acuity to analyze the presence of these signs—especially the more covert they were—also became a higher-order sign of his institutional knowledge, an icon of the expert analyst quality that some Sangdo holding company managers saw in themselves.

New Countercultures

In 2010, the national Ministry of Gender Equality and Family promoted a new office policy known as Family Day (*gajogui nal*). On Family Day, typically every Wednesday, government employees were forced to leave work at the official stopping time (usually 5:30 p.m.) to go home and spend time with their families. Many corporations also adopted the policy as a sign of alignment with government goals and an indication of their progressive work cultures. A few of the Sangdo Group companies had also adopted the policy. One office I observed played a song over the company loudspeaker at 5:30 p.m.

sharp to remind employees to leave. A few minutes later, employees from the HR department circled the floor to encourage stragglers to get out. By forcing employees to leave early, this policy appears to combat South Korea's global reputation for long work hours (which, since the time of my research, has witnessed even further legal and technocratic interventions into leaving on time). The particular shape of the policy and the way it was enforced, however, provide a clue as to what the underlying cause of these long hours seemed to be. The policy encourages being away from work and the pressures of being attuned to one's superiors, which might occur as one's obligations are torn. On one hand, there are legal or contractual allowances to leave when work is deemed to be finished (at 5:30 p.m.), and on the other hand are one's personal obligations to a boss to leave when the boss's work is finished. To leave at the precise time that work is finished (*kal-twoegeun*) or to leave when one might not have any work tasks can be considered an act of selfishness or even recalcitrance.[26] Thus, when HR employees walked through an office, they were severing the invisible chains of authority between team manager and team member that link signs of visible self-sacrifice to relations of fealty between boss and subordinate.[27] The Family Day policy created a contrast through a poetic reversal; instead of staying late with fictive kin coworkers, the policy emphasized going home early to be with one's real kin.

Other corporate culture reforms pick up more subtle cues around where to locate office improvements. When I spoke with the HR director of Sangdo South, another subsidiary in the Sangdo Group, he told me of the myriad of new office policies his department had initiated for improving what is called *sanae munhwa* (internal company culture). These included the following: (1) an eco-office program that installed indoor plants in each team area; (2) the institution of after-work sports leagues such as bowling, hiking, and soccer; (3) a billiards tournament; (4) small-group meetups for workers of similar ranks; and (5) new guidelines for company after-hours socializing (*hoesik*). The first, the eco-office, is an attempt to bring nature into the office space itself, an otherwise bare arrangement of desks that might follow an implicit rank-stratified pattern of desks and computers. The second, third, and fourth policies, however, were meant to promote alternative socializing activities that emphasize collective, fun, team-based activities. It is these activities that exhibit a degree of distinction from older manager-marked activities, like drinking at night, that are unhealthy, hierarchical, and parasitic for team-based relations. And in the fifth policy, HR managers redefined *hoesik*, an activity that generally connotes South Korea's corporate drinking culture, around its literal meaning of company dining. The guidelines his team made suggested that teams and managers could consider *hoesik* as doing volunteer work, reading books together, or going to the movies with coworkers as possible substitutes. This image of wholesome activities was reinforced in the Sangdo employee magazine, where colorful spreads in every issue portrayed two or three employees (usually a young male and a young female employee together) engaged in small-group activities such as cooking, coffee tasting, or paper making, reinforcing an image in complete contrast to typical drinking events—nonalcoholic, gender-equal, pro-social, and creative (rather than destructive) forms of *hoesik* done during the daytime.

One of the most public policies adopted by large corporate groups during my research was the "119 policy." This number, 119, is the national emergency telephone number in South Korea. The policy stipulates that company credit cards should only be used to pay for "1" restaurant, with "1" type of alcohol, until "9" p.m. Anything beyond those conditions should not be covered by company credit cards. (Some companies instituted their own variations, such as "111" or "112" to express some creative difference.) The effect was to officially minimize time in quasi office-related activities by cutting off managerial authority to use discretionary funds excessively. Similarly, another program known as *keullinkadeu* (clean card) was also widely adopted among South Korean companies, in which attempts to use company cards at bars with illicit names or any attempt to swipe a company card after midnight would be refused electronically and then flagged for auditing (late-night bars have coded, but recognizable, names). Together with these policies, a new lexicon of descriptors for *hoesik* also emerged, distancing it from its more illicit connotations of excessive drinking and sponsoring trips to hostess bars. These terms describe it as *geon-ganghan* (healthy), *geonjeonhan* (wholesome), or simply *isaek hoesik* (alternative).

The older managerial stereotype is not directly named in these policies but is indirectly cued by mere mention (such as *hoesik*) or topical focus (such as emphasis on leaving on time). This indirectness resembles forms of corporate doublespeak or oxymorons usually signaled to the public as part of virtuous PR campaigns.[28] Given that campaigns in South Korea are equally directed to employees, such indirectness reflects the delicate nature of castigating a perceived subgroup of current employees. Attempts to restrict or punish drinking may be seen as overtly targeting a certain group, but positively encouraging

Table 3.2 Indirect references to activities or actions surrounding older managers

Korean	Direct translation	Actual policy
myeong-ye toejik	emeritus retirement	incentivized early retirement
isaek hoesik	alternative company dining	non-drinking work events
hoching supyeonghwa	title horizontalization	rank reductions
samjin auteu	three strikes [and you're] out	performance-review based dismissal
illyeok jeokchae haeso	workforce accumulation resolution	fixing overstaffing
keullin kadeu	clean card	ban on illicit use of company credit card

movie watching or book clubs cannot be easily misattributed. Internal phrasing and narratives contrast with treatment of managers in the public realm, where harsh and moralizing descriptors of specific individuals circulate. This is also visible in the basic distinction between words for old men that circulate in public (*oldeuboi*, *gocham*, or *ggondae*) that place emphasis on their age, versus their internal reference where managers are referred to neutrally, as *wit-saram* (those above), or even affectionately, as *seonbae* (seniors), akin to a university mentor. This pattern of reference—critical in the public sphere, indirect in the company sphere—does not mean that such policies merely acquiesce to older male managers. In fact, this antiregister directly targets personnel issues surrounding older managers using flowery, positive, or neutral terms, as listed in table 3.2. Terms such as *myeong-ye toejik* (emeritus retirement) refer to programs for coerced early retirement, while a term such as *samjin auteu* (three strikes and [you're] out), a baseball term that refers to a general policy for all employee evaluations, is one specifically geared to those who might receive bad evaluations as managers over multiple years.

Corporate policies like these suggest a stance against proverbial father figures, both from a labor standpoint (as seen by a number of early retirement policies and new evaluation schemes discussed in the next section) and from a social standpoint (as seen by the internal crackdowns on illicit activities). But what is important to note is that these terms put the problems of older male managers within a register of conventional corporate management distinctions like labor management, proper financial accounting, or company-culture promotions rather than social categories of castigation. As I discuss in the next section, however, creating corporate-level distinctions instead of complete differentiations generated its own problems in terms of cleanly separating older male managers from others.

Modeling Managerial Qualities

Executive Cho's HR team in the Sangdo holding company had the task of implementing new policies that would create objective evaluations for executives and team managers across the entire group. (Executives and team managers were the only two levels at which the headquarters department had the authority to operate within the bounds of labor laws.) Modeling of distinctions among executives and managers can lend more legitimacy to efforts to separate out their imagined qualities. For executive Cho and team manager Jang, this was a matter of their professional expertise in HR planning. Even though they both had intuitive senses of which men on their floor or in the broader group constituted old boys, any formal assessment of them—either to demote them as team managers or to build a case for their dismissal—would have to be mediated through a rational and objective process divorced from their own opinions and biases and based on recognizable and legitimate techniques. This reflects a heightened attention in South Korean bureaucratic genres and techniques to appear as neutral as possible on paper. This is not necessarily to achieve scientific objectivity per se but to avoid counter claims of bias or targeting. To separate good and bad managers would require the creation of a technique that could actually enact such objective distinctions that might align with their perceptions of social differences—but it would also have to be applied to every executive and team manager equally, including themselves.

The program they created, called (as a pseudonym) the New Sangdo Development Program (NSDP), provided a new model for evaluating team managers and executives based on a range of factors. This was created with the particular idea that there were many executives and team managers who had been promoted as a matter of seniority but were not fit to be managers. The basis of this model was not financial performance or career history but the abstract notion of fitness or appropriateness (*jeokjeolseong*) that a team manager or executive would possess as a condition for maintaining their managerial responsibility (but not necessarily their position as an employee). Evaluations as part of NSDP at Sangdo were intended to draw a comprehensive picture of managerial qualities that captured different aspects of leadership behavior with the goal of creating a robust set of metrics that could objectively adjudicate between well-fitting and ill-fitting leadership types. Because the process of the NSDP evaluation had to be comprehensive and objective, however, it could not show any sign of favoritism or interpretive subjectivity. Of further difficulty was that the method also had to properly capture regularities in interactional behavior, over a period of one year, in a clearly metricized way. After conferring with different consulting companies and scouring books and websites for appropriate methods, surveys, and visualization techniques, the HR team eventually decided to use its own customized 360-degree feedback survey and platform.

Originally developed in the US in the 1950s, 360-degree feedback (*360-do pyeong-ga* or *damyeon pyeong-ga*) is a personal development technique that spread throughout the American business community beginning in the 1990s. With the increase in South Korean businessmen attending US business schools, the global spread of US management consulting firms in South Korea, and the shock of the Asian Financial Crisis of 1997, South Korean companies also began to use 360-degree feedback to evaluate managers and executives. In 1998, even progressive President Roh Moo-hyun mandated 360-degree feedback to be used to evaluate upper-level government bureaucrats.[29] A typical 360-degree process involves the distribution of a standardized survey to an individual's superiors, peers, and subordinates with whom they interact frequently and who can comment on their behavior and aptitude. Survey questions often ask about qualities of work, such as teamwork, leadership, decision-making, or problem-solving. Once results are collected and tabulated, an individual is shown the aggregate and anonymized results so they may become aware of their own weaknesses and begin to improve them.

The HR team developed three different survey question types: the first method utilized 5-point Likert scale questions that asked respondents to note how often they had observed certain behaviors of their team manager or executive, from "always observed" to "almost never observed." The second method was a forced-choice method between two contrasting but positive qualities, again based on their observational experience. The third method asked evaluators to grade subject-area competency in a range of areas such as business knowledge, analytical skills, and strategic planning ability. Throughout, the survey questions embedded seemingly neutral distinctions between different types, such as those who "allow open thinking" versus those who "play by the rules," those who "emphasize new ideas" versus those who "emphasize efficiency." These categories, unwittingly or intentionally, recreated a basic imagined distinction between the style of experts at the holding company (as knowledge workers) and the opposing skills of subsidiary managers or older executives (as bureaucratic rule followers).

Each of these three areas concealed any higher-order characterization of bad managers by avoiding direct questions while also forcing employees to choose between obviously preferred types, preventing any tendency for score inflation. Only after the survey results were complete were answers rendered into superordinate categories. The first set of questions correlated to values by using behavioral observations to assess whether the manager or executive was living up to the ideals of the group. The second correlated with leadership style to indicate what kind of leader one was, based on contrasting features. And third, work execution, judged managerial aptitude against a standard set of processes involved in managing. Each of these selected different managerial qualities that could scale up to create a composite image of managerial ability, whose different metrics might indicate relative fitness for their position. Taken together, these qualities captured the comprehensive features of an ideal manager. The potential uses of these were not as blatant as simple evaluation and dismissal, however. The HR team envisioned creating ideal-type manager styles for different office functions, such as finance or strategy, so that a manager who was a controlling type in a department that needed a forward-looking type might be seen to be the wrong fit and justify the relegation of the team manager title to another or a transfer them to the right team.

As a form of 360-degree feedback, the NSDP could rely on the voices of those in the surround to effectively weigh in on a manager's appropriateness on a range of levels, thereby removing HR or ownership as the evaluation's source. In order to ensure that these observations were accurate, however, the survey was also framed as a feedback survey meant to help an executive or manager improve his or her skills, not necessarily as a device that would directly impact the evaluation of a superior. This neutrality then had to be partially concealed through the neutral language that employees were given when filling out the survey. The impact of the survey depended on secrecy of its ultimate purpose, a fact that was awkwardly revealed to me one day in the elevator with team manager Jang and another holding company member on the strategy team. I was asking Jang about what the point of such questions would be. Jang suggested that they were just for improving executives' skillsets and leadership. However, as we got out of the elevator and were out of sight of the other strategy team member, Jang pulled me into a small room to tell me to be careful about revealing the evaluative purposes of NSDP even among younger coworkers. If those filling out the survey, including peers and subordinates, knew their opinions would result in something negative for their boss, they might change their answers—a moral hazard for subordinates who might fear retribution or attempt to curry favor.[30]

After the initial run of the 360-degree feedback results and analysis, I am not certain how the NSDP ultimately affected specific team managers or executives across the group, as individual personnel records were kept confidential and executive decisions were made behind closed doors. I had heard one passing mention that a number of executives at one subsidiary were let go as they had received poor results. (Executive contracts, despite their high positions, are not protected employee categories like regular managers who cannot be fired due to poor results.) It was not clear if they were let go because of revenues or the NSDP results. Nevertheless, I wondered if employees in that subsidiary would be happier without those particular executives. One unexpected issue was that the survey generated results for those who were not expected to receive bad results. A minor commotion ensued among one team when an executive in the headquarters, himself decidedly not an old boy, received some of the lowest evaluations in the whole group, reflecting the fact that bad managerial distinctions could cohere in persons outside of the figure of alterity itself.

From Differentiation to Distinction

This chapter has discussed the ways that the figure of the South Korean older male manager has become a differentiated figure or a figure of alterity. Older male managers are not only seen as outdated but as parasitic on future forms of merit-worthy capitalism. This figure of alterity is not a social outcast but precisely one who lies at the heart of contemporary capitalism's most desired positions. While publicly circulating, media discourses configure the older manager as a coherent person who reacts emotionally and abuses others through a limited set of recognizable behavioral traits (usually enacting the role of the villain), the coherency of the figure is more complex within actual organizations, where it might appear as a form of represented discourse, office commentary or as an indirect target of office culture programming. This complexity produces a less coherent figure but, strangely, one that also seems to permeate all dimensions of office life, making the process of ridding corporate life of the negative influences that seem to cohere in older male managers an ongoing effort, as any individual instance of office relations gone awry can be taken as a sign of older manager influence or a reversion back to old norms and social control.

South Korea supposedly entered the performance era in the period after the Asian Financial Crisis when a host of new changes was supposed to have brought the new spirit of capitalism from the West to them. Why then are the ghosts of the office place past still being fought, especially when similar social and labor divisions seemed to emerge at the turn of the new millennium? Certainly, any total change to office life and the eradication of negative elements is a slow, uneven process, especially in a country where the floor of labor protections for regular work is still quite high and the elaborations of corporate life in society are wide. Another answer may be that old figures are perennially a useful target as a basis for differentiation, and that the old-new binary will always be productive for articulating change, especially in a place such as South Korea where developmental narratives around regressing into the past weigh heavily on the national conscience. In other words, there will always be some semiotic variety of "old" that might be blamed for social and economic problems as long as old age continues to remain a marked social status in capitalist societies more generally. However, there is also a subtle tension that directs attention and causality toward the problems and problematic characters of office life from whom new ideas are crafted and new programs are created. They take attention away from the fact that workplace distinctions and the various infrastructures that organize them, however meritocratically, are in the service of creating stratified persons in organizational ranks, titles, and grades. In other words, a focus on particularly negative forms of hierarchy as a moral, cultural, or simply interpersonal problem can sanitize the more generally accepted pursuit of desired corporate positions, which has come to be seen as separate from issues of negative hierarchy and not, perhaps, their cause.

The relationship between differentiation and distinction, as I have discussed them here, is an important one. On one hand, it captures two ways of conceptualizing how modern institutions sort people. Michel Foucault in *Madness and Civilization* understood that at the heart of modern institutions, including education, prisons, psychiatric practice, and legal systems, lies a fundamental differentiation between the normal or abnormal or the reasoned or the mad.[31] In the context of the office, modern distinctions around merit and achievement are premised on including those who are not figuratively "mad"— precisely the kind of manager who does not have a fundamental defect or live with the norms or standards of a previous era. Images of older managers being out of step with interactional norms, being emotionally volatile, and indulging in excessive behavior can be thought of as one form of modern economic madness for which such actors should be relegated elsewhere because they do not categorically fit. (Indeed, for some team managers who left Sangdo, I rarely heard of what happened to them or where they went.) On the other hand, distinction as a set of gradations, ranks, or scalable marks that resonate with class markers reflects Pierre Bourdieu's concerns in his classic work *Distinction*.[32] For Bourdieu, forms of evaluation, promotional marks, prestige brands, and company-sponsored activities are ways that the middle classes come to distinguish among themselves through the accrual of various forms of symbolic capital (along with their judgments on consumer and cultural goods). The great machinery of distinction-making techniques and policies organized and managed by HR provides the distinctions appropriate to those only who are seen to have the proper class (aspirational) qualifications. This is why contract workers, cleaning staff, personal drivers, and other labor categories are often excluded from such distinction granting mechanisms in the first place.

While older manager types might be thoroughly recategorized as a different social type worthy of social criticism, official judgments about them must nevertheless be channeled through various infrastructures of distinction. This is why the HR department at the Sangdo holding company had to develop evaluations for all executives and team managers that had to be couched in best practice forms of evaluation such as 360-degree feedback, and why additional efforts had to conceal the hoped-for goals of the program. The fact that the program, at least in its first running, partially had contradictory results reflects the way that the expert managers were also beholden to legitimated techniques of distinction. As I take up in the next chapter, there were other risks that could befall the holding company as it attempted to redefine the basis for distinction within the group. The potential failure of such sociotechnical projects could also reveal them to be less the experts than the were purported be.

4

Surveying Sangdo

SURVEYING IS A UBIQUITOUS TECHNIQUE in South Korea for gathering and narrating sentiment about the internal thoughts of citizens, employees, students, and others.[1] This is particularly true across the corporate sector: job recruitment websites such as JobKorea and Incruit regularly conduct and publish surveys on the attitudes of job seekers to give a sense of changing attitudes toward work culture: "What do workers think of end-of-year parties?" "What are common reasons people leave their companies?" "What do workers think of work-life balance at their companies?" Surveys act as key points of reference for evidence-based decision-making, management, and policymaking. The HR departments of the Sangdo Group regularly conducted their own annual and semiannual employee surveys in the form of satisfaction or engagement surveys. Similarly, the PR department conducted surveys and focus groups on Sangdo brand awareness, and the internal magazine group published internal surveys related to its quarterly themes.

Surveys offer formalized methods for reading various aspects of behavior, opinion, or politics, but this does not mean that they operate without artifice. "The opinion survey," Pierre Bourdieu wrote, "treats public opinion like the simple sum of individual opinions, gathered in an isolated situation where the individual furtively expresses an isolated opinion. In real situations, opinions are forces and relations of opinions are conflicts of forces. Taking a position on any particular problem means choosing between real groups."[2] For Bourdieu, the use of majority public opinion was not just a reflection of an existing public but had taken on its own quasi-religious political force in its ability to assert certainty of a collective will.[3] Even if surveys or opinion polls are a reduction of politics to matters of checking a box, they nevertheless have come to mediate how different kinds of organizations and institutions read themselves back to each other. As surveys have become legitimated points of collective truth claiming, they have become a valued genre for offering technocratic participation. That is, they are both a genre of distinguishing (and ranking) opinions through numbers and a form of democracy—from which majority opinion might be gleaned from a sum of numbers. They have also become a powerful channel for determining who can represent the collective sentiments of "the people" to make truth claims within institutions. Things like satisfaction or engagement surveys may be clichéd—particularly because of their use across the consumer and retail spectrum—but they are powerful institutional techniques because they not only collect opinions and numbers, they also seemingly convert one into the other without the need of human interference.[4]

The HR team at the Sangdo holding company had permission to run its own group-wide employee survey during my research in which they surveyed non-manager white-collar employees across all of the group's South Korean employees.[5] The survey had been carried out sporadically before, with different personnel in charge, in 2007, 2009, 2012, and 2013. The prior year's survey was led by a previous team manager whose survey according to team manager Jang was largely ineffectual. Jang noted that were problems with how that survey was structured and how the numbers were presented: it produced accurate numerical distinctions like "3.6" or "4.2" satisfaction ratings, but no one knew how to anchor those as good or bad. That year's survey, now under Jang's direction, was to be redesigned under a new format in both structure and analytical method. The team saw the survey as a chance to technically improve over the previous year's methods. They were also concerned with wanting to improve the work cultures at Sangdo's subsidiaries, especially at offices or factories where employees were known to work long hours, had particularly stern bosses, or had subpar office conditions. The survey also played other roles in mediating an imagined structure between the holding company and the rest of the conglomerate.

The survey was one of the few mechanisms by which the holding company could hear from subsidiary employees without going through their managers or executives (who were also excluded from taking the survey). The survey held two key promises: First, it was a mechanism by which the HR team could gather the evidence necessary to build an indirect case against the older male manager figures they saw as the root of many problems. That is, they were hoping to collect clear accounts of dissatisfaction that might prompt intervention or greater oversight by the holding company in subsidiary personnel management. By collecting the anonymized voices of others' employees, this would deliver irrefutable empirical evidence for highlighting problems on the ground that required fixing from the bottom up, not the top down. Second, it was also a mode of demonstrating the expertise of the holding company and the outside-hired crop of managers brought in by ownership to use innovative techniques. A sign of this was the fact that the survey they developed was called an engagement survey (*muripdo seolmunjosa*) in contrast to the more conventional satisfaction survey (*manjokdo seolmunjosa*), suggesting a higher plane of work (engaged workers, not just satisfied ones) and a higher plane of analysis.

To perform such a survey would require months of work and acts of calibration that spanned numbers on screens, visual graphics and analytic reports as well as meetings to analyze and present the results. At stake was the fact that the survey ultimately served as a form of participation for the whole conglomerate but also acted as a new form of distinction between subsidiaries (such as which office had the best engagement) as well as a form of distinction for the experts themselves. This reflects the way that distinction operates as both a first-order and a second-order phenomenon.[6]

First-order distinctions refers to numbers or grades that classify people or things into discrete categories such as satisfaction, quality, or experience. Titles, ranks, and salaries might be overt forms of first-order distinctions within organizations. Second-order distinctions reflect judgments about certain kinds of conduct that may themselves not be visible form of distinction. Sloppy handwriting might indicate that a person is sloppy; conversely, a clean presentation might indicate that a person is organized, competent, or prepared.[7] Contemporary office work presents an interesting zone to explore the relationship between first-order distinctions and second-order forms of distinction because employees and other actors both encounter and produce different combinations. Some office practices might appear to disavow overt forms of distinction at a first-order level (say, having a meeting and discussing ideas democratically), but these might fit into a larger notion of cultural distinction at a second-order level (because democracy is valued higher). Second-order distinctions are shaped by wider notions of prestige, quality, and taste, such as ideas about what constitutes "best practice." In this sense, they can be harder to pin down or reform, but they are no less salient as matters of distinction. First- and second-order distinctions are often the site of change and conflict within and across corporate organizations. What may make workplaces feel distinct (special or valued) are the seemingly intangible differences in (second-order) forms of conduct that are distinct from the material qualities of a job: the way colleagues treat each other, the diversity of work people do every day, or the personalities of ownership. At the same time, first- and second-order distinctions can also converge in curious ways in managerial projects where seemingly neutral tasks may be part of projects of second-order distinction making (such as helping someone get a promotion via a project that appears as participatory or progressive).[8] As I will discuss, for South Korean employees, everyday workplace decisions, even simple ones like participating in a survey, can pose complex dilemmas.

In carrying out the employee survey, the HR managers at the Sangdo holding company were ostensibly carrying out a duty of their office and reporting the results to the chairman about the collective state of "his" employees. They were also trying to institute or regiment a particular second-order association with them as experts in such a process, distinguishing their survey from others, and distinguishing themselves from others. This chapter suggests that part of what the Sangdo managers managed was the relationships between first-order and second-order distinctions afforded by the survey. This includes a link between the scope of the survey and the scope of expertise (more people surveyed = more knowledge expertise). However, it also included avoiding the negative second-order distinctions that might threaten their claims of expertise. To carry out a survey might create first-order distinctions among companies, but it did not necessarily guarantee that the surveyors themselves would be recognized as knowledgeable experts. In their way stood employees that tried to game their answers, numbers that did not cohere statistically, and the possibility that a survey could reflect on the surveyors themselves.

Distinct Expertise

In the fall of 2014, assistant manager Ji-soon and I had brainstormed a first set of questions for the survey along with a set of categories in which the questions would be grouped. We presented these to team manager Jang and assistant manager Min-sup for review at a meeting in October. Team manager Jang led the meeting and asked us to project the draft survey onto the wall from our computer as he evaluated the range of questions. Our initial questions were an amalgam of conventional survey questions we had found from sources such as the American Society for Human Resources Management, the off-the-shelf Great Place to Work Survey, and other subsidiaries' past surveys. Ji-soon and I divided these conventional questions into three areas: My Job, My Company, and My Sangdo that each comprised five questions; the average of each would then create a numerical index of generalized engagement in each of the three areas. These categories encapsulated a basic grouping of South Korean organizational worlds (employees belonged to working teams, teams were part of companies, and companies were part of the Sangdo conglomerate). Sensing a tendency toward conventionality, Jang began to suggest new question formats such as a fill-in-the-blank that he wrote out in English on the whiteboard: "Everyday I wanna _____my boss." He sardonically wrote "kill" as one potential answer that employees might fill in.

As the meeting progressed, we began to venture into new topical questions that might have been otherwise taboo to ask: "How many nights a week do you work late?" "How often do you go drinking (*hoesik*) per week?" "Are you given opportunities to share your opinion in meetings?" We came up with proxy questions such as "What time do you usually go home?" as a way to understand whether employees were overworking without asking directly. Jang insisted we include questions about whether workers were satisfied with compensation—presumably because no one would be happy with their compensation. At one point, when evaluating a question about the quality of internal training programs (*sanae gyoyuk*), Jang suggested that it was not worth including. In his view, all programs were pointless so there was no point in trying to improve them.[9] When creating a question about the Sangdo Group, someone proposed asking what employees thought about the holding company itself. That proposition received a resounding "No." At more banal moments, Jang and Min-sup debated the merits of a 4-point versus a 5-point Likert scale, suggesting that executives preferred surveys with 5-point scales but that a 4-point scale might force employees to pick a side.

After the meeting, team manager Jang confessed on a break that after a negative interaction with another subsidiary manager earlier that morning, he was starting to think that the broader HR environment of Sangdo would be resistant to any changes and that this fact would stunt the possibility of any new HR programs he and his team were developing. However, he was upbeat about the possibility that the engagement survey, which we were writing from scratch, would circumvent the same subsidiary managers and go directly to their employees. This might make possible a new kind of system that would mark the holding company's approach as unique. Moreover, it would give validation to Jang's personal mission to bring an innovative HR program to a midlevel conglomerate.

In the beginning, it seemed that the survey might achieve such ambitious goals. Executive Cho had proposed sending it out to white-collar employees in the entire Sangdo Group, including overseas office workers, meaning it would need to be translated into English and Chinese, the two largest language blocs other than Korean. Team manager Jang seemed particularly excited by this potential, even though he disliked surveys themselves. He often told me of the inherent statistical problems and vapid results that came from high-profile employee surveys, especially when they were conducted by high-priced HR or management consulting firms. Not hiring an outside consulting company to run the survey was not just a matter of cost-savings. Doing so was a mark of the team's expertise in the eyes of the owners and chairman who would receive the final reports directly. Even I, an American doctoral student putatively interested in the kind of measurable organizational culture analysis they sought, fit into the plan of building up the expertise of the survey and the surveyors.

In developing the survey as a proposal, HR managers drew on ways of differentiating their survey from those of subsidiaries: where subsidiaries studied satisfaction (*manjokdo*), the holding company studied engagement (*muripdo*); where the subsidiaries did analysis (*bunseok*), the holding company did diagnostics (*jindan*) with regression models (*hoe-gwi*) and indexes (*jisu*) that could create new aggregate measures. Newly created culture maps (in English) would provide visualizations for what kind of relationships certain team types (finance, sales, procurement) were likely to have. The culture maps were meant to describe all office cultures as fitting within a two-axis diagram based on two opposing qualities with opposite poles at each one: one axis based on working style would indicate whether teams were work centered (*eommujungsim*) or organization centered (*jojikjungsim*) in their organizational structure; the opposite axis based on team relations would indicate whether they they had cool (*naengjeong*) or warm (*onjeong*) relations within their teams. Cool teams might refer to ones that did not have strong interpersonal relationships; warm teams referred to those where employees considered themselves friends.

Likewise, work-centered teams had actors with work that was independent from each other (such as sales), whereas organization-centered teams operated within a coordinated team structure.[10]

The team also agreed to hire a statistician to run a correlational analysis (*sang-gwan gwan-gye bunseok*) linking variables around team culture to rates of workplace engagement levels. The idea would be to prove scientifically what kind of team culture (along the four axes of work-centered, organization-centered, cool, or warm) would correlate best with workplace engagement. Moreover, each subsidiary would receive a special diagnostic report (*jindan bogoseo*) with graphics and individual insights divided by team, function, gender, rank, age, and office location. These would lead to the creation of new action plans created after the survey to track some of their specific issues. In this sense, the HR team drew on a wide-ranging assemblage of expert genres, terms, and techniques to demonstrate its expertise—forms that mimicked the outside consultancies' language that they otherwise thought they could improve on.

The holding company managers were averse to what we might consider a kind of generic managerial expertise, which could include forms, modes of knowledge, systems, or programs that were used in the past, that were used by other South Korean companies, or that simply did not deliver what they saw as interesting insights. The buzzword insight (*tongchallyeok*) itself had been inscribed as part of the new values at Sangdo a few years prior to my arrival. Insight, as both a description and an aspiration, would allow Sangdo as a whole to "grasp the essence of phenomena and seek out the right solutions for optimizing as a whole," according to the core values pamphlet. In a survey conducted by the job training site Hunet in 2014, "insightfulness" was the top result when employees were asked what qualities they looked for in a company leader. As executive Cho noted once in a meeting when reviewing the survey questions, "we [the HR team] need to ask these questions 'smartly' (*smateuhage*)," reflecting the blurry boundary between the quality of the questions and the qualities of the people asking them. Because the results would ultimately be read by the chairman, there was an extra incentive to perform insight for the chairman. An insightful expert was often viewed in contrast with a bureaucratic (*gwallyojeok*) type of corporate employee who simply fulfilled his or her job requirements without striving to improve, collaborate, or advance the organization. This was redolent of the marked older manager style described in the previous chapter in which expertise was simply a function of one's position in the corporate hierarchy, not a reflection of one's intellectual capacity.[11]

Insight, however, as a specific quality of persons is not easy to define in practice; it is a socially constructed and relational quality that often figures as a business community mantra in corporate recruiting rituals, innovation training, and expert displays, such as with PowerPoint presentations where expertise can be artfully put on display.[12] In this sense, like other forms of expertise, insight is an institutionally valued quality (as a high marker of distinction) but nevertheless must be continuously demonstrated and displayed to others. The risk of not having insight is not its lack, necessarily, but the appearance of being generic—that is the quality of showing no distinction— much in the same way that brands aim to differentiate from generic commodities to avoid being seen as generic goods.[13] For the HR managers, to lack insight would be to perform generic knowledge or information without distinction. To be unique as experts was a matter of distinguishing from what they saw as generic forms of expertise that they imagined the subsidiary managers produced.

Surveys conducted by the subsidiaries, which I was able to review for inspiration, were indeed simpler in construction, asking employees about various categories of satisfaction without any higher-order categorization or correlation. Compared to the subsidiaries, however, the holding company depended on such acts of expertise because they lacked many of the other institutional forms of knowledge or oversight. For example, when I visited Sangdo First's HR team, which I had been told had an outdated view of HR, the managers there revealed an elaborate and sophisticated computer system for keeping a record of the subsidiaries' workforce of several thousands. A low-level staff member, Jin-woo, gave me an introduction to their company's Human Resources Information System (HRIS). Though a junior worker, Jin-woo had been trained in the kinds of coding necessary to input, navigate, and analyze personnel data in the highly elaborate system that contained personal information, salary, insurance, and annual reviews for thousands of employees. The multimillion-dollar platform gave them a way to manage many details about their workforce in one system, both domestically and abroad.

The holding company, in contrast, had no HRIS and largely relied on individual forms that were stored in a locked cabinet or simply as files on individual computers. To track personnel records and conduct other HR projects, they had to rely on Excel spreadsheets, lengthy PowerPoint reports, older intranet forms, and low-cost ERP applications made in collaboration with an internal IT team.[14] Assistant manager Min-sup described the assemblage of the holding company as manual labor *(sujageop)* because of the need to input data by hand, ask subsidiaries for information, double check for errors with pen and paper, and create generic forms on a one-off basis. Furthermore, because subsidiary ERP systems were established only for use on their own computers with their own data and coding structures, they were not mutually compatible and the holding company managers could not have the digital access to the company systems that they saw might befit their position as upper-level managers.

The Non-Surveyed

On the eve of the survey launching in December 2014, one subsidiary CEO called the holding company HR team to ask if his company could be exempted from the survey. They had just conducted their own internal survey and found employees to be unhappy due to new revenue-target demands, a fact the CEO did not want conveyed to the chairman. They were not granted an exemption. However, one subsidiary remained completely off the books, numbers, and ranks without any overt discussion, nor did its CEO make a formal request. This was Sangdo NET, the subsidiary that provided the hardware and software services and maintained the IT infrastructure for the entire group.

Though a fully owned subsidiary of the holding company and a vital part of the operations of the conglomerate, Sangdo NET remained an elusive figure in the wider group structure. Its head office was relegated to the bottommost floor of the Sangdo tower, and its employees were only loosely considered as regular Sangdo-ites as they largely operated as on-location tech support for other subsidiaries, factories, and data centers. Across from my desk in a windowless office sat three IT managers from Sangdo NET. They were officially contracted to work on computer issues for the holding company, and their coworkers were based on other floors helping other companies. While all teams in the holding company were socially considered part of the same company, the IT workers were never included in interteam dinner events, shared snacks, or impromptu lunches. Where other teams collaborated *(hyeob-eop)* with each other on special projects, the IT managers were specifically contracted *(gyeyak)* to projects for teams in formal and explicit ways. They were contracted to work on the employee survey itself, converting it from a document of questions into an interactive object that would launch on the group intranet and produce raw data for our analysis. It was thus with some irony that Sangdo NET employees were excluded from the survey that they helped to launch.

The reasons for their exclusion reflected one area of taboo: one of the members of the owning family also was an executive with Sangdo NET. This person was not, by profession, trained in IT and frequently had clashes with the executives of Sangdo NET. Furthermore, executive Cho and team manager Jang knew that it might be politically risky to collect data that might show bad results to the chairman, such as employees' true opinions of ownership or engagement results that were exceptionally low. For example, if the survey created a question that asked employees if they felt like staying at Sangdo for a long time (and if employees answered in the negative), then this would potentially insult the chairman for overseeing a conglomerate where no one wanted, in theory, to work. (The previous year's survey had included the curious statement, "I am *not* considering or preparing to quit or move to another company.") Bad answers to such a question might signal that there were deeper cracks within the Sangdo Group. Whether or not it was true, it would create an unwanted form of hyperdistinction that might otherwise prove problematic.

Even though Sandgo NET was formally excluded from the survey, it was not technologically excluded; the Sangdo intranet was open to anyone with Sangdo email and any employee could click on the survey link. A few dozen Sangdo NET employees took the survey unwittingly, completing each section, including the free response. They only became aware of their exclusion when asked to select their company name from a list at the end of the survey. One wrote in the free response, aware of their possible exclusion, "Sangdo NET is not on the list for company selection. It seems that it is not part of the Sangdo Group which makes me sad (*seopseophan ma-eum*)." When their partial answers came through in the raw data, they were left uncounted in the aggregate figures and tables and remained largely unmentioned in league tables and analytics reports. (Similarly, a number of blue-collar workers also filled out the survey seemingly by mistake. The survey was launched via the company intranet and the HR team assumed that those who worked in factories and were on the blue-collar side did not even have access to computers, the intranet, or company mail. Those results were also filtered out.)

Free-response answers, provided as an option for respondents at the end of the survey, were also largely excluded from analysis. Free responses allow employees to offer their own diagnoses but are generally a psychologically comforting technique to make one's voice feel heard in what is, otherwise, a statistical data-collecting encounter.[15] The HR managers understood that free-response answers were a way for employees to vent about things such as Sangdo's rotten culture (*gorittabun munhwa*) or military culture (*gundae munhwa*). They also had complex forms of response, such as employees who offered their own diagnoses on what the group's business strategy should be. One suggested that Sangdo abandon overseas development projects and focus new attention on the Chinese market so that it would be more competitive. Others seemingly believed that their responses would go to the chairman or might be linked to their personal identities and thus offered slavish, pro-corporate messages. One echoed that "our Sangdo Group should go beyond South Korea and be the most beautiful company in the world, excellent in all aspects." The same comment listed a number of diagnostic reasons that Sangdo's corporate culture was lacking, including its responsibility-blaming (*chaegim chugungseong*) culture, command-giving meetings (*jisiha-dal hoe-ui*), the conservative steel industry culture, and the lack of respect for opinion sharing. These comprehensive diagnostic accounts are their own kinds of insider performance, reflecting a deep familiarity with one's own organization and the key structural problems that affect it. The effusive echoing of generic corporate slogans in some instances, however, reflects an awareness, perhaps, that the respondent was tailoring his or her comments to ownership or holding company managers as the imagined recipients who might be monitoring who said what. In this sense, employees were navigating between their own understanding of first-order meanings (literal answers on the survey) and second-order judgments about their conduct on surveys (and what that might say about them as Sangdo employees).

Part of running a survey is controlling the experiment-like conditions around it to control not only the populations who take it but the idealized kinds of first-order responses that are necessary to create proper second-order readings, much like scientists collecting uncontaminated samples. The idealized second-order reading was that the holding company would become seen as an expert analyst vis-à-vis the subsidiaries and their employees as subjects, enacting a higher-order distinction around expertise. One of the simplest ways of doing this was purifying responses through certain forms of exclusion— such as excluding problematic companies or problematic categories of response. These responses are not problematic in and of themselves— arguably, from the perspective of organizational knowledge, they are quite useful—but they interfere with the goals that are layered on top of even relatively benign genres of office work like satisfaction or engagement surveys.

There was one first-order interference seen within the data that the HR managers neither could have predicted nor excluded. One of the subsidiaries that was generally understood to be the most male-dominated and military-like in its corporate culture, Sangdo South, reported the highest engagement rate in the whole group. This came as a particular surprise as HR team members thought the subsidiary's employees might have expressed more honest individual opinions about their conditions. The results were so positive in some cases that they seemed to be an example of straightlining (filling in the same answer through the whole survey), which is a case either of carelessness, a rush to finish, or an awareness of being judged for making honest judgments.[16] For team manager Jang, such responses were indirect signs not of the failure of individual subsidiary employees but of the older male managers: he surmised that the Sangdo South employees knew the normative way to answer when asked about their bosses or company, which was to give that company's engagement rating a boost. To him this was an effect of the older male managers at Sangdo South who had implicitly or explicitly influenced the younger employees in one way or another. However, because their answers were produced honestly and did not appear to overtly straightline, the answers to the survey were kept as part of the analysis. And it is certainly possible that employees were, in fact, satisfied with their jobs.

Hinterlands of Authority

Sociologist John Law has described how surveys, such as the European Union's Eurobarometer, construct ways of seeing a population or a community because they create the realities that they purport to be measuring. Such realities do not emerge out of thin air: they rely on what Law describes as "hinterlands" of practices and evidence that can be traced back, undergirding and lying behind such realities. Corporate expertise relies on the hinterlands of traceable practices in order to be properly enacted: the veracity of information in a report relies as much on the fact that it might have passed through multiple hands, that it has multiple signatures on the top, or that it contains a detailed appendix as it does on the aesthetics of information itself. For the holding company experts at Sangdo, it was necessary to create the appropriate hinterlands that would make the survey reliable as an object of scientific knowledge and carry weight across the Sangdo Group.[17]

The HR team received the results of the engagement survey in early January, two days after the survey closed on the company intranet. The numbers came out perfectly ordered in an Excel spreadsheet, but the team would spend the next three months trying to figure out how to properly calibrate the calculations within the results to convey both the (true) opinions of employees and the expertise of the holding company. The survey had been sold on its ability to execute a high-level correlational analysis between employee satisfaction and employees' reported behaviors on their teams. This was captured in a diagram on a PowerPoint slide that promised to identify the causal relationships among three areas: engagement indices, drivers, and reported behaviors. Though the survey had actually shown a drop-off in the number of employees who completed it compared to the prior year, it appeared at first that the survey might have revealed the holy grail of managerial phenomena: a causal link between work behavior and engagement. Causal certainty, backed up through regression analysis and numerical fact, would provide what the team was looking for (and make up for the general lack of enthusiasm among employees to complete the survey). This elation was short-lived.

The results were first sent to a statistician in the US, a PhD student I had contacted. His initial report came back with regression analysis and there seemed to be a correlation between positive behaviors and high engagement at the aggregate level. This meant that there was proof that reportedly happier workers were more engaged at their jobs. However, this initial promise dwindled when we realized that a statistician's level of certainty is much different from a manager's certainty. To a statistician, positive correlations still suggest some range of error and level of confidence about the strength of correlation based on R values. The statistician had ultimately made those decisions based on his own judgment, so the results were considered too subjective and variable as proper evidence for the Sangdo managers. Furthermore, a correlation could be said to exist for the aggregate of a few thousand respondents, for which the margin of error was small, but for each individual subsidiary, whose samples ranged from a dozen to hundreds of workers, the margin of error eclipsed nearly 40 percent in some cases. Anticipating future rebuttals from subsidiary CEOs to whom these results would eventually be presented, team manager Jang reluctantly admitted that the correlational analysis would not pass muster and we had to abandon the results.

If advanced statistics proved too messy for corporate use, even simpler kinds of analysis embedded in the survey design itself ran into problems. When employees were asked about specific drivers (*yoin*) or factors that motivate or demotivate people, employees selected that they were motivated by salary and also demotivated by it. Were they motivated by salary in general but not their current salary? Or did they misunderstand the question? No one on the team could figure out how to make the logical connections between what were negative and positive responses nor what the referent of salary was (salary in the abstract or their own salary). With competing results, no one could figure out which aspects of office culture had to be improved—such as team internal relations, overtime, or benefits—versus what had no impact on satisfaction, such as vacation days. Employee opinions began to look equivocal, though because they were an artifact of the survey design itself, they started to seem less like calculated confusion and more like poor question design. (To navigate this dilemma, results were ultimately presented on a slide without any overt interpretation of their correlation or larger meaning; subsidiaries would have to interpret what they meant.)

Alignment between numbers was also vital for drawing inferences about broader behaviors that could be used for analysis. The team had created a two-axis model for mapping corporate culture by each office: these modeled what we took to be a basic distinction that could map every team in the entire group—work centered (*eommujungsim*) versus organization centered (*jojigjungsim*) and cool (*naengjeong*) versus warm (*onjeong*) relations within their teams. Respondents had to fill in what they thought their current behaviors on their team were and what they desired them to be, using a common survey technique in South Korea (*as is* and *to be* categories). These basic oppositions (that were imagined to be paired together to reflect four mutually exclusive styles of work, such as work centered + cool or organization centered + warm) were meant to encapsulate discrete poles of team identities that loosely alluded to perceived differences, without castigating any of them in a negative light. We had suspected that some teams would fall to one side or the other, giving empirical proof to diversities in professions, styles, and tastes. This format was also imagined as a technocratic way of sorting people with different working styles and preferences around participation—by putting them with people of their own behavioral kind. In the end, however, every team answered that their *to be* side was composed of cool relations and was organization focused. This seemed to suggest that all employees had the same idea: they did not want to be burdened by the shared responsibility of team relations, but they also wanted to work for broader organizational goals, not necessarily ones focused on their individual work goals. Because the survey generated no clear distinctions among behavioral types, the use of cultural distinctions to analyze and categorize each team—creating static culture maps—fell by the wayside, along with the higher-order categorizations that had been built into the survey design such as causal analysis.

In retrospect, it is clear that the ambiguous results of the survey revealed something about the contradictions at the heart of a supercorporate ideal itself. If the supercorporate ideal marks corporations as sites of objective distinction for individual merit as well as positive group interactions, the embedded realities of distinction and participation in office life itself complicates efforts to sort these clearly, especially when work is expressed in different forms of collaboration with other teams and is the subject of other people's evaluations. For example, on the survey, 52 percent of employees said they had shared goals (*gongtong mokpyo*) with other teams, but 85 percent said they ideally would like to have more of them. Similarly, 46 percent said that promotion was currently based on their own abilities (*gein neung-yeok*), while 92 percent said they desired such promotions. To the HR managers, these were set up to be contradictory positions—they expected certain people to be more individually oriented and less interested in cooperative work, while others might enjoy collaborating with others. Thus, they expected the differences to be between different person types (who had different professional experiences or generational differences) rather than as a contradiction within persons or within modern work ideals. Indeed, one free response noted that "when our annual results [*seong-gwa*] get evaluated, 'evaluations by department' are important but some departments collaborate more than others, and for others, their collaboration is not seen. It would be good if there were a system that could understand this." This reflects an idealization of rational corporate systems that could both involve participatory work with others and also evaluate that cooperative work such that it might be divided individually—that is, that it could easily disentangle collective projects into their individual components without the mediation of a boss (a system). This represents what anthropologist Kelty has described about the paradox at the heart of popular and celebratory discourses on participation. In popular discourses, participation is imagined to be both about losing oneself in the crowd (or the team) and marking oneself from the crowd (or the team). That is, people should be recognized for their individual participation even though such participation is premised on losing one's individuality.[18]

The survey's inherent faults were not an occasion to ruminate philosophically about the contradictions inherent in employees' self-understandings or in contemporary capitalism that promotes participation. The team had to submit an analysis report to the chairman and to subsidiaries about its findings as part of its professional duties. After various failed attempts at resolving the analytic conundrums located in the structure of the survey and the data (including attempting to recategorize basic survey questions into new behavioral types such as "flat" and "vertical"), the team decided it was better to focus on the precise presentation of results that subsidiaries could interpret for themselves. The survey captured a bevy of demographic data from employees on age, gender, location, rank, and professional area that allowed them to present the same data as detailed and elaborate quasi-scientific breakdowns of behavioral patterns of each subsidiary. Added to this, Jang and assistant manager Jisoon developed a sharp visual language through PowerPoint to depict the information with Sangdo-themed graphics and colors that presented slide after slide of detailed data and cross-sectional analysis by rank, gender, workplace, and team. A few selections from the open response section were included to add human voices at the end of each report, but they were cleaned of the most critical responses.

Where the survey became a generic set of data and not the elaborate expert technique the HR managers hoped, the distribution of the results almost five months after the survey had been completed nevertheless offered an opportunity to mark off the holding company's position vis-à-vis the subsidiaries based on their engagement scores. In his ethnography of management at a British bank, John Weeks described how satisfaction surveys were used to create new forms of competition within segments of the large bank.[19] By sending individual directors or executives the results for their unit that ranked them relative to other units, the headquarters of the bank created an internal competition around satisfaction indicators, with regional directors eager to bump up their scores, even though, as one surveyor noted, the differences between the scores were statistically insignificant. Similarly at Sangdo, the various engagement indices and tabulated responses were ranked against other subsidiaries' scores. The results only showed a company's own employee score against other anonymized subsidiaries whom they might be above or below. For instance, a company might know they had the third highest engagement rate in the group without knowing which company was first or last. (The chairman of Sangdo received a full report on all the companies that had information for each subsidiary, deanonymized.) The individual reports turned into occasions for the HR team to go over the results with the respective HR counterparts from each subsidiary. Jang scheduled meetings with team managers to walk through their individual reports.

I was able to sit in on a few of these meetings toward the end of my time at Sangdo. It was clear that the issues for each subsidiary were more complicated than the survey indicators or even free responses alone could capture. For instance, at Sangdo First, office workers from one regional location had particularly low engagement scores. The HR manager there, team manager Chun, explained that they were aware of that factory that also produced the highest revenues in the whole subsidiary. This was due in part to the factory foreman (*gongjangjang*) who was a reputed figure within the subsidiary, said to arrive at work at 7 a.m. seven days a week. Though employees there complained of their inability to use vacation time and to leave on time, Chun was reluctant to use the results of the survey to attempt to upset the authority of the factory boss, as that would possibly make his CEO upset over the threat to revenues in a particularly competitive industry during a down year. Furthermore, as a longtime Sangdo First worker, Chun knew that workers attached to factories (even if they had office jobs) did not necessarily think about work the same way as Seoul people did—that is, he was aware of their local culture (at least in its sense of difference in norms) from his own experience, not a model produced on a survey. According to Chun, even if the head office of Sangdo First forced employees to go home on time or take their vacation days, employees would likely refuse because of the norms at that factory. In this sense, Chun was pointing out his own expertise and insights around Sangdo First's internal dynamics and resituating the holding company managers as out-of-touch with the broader Sangdo world. In some ways, the problem of the HR department at the holding company was mirrored at the subsidiary level: Chun himself was managing a different set of relationships within his own infrastructure of distinction.[20]

Distinction Delayed

After the meetings, each subsidiary was given a template for an action plan. The subsidiaries were meant to identify the issues in the survey results to indicate what areas they would improve on among their problem areas. The blank template, with column headings listing out areas of concern, plan of action, date of start, and end date, was not necessarily an object of expertise a but new kind of organizational obligation in which the subsidiaries had to make obligations on paper, handled by the holding company and reported to the chairman. Because of this, subsidiaries would not be able to ignore it and would have to make time to identify their issues, shape what ways they would fix them, and write an action plan for how and when they would resolve them. By the time I finished my fieldwork in late June, the subsidiaries had begun individually filling out their forms and creating their plans for the end of the year. The action plan is nominally a form of indirect control through the establishment of a new report and a chain of commitments, but even if subsidiaries had filled out their forms, it was not entirely clear if the survey had dramatically changed either the conditions on the ground for employees. Less clear was also the shift in expertise between the holding company and the subsidiaries—the recognition of second-order distinctions can be difficult to assess.

When I visited team manager Chun at Sangdo First after they had received the results of the survey, managers there extracted the figures from the holding company survey report and began to develop their own PowerPoint report to give to their own CEO, as if the data were produced by an outside company. They linked the data and used it to trace their own progress with surveys they had done internally. Working within a different milieu in which their authority was not as fragile and absolute precision and aesthetic pleasantness were not as valued the HR managers of Sangdo First reworked the holding company survey to come up with their own conclusions, such that satisfaction actually had gone up from one survey to another (even though the surveys were completely different). They seemed little bothered by the fact that they were reporting to the holding company in this process. Team manager Chun even conducted a focus group at a regional factory site where various foremen aired their grievances about office problems. While Chun may have been reporting for the sake of the action plan, he was also creating a new node of expertise for himself by which he had greater position vis-à-vis workers in his own company whom they more closely monitored. But even when compelled to fill out the action plan and report it to the holding company, they were, somewhat ironically, able to reposition their own roles as experts within their workplace.

The employee survey was an indirect and covert means of wresting information from the subsidiaries to use against their own management. The

neutrality of the request, the objective analysis of the data, the equality premised in face-to-face meetings, and the documentary mediation of the fol-
low-up together made the distinction-generating nature of such a project less
salient. This kind of project depended on the stability of numbers and data
to stand in for employee voices, especially unsatisfied ones. Where managers
originally sought to use causality as a quasi-scientific tool, the holding company HR team eventually resorted to a number of other expert techniques
to both differentiate their approach from others and develop the appropriate hinterlands to justify their claims. The bevy of techniques, methods, and
strategies reflected the fragility of such expertise, not its strength—especially
within a context of competing experts and second-order forms of distinction.[21]

Amid such neverending status competitions among experts, it is crucial
to see the way that employees, their voices, and notions of participation also
play a part. Many of the free-response comments in the survey mentioned the
concepts *daehwa*, *(uisa)sotong*, *non-ui*,—conversation, communication, discussion—as things that were desperately needed or missing between top managers and lower-level employees or between teams and subsidiaries. Unlike
the unmarked term "conversation" in English, which is framed as a natural
activity with any number of people speaking, these terms refer to a marked
activity that places emphasis on the bidirectional quality of two people communicating both word and sentiment. It lies in contrast to other forms of communication that are seen as unidirectional (*ilbanghyang*), which are more like
directives or done without the care of the other person. These terms for communication, which had become in vogue in wider South Korean management circles at the time of my research, were premised not just on the clear
transmission of information but on the reestablishment of a moral community through mutual understanding, much like ideas of conversation between
generations discussed in the previous chapter.[22] In particular, *sotong* (conversation) was operationalized in events such as town halls (*taunhol*), which became popular during my research, in which CEOs or chairmen met with their
employees face-to-face to talk about company and employment issues.[23] These
events were largely staged encounters to interactionally and communicatively
represent equivalence between those who question and those who answer, a
flip of the normal communicative assumptions about how people of different
ranks are meant to speak to each other in South Korea.

Such examples represent a corporate co-optation of the idea of *sotong* in
its more empty guises as staged events or as part of company fanfare, what

organization scholar Catherine Turco described as an effort to overcome hierarchical perceptions by becoming what she calls a conversational firm.[24] By focusing on conversation as an ideological form opposed to negative notions of hierarchy, Turco suggests that the American tech firm she studied overcame linguistic stereotypes of bureaucracy as being top-down organizations by having employees openly debate and decide company policy on a company wiki without fear of managerial retribution. Such ways of rethinking communication nevertheless were always threatened by appearing to serve merely as public relations displays or as forms of labor placation.

The Sangdo case, indicative of broader discussions in South Korea, highlights the move toward communication and conversation as a quasi-cultural movement to overcome not just organizational inefficiencies but the affective gap between alienated coworkers. In the engagement survey, the HR team also borrowed these assumptions about conversation for metricized survey questions, asking employees whether "I can freely share my opinion in meetings" and whether "age and rank do not strongly affect how I communicate with my team members." These questions were answerable on a five-point scale in the service of an effort to generate data for a culture map that could be used to classify different teams and professional functions by their communicative style. The broader goal of such questions was to use data points to help invert one perceived hierarchical order to institute a different one between the holding company and the subsidiaries that differentiated subsidiaries via their engagement rates. Where *sotong* discourse emphasizes overcoming one-sided hierarchy through two-way or mutual communication, the holding company would now be the arbiter of good workplaces. For managers like Jang, with their own histories and experiences of workplace complaint in South Korea, such a technocratic solution might be the only way that the more inveterate problems of workplace complaint could be solved. Where mild employee complaints could be dismissed, a mass of data with advanced analytics could provide a new kind of evidentiary hinterlands, a new kind of communication, and a new kind of organizational order based around company-level engagement and expert insight—even if such an idea co-opted the idea of communication via a survey instead of encouraging actual communication, whatever that might look like.

As the exclusion of Sangdo NET, blue-collar workers, non-office-based positions, contract workers, and non-Korean speaking overseas workers suggests, only certain kinds of sentiments were needed to constitute this new order. This reflects the fact that though the managers were attempting to construct a kind of scientific hinterlands of data and evidence to change the footing on which subsidiaries were evaluated and on which their own expertise rested, they also relied on assumptions on which kinds of organizational order their expertise could apply to. Some existing organizational relationships had to be kept at bay, lest radical new kinds of difference or distinction were to come to light (such as finding truly disgruntled workers or those who might really want to leave). This bears much in common with the notion of the public sphere. In Habermas's classic discussion of the public sphere, sites and interactions outside of the state act as important communicative zones for debating the state among private citizens who could self-authorize as the people. This public sphere was nevertheless premised on the exclusion of many others—namely women and other non-normative groups.[25] In other words, even seemingly radical changes inside corporate organizations can be premised on rather conventional or normative understandings that do not threaten too much change.

5

Interrupting Democracy

ON FRIDAY MARCH 27, 2015, the South Korean economy witnessed an unusual form of cross-corporate coordination. Nearly eight hundred shareholder meetings took place precisely at 10 a.m. across the country. Most meetings wrapped up quickly, often within thirty minutes, without any formal acknowledgment of their co-occurrence. That Friday in March has come to be known in the media as Super Shareholder Meeting Day (*syupeo juchong dei*). On the surface, the coordination of companies on Super Shareholder Meeting Day appears to disrupt the formal governance mechanisms of a properly running securities market in which shareholders, analysts, and journalists are prevented from attending and voting at multiple meetings. Since as early as 2005 when the term became commonly used, newspaper editorials, minority shareholder groups, and anti-corporate critics annually announce and frequently denounce the practice of meeting clustering as it is known in other countries. The Sangdo holding company, as a publicly traded company, also had its meeting on March 27. For the corporate directors and managers in charge of the meeting, the goal of the meeting was partly a defensive effort. They were staving off potential disruptions from *chonghoe-ggun* or meeting extortionists. *Chonghoe-ggun* are individual shareholders who try to disrupt meetings through aggressive questioning with the hopes of receiving a payoff from a single company or multiple companies. Described in the media as ants (*gaemi*) that are impossible to keep out of meetings, these individual shareholders bring fear to some of the country's largest and most powerful economic organizations year after year, simply through the risk of asking uncomfortable questions at meetings.

This chapter explores the dynamics of shareholder meetings at Sangdo and in South Korea more broadly to understand a possible rupture in the supercorporate ideal that is managed by internal actors. Shareholder meetings are significant annual rituals in governance, auditing, and financial transparency. At the same time, they are also small-scale laboratories of democratic practice through mechanisms of elections, deliberations, the use of quorums, and protections for minority rights. Even as the classic Berle and Means company of the twentieth century—marked by an adversarial division between shareholders and professional managers—has faded and new economic actors have emerged with new claims to corporate profit and corporate existence, the shareholder meeting has endured, a relic of nineteenth-century parliamentary practice in which internal actors (directors and executives) must face their critics (shareholders) in a mandated face-to-face format. The shareholder meeting remains a legitimized site for enacting change at the level of corporate management and for the distribution of corporate profit, as much as other aspects of corporate systems, commercial technologies, and financial powers have shifted. Meetings represent a fundamentally parliamentary genre of democracy, right at the heart of corporate practice, albeit once a year. In this sense, they carry their own ideal around both how people should be distinguished (minority and majority shareholders) and how they should participate (discussion and voting), which came to clash with other infrastructures of distinction in everyday office work.

As much as these governance mechanisms are meant to restrict inside actors and allow participation by interested investors and the public, they have also become sites of interruption that stifle the otherwise smooth flow of corporate presentation. But it is precisely because of these interruptions, and the formidable parliamentary rules that ensure their place, that they present a different understanding of what the fundamental purpose of corporate life is, who it is for, and how it should be mediated. As a genre, grounded in historical conventions, shareholder meetings are venues for conflict. Meetings enact a particular kind of democratic theater with courts, professional associations, and parliamentary societies encouraging their proper functioning. To managers at Sangdo and elsewhere, shareholder meetings could become distorted by illegitimate interruptions, particularly as nonlegitimate members make claims

through extortion, activism, or foreign tampering. Yet what counts as an illegitimate disruption in these cases, or a disproportionate response, for that
matter? I suggest in this chapter that shareholder meetings and their interruptions can be understood as a form of radical democratic practice that does not
mesh with the kinds of civilized, office-based forms of polite participation and
communication premised on incremental forms of HR-based distinction. It is
precisely because this is not an idea shared by everyone that makes it relevant
for understanding different definitions of the supercorporate ideal. Minority
investors, financial institutions, political activists, and even *chonghoe-ggun*
see such shareholder meetings as venues gamed by corporate actors seeking to
disrupt a state-sanctioned financial governance event while nevertheless using such events for particular kinds of distinction making of their own. From
all sides, competing ideas abound about what constitutes proper and improper
conduct in a corporate democratic theater.

In contrast to their parliamentary democratic bases, shareholder meetings
have often been framed as what anthropologist Dinah Rajak has called "the-
aters of virtue" and anthropologist Annette Nyqvist has described as "front-
stage performances," where company management can project wholesome or
coherent images to the public and to investors.[1] They can be elaborate theat-
rical events in which the scales of company myth making and nationalist values become intertwined, such as in the case of Walmart's shareholder meetings that presented an image of Walmart that reaffirmed "the mythic values
upon which the greatness of America is based."[2] In anthropologist Mary Jo
Schneider's understanding, meetings serve as liminal spaces where meanings
are radically reworked, and corporate giants can promote mythic, patriotic,
and utopian images of corporate practices, national(ist) capitalism, and workplace relations.[3] When shareholder-minded management and shareholders
themselves come together, the effect can be a performative alignment around
value creation and profit making. Indeed, much attention has been dedicated
to meetings that generate spectacle, either as corporate entertainment (such as
Berkshire Hathaway's festival-like meetings) or large-scale activist gatherings
(such as anti-Coca-Cola protests), in which visual or auditory displays distract
from the parliamentary aspects of the meeting.

As a governance mechanism among corporate executives, auditors, and
shareholders, including both minority and majority, meetings are also sites
where different claims to institutional power seek to prevail over others, including ethical activists who have used the very rules of meetings against

corporate executives—for example, the American activists Sisters of St. Francis have used a religious moral authority to bring attention to corporate ethics issues—and financial actors who use them to wrest control, such as what the American T. Boone Pickens did in Japan.[4] In this sense, the powers that converge at such meetings are not binary (such as corporations versus investors or corporations against communities). Various competing groups have differing interests in company governance and profits, such as unions, banks, hedge funds, pension funds, other corporations, institutional investors, activists, and individual investors, not to mention competing factions within a given company. In South Korea, shareholder meetings can be places where internecine family battles take place, such as the feud among brothers and a father over control of the Korean-Japanese multinational Lotte Group in 2015.[5] These diverse actors take advantage of the unique potentialities of shareholder meetings for governance decisions and the singular stage they offer for heightened performances of both corporate and individual reputation making.

It is worth asking why the rather dry process of the shareholder meeting—and not other sites or modes such as corporate espionage, power brokering, general bribery, or even militaristic takeovers—has become the privileged site for actors to converge and make different kinds of economic and sometimes political claims. As a parliamentary-style meeting in which the right to ask questions, criticize majority positions, and hold contentious debate in person are enshrined and legally protected as core principles, criticism is promoted while those who run meetings are restrained. Corporations have the responsibility to organize meetings as they see fit, but they are also obligated to ensure that the minimal requirements for meetings are met. This makes them particularly privileged sites for minority groups to openly criticize majority powers. However, because the rights of minority shareholders are enshrined and because corporate managers and employees oversee meetings, distinguishing legitimate criticism from illegitimate organization is a difficult task, especially when different parties follow the norms of parliamentary decorum. Cases of interruption in contemporary South Korea bring attention to the ways that claims to corporate property are in flux and subject to different forms of legitimized disruption.

The shareholder meeting, the "black box" of corporate history, in the words of historian Colleen Dunlavy, is the singular channel through which organizational outsiders' claims are made, legitimized, and exercised.[6] More than just discursive control over the content or framing of corporate activity, the very nature of meetings, in which participants are allowed to criticize and even oust those who run the meetings, allows for certain parties to create what we might think of as interruption rackets within perfectly democratic systems. Interruption rackets are regularized modes of extortion or control that work in part by threatening future interruptions. *Chonghoe-ggun*, the meeting extortionists in South Korea, operate one kind of racket premised on uncomfortable questions launched at company directors. However, other kinds of rackets also attempt to legitimize economic claims to corporate control and profit by playing within, and with, the rules. Interruption rackets are difficult to unseat precisely because they operate within legitimate norms of conduct and promise ever greater interruptions in the future. This is similar to but less visibly dramatic than the dynamics that Japanese shareholder meetings encountered in the 1980s and 1990s in which organized crime groups (yakuza) had become extortionists by buying shares in publicly traded Japanese firms and eventually offering mafia-like protection to publicly traded companies. *Sokaiya*, the Japanese linguistic equivalent of *chonghoe-ggun*, also used similar strategies of prolonging meetings through discussion and harassment of managers over corporate expenditures and through personal insults. Companies reckoned with them through various forms of payout, legal reform, and organizational maneuvering. By the 1990s, the extortion relationships became so extreme that company executives were physically attacked when they did not want to pay bribes. (On one occasion an executive was even killed when his company did not pay.) Japanese corporate executives eventually had to be escorted by police to attend shareholder meetings and many in the Japanese media wondered if any measure would be able to rid corporate markets of such embedded parasites.[7]

The South Korean case, with less obvious victims and villains, offers some subtleties around the nature of participation and the substance of claims. In this sense, it fits within a movement to think about the pluralities of shareholding, as the figure of the passive shareholder has given way to varieties of action and activism, particularly around topical issues such as environmentalism. Empirical cases in which company managers and shareholders, both small and large, make claims for the right to speak in different ways bear significance for conceptualizing formal forms of participation in the form of "voice rights" or "voice hierarchies."[8] Company delegates (employees or executives) control the right to speak through PR and through contracts in the conduct of business, but the right to speak for the corporation is disassembled and reversed during shareholder meetings. While the power of meetings is typically associated with their democratic functions such as majority voting (and associated concepts such as proxy fights), the translation of a financial right into a speaking right allows for simpler discursive techniques in making claims to corporate management or profits. Shareholders, often irrespective of their shareholding amount, have the potential to claim speaking rights (*bareon-gwon*) at meetings and can shift corporate reputations with a minimal amount of shares and a few comments. Given that the shareholder meeting is not just theater but a process in which corporate surplus is accounted for and distributed (or not) in the form of dividends, stock splits, and so on, these interruptions can have significant legal and financial stakes. Yet not all claims are similar nor are all forms of interruption equal. The persistent problem of interruptions cannot be solved by more enforcement, more democratic practice, or abstract ideas of dialogue. A focus on meetings reveals that rights and claims to corporate property and the (non-)distribution of profits are, at their core, ambiguous and subject to contention—much like other kinds of ideas around the proper form of marking distinction in other areas of the corporation. Given that such rights are mediated through a nineteenth-century parliamentary ritual premised on face-to-face deliberation, the threat of interruption and discord, even by small actors, proves as powerful a method as financial or managerial power abstractly conceived.

Translational Events

In one perspective, shareholder meetings are basic interruptions in the workaday corporate order, foregrounding the state's ability to regulate and subordinate publicly traded corporations to ensure property rights, particularly minority property rights. In contrast to other varieties of everyday or repetitive business, shareholder meetings are marked as rituals in both their internal sequencing and broader bearing on institutional governance and property relations. In this regard, shareholding meetings have a particular temporal structure and are vested with unique rights. They occur after the end of a fiscal year when annualized financial statements must be disclosed and approved, corporate performance can be assessed, and director-level decisions made. Shareholder meetings are what accounting scholar Michael Power has termed a "ritual of verification" in which managerial authority is offered up to be validated by a representative quorum of shareholders.[9] This ritual translates an ownership claim (via a share) into a discursive claim (via a presence and a vote) as a way of marking accountability between shareholders and corporate directors. While much scholarly attention has been paid to the articulation of these rights, what is known as plutocratic voting rights (voting based on proportion), types or classes of shares, or voting by proxy, the interactional dynamics afforded by meetings themselves have a formative effect on the qualities of the meeting as distinct from everyday work activity.

Shareholder meetings are upheld with rigid rules, new roles, and strict rules of conduct. They uphold the virtues of a civilized, parliamentary culture and are a space for rational economic interests to rein over irrational passions.[10] In this sense, more than just an accounting or governance procedure, shareholder meetings are a translational event, allowing otherwise outsider shareholders a ratified insider role via a voice (to ask questions, complain, or vote). The proper conduct of and in such meetings becomes a sign of properly functioning securities markets and the upholding of minority property rights. While it is common to think about corporations as bounded legal or market entities that, the necessity (and burden) of conducting shareholder meetings brings to the foreground both their communicative constitution and the contingency of their power relations.

This happens through a process of disassembling the corporation down to its basic political components: human (shareholders and directors), fiscal (assets and liabilities), and constitutional (resolutions). This does not mean that other attempts to present a unified image or efforts to control impressions by certain actors, such as through glossy annual reports, are absent. However, the parliamentary dimension of corporate shareholder meetings is key as a site of contestation through which property rights become manifest. Actors with plural interests are funneled through different participatory roles: directors present meetings to shareholders and shareholders in turn exercise votes and ask questions of management, among other rights.[11] Auditors, acting in theory on behalf of shareholders, ensure the validity of financial statements. In this light, the voice rights of the corporation, normally reserved by management or delegated to public relations offices, are entirely reversed: a simple property claim generally guarantees the right to speak. Thus, meetings provide shareholders momentary situational power over corporate directors, CEOs, chief financial officers, and other executives who must answer to the audience as part of their fiduciary duties as state-sanctioned officers. As such, meetings circumscribe otherwise politically or sociologically powerful corporations and directors into highly constrained roles whose duties carry significant consequences if not met (such as a lawsuit to the company or the stripping of one's director status).

These duties, of both the corporation as a legal entity and the directors, are buttressed by two formal apparatuses: commercial codes and parliamentary norms. National commercial codes specify what must be presented at a given meeting, how that information should be audited, what directors are obligated to do, and what rights minority shareholders are entitled to. Parliamentary norms, on the other hand, dictate the conduct of actors during such meetings. Modern parliamentary norms are based largely on Robert's Rules of Order, a set of widely adopted parliamentary guidelines developed in the United States in the late nineteenth century. The rules provide instruction on how to ensure that "assemblies of any size, with due regard for every member's opinion . . . arrive at the general will on the maximum number of questions of varying complexity in a minimum amount of time."[12] Commonplace meeting mechanisms such as proposals, voice votes, ratifications, and motions are key elements of the rules that exist in a variety of deliberative bodies, from student councils to shareholder meetings.[13]

In South Korea, the commercial code (*sangbeop*) was originally borrowed from Japanese commercial code during the colonial period (1910–45). The Japanese code was largely modeled on German commercial law. Attempts to revise the South Korean commercial code after decolonization incorporated many aspects of American corporate governance, such as the right to elect directors, establishment of fiduciary duties, the right of inspection, and majority voting, among others.[14] After the Asian Financial Crisis of 1997, in which the failures of proper corporate governance were blamed for over-leveraged corporate investments, various mechanisms were introduced to the corporate code to ensure tighter control (such as outsider directors, facilitation of lawsuits, and increased director liability).[15] On the procedural side, Robert's Rules are widely used in South Korea, including in the National Assembly and in shareholder meetings, where they are said to preserve the principles of freedom of debate (*toronjayu*), member equality (*hoewonpyeongdeung*), and majority decision (*dasugyeol*).[16] The Korean Parliamentarian Association provides guidance on parliamentary norms and procedures to various public and private institutions. The Korean Listed Companies Association (KLCA, or *hanguk sangjangsa hyeobuihoe*), the group that represents publicly traded companies, recommends its members follow the guidelines listed by parliamentarians or simply follow Robert's Rules directly.

Significant about Robert's Rules is that criticism and questioning are baked into the procedures as a means of preserving minority rights and debate; in this sense, interruptions are a basic and even necessary aspect of shareholder meetings. In fact, meetings held without deliberation before voting, for instance, can be considered null and void. Part of what makes these interruptions protected is concomitant norms of conduct on directors themselves during meetings. Robert's Rules specifically notes that debaters should show a basic respect to the meeting and to the chairperson:

> If one desires to ask a question of the member speaking, he should rise, and without waiting to be recognized, say, "Mr. Chairman, I should like to ask the gentleman a question." (RR VII.43)
>
> During debate, and while the chairman is speaking, or the assembly is engaged in voting, no member is permitted to disturb the assembly by whispering, or walking across the floor, or in any other way. (RR VII.43)

While Robert's Rules outlines an "order of precedence" granting differential powers to roles (such as who can introduce a motion), the rules are explicit in constraining the powers of those with situational authority from abusing the rights of the minority via debate:

> The right of members to debate and, make motions cannot be cut off by the chair's putting a question to vote with such rapidity as to prevent the members getting the floor after the chair has inquired if the assembly is ready for the question. (RR VII.44)

The rules thus constrain those running debates and those participating in debate.[17] While "disorderly" comments are proscribed, the rules offer no clear categorical distinction over what constitutes such speech or action. Disorderly comments, for instance, "should be taken down [in writing] by the member who objects to them, or by the secretary, and then read to the member" and should not be of a "personal nature" (RR VII.43). The rules thus provide guidelines on polite conduct, but not on proper content. In a 2017 shareholder meeting at the American bank Wells Fargo, for instance, a protester loudly interrupted the proceedings to scold the presiding CEO over an unfurling scandal at the bank. The CEO thanked the disrupter for his comments, calmly commented that he was out of order, issued a warning of consequences, and made subsequent warnings that he was interrupting the next shareholder, all before asking him to be removed by meeting security. The next speaker was Sister

Nora Nash, a well-known religious activist who had prepared formal remarks for a proposal to investigate the scandal. While the male protester was ejected from the meaning, the CEO could do little to curtail Sister Nash from introducing her proposal, which was passed by shareholders and significantly disrupted the bank's image as facts from the scandal emerged. At South Korean meetings, people who take over the microphone and earn speaking rights can extend meetings for hours while castigating company directors who have little procedural recourse to stop them.

Under notions of deliberative democracy such as from Jurgen Habermas's conception of the public sphere or Paul Grice's cooperative principle, comments and discussion are premised on shared interest in civil discourse and shared intent.[18] These ideas generally focus on the notion that truth and intent can be understood through sentence-level meaning, in which lies and deceit are similarly seen as noncooperative. Yet such theories have trouble accounting for kinds of speech that manipulate other aspects of the linguistic context. There are numerous kinds of political interruption that can happen within authorized speech varieties, such as polite humor or covert teasing, that act to insult a listener while concealing the intent of the speaker or concealing the intent itself. Furthermore, there are interruptions that can happen outside of the act of speaking itself, such as the formatting of speaking rules, that significantly frame how such deliberations take place: certain actors might be excluded, speaking turns may be predetermined, or formal registers may exclude those who do not have access to such ways of speaking. Thus, even when the discursive conditions of parliamentary practice are present, other kinds of interruptions can still take place—and gain hold, given that parliamentary norms can only restrict certain kinds of explicit disruptive behavior and not others. There is an exploitable zone between what is considered a legitimate questioning of management and potential extortion, especially when those questions may be uncomfortable and critical in the first place, such as harsh critiques of management practices, low dividends, or executive compensation.[19]

The Tyranny of Small Shareholders

Meeting extortionists in South Korea are generally unaffiliated individual shareholders who own a minimal number of shares in multiple companies.[20] Largely unknown figures, they are believed to be former corporate employees, finance managers, or otherwise well-informed older men who are familiar with commercial codes, corporate finance, and the recent activities of individual companies such that they can go to companies to extort money or other goods during shareholder meetings. Where shareholder activists consciously aim to bring change to corporate governance and society at large, meeting extortionists disrupt meetings with the goal of blackmailing companies for personal gain in the form of a monetary or material payoff. They succeed in this racket primarily by making a literal racket: during the requisite question-and-answer time allotted at meetings reserved for minority shareholders to question managers or propose resolutions, at which time they are allowed to claim speaking rights that cannot be infringed on, they "hog the stage" (*dokchajihae beorida*) in the words of a report from 1981 detailing their tyranny (*hwingpo*).[21] These questions are not rambles or mere noise but highly relevant and pointed questions: one account described a *chonghoe-ggun* as questioning directors based on specific decisions such as, "Why did you expand the headquarters without making that news public?" and "Why have you borrowed so much money from the majority shareholder?"[22] One anonymous online message board writer, a worker at a large listed company, wrote a lengthy post entitled, "Do you know *chonghoe-ggun*?" describing their presence in the following way:

> If everything goes to script and everyone plays their part, shareholder meetings should finish in ten minutes. However, someone from the audience will shout, "Mr. Speaker, I have a different opinion." At that moment, you have to be ready for five to six hours, as the normally stern CEO starts to sweat while getting rebuked. While voting rights are proportional to one's shares, speaking rights [*bareon-gwon*] are not.[23]

Their actions are often dramatically characterized in media reports by other investors as emotive or irritable: *hang-ui* (a disruption), *soran* (a fuss), *hwoebang* (a disturbance), or *murihan yogu* (unreasonable requests). A 2018 petition submitted to the President of South Korea's online citizen petition website, categorized under "economic democratization" (*gyeongje minjuhwa*), asked the government to create a policy against extortionists, labeling them as disturbers (*gyoryanja*). The petition lamented that their continued presence at meetings renders the Korean securities market like a black market that made the country look backward (*hujinguk*).[24]

In a 2007 anonymous survey, more than 40 percent of publicly listed companies in South Korea admitted they dealt with problems from *chonghoe-ggun* at their annual meetings and 13 percent reported they dealt with between eleven and twenty separate individuals.[25] A typical strategy of extortion is to return to the same company or set of companies year after year for continued profits (a racket in the criminal sense). At Sangdo, the handful of publicly traded companies within the conglomerate each dealt with their own extortionists. Midlevel finance managers I spoke with lamented the burden that these extortionists placed on organizing complex meetings. For many companies or finance managers, participating in the racket by paying them off is easier than dealing with them at a time- and decorum-restricted meeting with company reputation, and the possibility of legal recourse, on the line.

A South Korean legal blog explaining the phenomenon admitted that if a company wanted to sue a disrupter for obstruction of work or even defamation, it would be difficult case to win because a disrupter can claim an infringement on shareholder rights while denying malicious intent.[26] Paying bribes to them is also illegal for companies—it is an unauthorized form of profit distribution and hence a breaking of fiduciary duty to other shareholders—so it is not overtly publicized or noted on company financial records, though it is widely known as a general phenomenon. According to the site, companies fearful of extortionists should "bite the bullet" and pay up money or material to avoid serious disruptions.

Beyond legal mechanisms for combating extortion, a practical problem extortionists pose is that it is difficult to distinguish a good shareholder from a bad one. Political scientist James Scott has described two tactics of resistance from weaker political groups to involve anonymity and ambiguity—the concealment of the identity of the speaker (with a clear message) or the concealment of the message (with a clear identity).[27] *Chonghoe-ggun* rely on both of these. One news article in Korean states this baldly in the headline: "Is it a Humble Shareholder or an Extortionist . . . the Best Make $100K!"[28] This ambiguity of identity was made apparent when I was talking to two senior managers at Sangdo following the 2015 shareholder meeting at the tower. At a meeting one of them attended years earlier, a disheveled man going into the meeting was carrying a simple black plastic bag from a convenience store. The manager did not assume him to be a wealthy investor, but when he happened to glance into the bag and noticed large stacks of shareholding bills, he suddenly realized that he was one of the company's largest minority share-holders. In this way, company employees have to treat potential extortion-ists just as they would other shareholders—as honored guests (*guibin*). Ex-tortion can only be interpolated as such during the act of disruption and even then it relies on its ambiguous position next to legitimate criticism; it is no crime to simply ask a question or even be present. In a news video from 1998 chronicling a tumultuous meeting at the Bank of Korea's shareholder meet-ing following the Asian Financial Crisis, the ambiguity of shareholder status becomes apparent as the event unfolds. As a number of individual sharehold-ers began to shout at the directors, it becomes unclear who is making a legiti-mate complaint, such as one man saying he spent his entire retirement savings on stock in the bank, or another who complained of the company's poor lead-ership. In the video, one suit-clad member of the company acting as a secu-rity guard tries to verbally mark one of them as an extortionist, shouting "I've seen you at other shareholder meetings!" By claiming that the shareholder at-tended other companies' meetings, he attempted to authenticate his claims as an insincere shareholder, rendering his criticism disingenuous.

One news article from 2001 notes that companies provide "hush money" in an envelope ahead of time to these men to ward off their physical presence at the meetings.[29] A television investigation in 2014 reported that companies are at the whim of extortionists, entertaining them regularly and providing them with gifts directly from the company's product lines. For extortionists that "know a company well," the reporter claimed that companies would de-liver whatever the men requested. The TV anchor listening to the reporter's account remarked in disbelief, "Are you saying that companies will listen to the absurd requests of just one shareholder?" The reporter confirmed, say-ing that companies who thought about reporting to the Financial Supervi-sory Service (the national financial regulator) were worried that the share-holder would come back next year to hurt them again with more ill will.[30] A Korean Broadcasting System (KBS) report from 2003 suggested that compa-nies even have different ranks (*deung-geup*) of A, B, and C to decide how much each should receive in payout—not unlike those ranks used to mark employee performances.

Paying off is a low-cost method of keeping potential agitators at bay.[31] Some companies make a payoff prior to the event, while others risk waiting until the event itself: one company was reported to prepare hundreds of dollars' worth of gift certificates to a department store at the door to their meeting in case some arrived. On the online message board cited earlier, the same employee notes how he can distinguish *chonghoe-ggun* on their arrival:

> Usually the people that come [to our meetings] are long-term shareholders who exchange greetings and then normally leave, but every year there are some new faces that show up. In these cases, it's almost the same process:
>
> 1. The person talks about their pride (usually about where they work)
> 2. Gives compliments about our company
> 3. Since it's a great company, it should logically keep its shareholders happy.
>
> If the conversation goes like that, I can tell that person's style (how much they know about commercial code and their likelihood for revenge) so I decide what to give to them based on that. All of the *chonghoe-ggun* who come to the company have different abilities, and based on such, I give them different amounts.[32]

Later he notes that if he does not give them what they want, they might come back to the next meeting to seek their revenge (using a metaphor for a spurned lover). Being a successful disrupter in this case is not merely a matter of a willingness for temporary public speaking; specific conditions must be met for one to be properly recognized—and rewarded—as a legitimate illegitimate shareholder. In contrast to other forms of interruption that rely on spectacle (such as noise protests), *chonghoe-ggun* forms of interruption rely on intimate knowledge and a specific kind of training in how to speak properly in parliamentary meetings about company proceedings. They can operate without any visible act of interruption at all.

At a Sangdo Group meeting in 2015, managers from one department had prepared a goody bag of company gifts (such as a USB stick) that they planned to give to known extortionists if they arrived. One did in fact arrive to the meeting, but it was after the meeting had begun. Because of rules for entering the meeting, the employees manning the doors were not obligated to let him in. Company actors drew on procedural rules and spatial access, not to mention the co-occurrence of other company meetings on Super Shareholder Meeting Day, to stave off a potential disrupter. Instead of polite questioning, company actors relied on different kinds of methods to interrupt the interrupters. It is no wonder that one commentator has described companies themselves as their own kind of *chonghoe-ggun*.[33]

Managing the Meeting

At the Sangdo holding company shareholder meeting in 2015, I sat next to assistant manager Ji-soon from the HR department. For Ji-soon, who had been to a few annual meetings before, the affair seemed ho-hum and predictable. From the first bang of the gavel to resolution voting at the end, the entire event was scripted, including the questions and answers. This is not so shocking given that meetings must follow a standard set of procedures and pronouncements in order to constitute a proper act of disclosure and voting. The script template had been provided by the KLCA and was modified for the context by members of the finance team, including filling in the financial figures and the contents of that meeting's resolutions. The meeting's convener discussed difficulties from the American steel tariffs, new branding plans, and the risk of potential downturns in the global steel market due to Chinese overproduction. However, beyond the formal oratory, other aspects of the meeting also went according to a different kind of script.

In the week prior to the meeting, the holding company was preparing for the meeting in different ways: roles were preassigned to employees around the office together with the script. Some employees at the holding company had jobs manning the welcome desk to greet shareholders and hand out the day's pamphlet with the enclosed financial statements. Others were in charge of making sure the microphones worked and VIP patrons were seated in front. Ji-soon and I did not have official roles but acted as anonymous shareholders. We took off the company pins on our lapels and ID badges from our necks and entered the meeting as would any shareholder.[34] We pretended not to recognize other coworkers when we entered the auditorium. Our primary job was to voice agreements during a voice vote in favor of company resolutions. Attending the meeting as undercover employees and participating in votes was not itself illegitimate: many employees at Sangdo owned some nominal shares in their employer.

More complex interactional roles during the meeting went to a half-dozen midlevel managers who had speaking parts. Since each of the resolutions had to be introduced by a shareholder, that task fell to those who were each assigned a different resolution to propose for ratification. Each of their parts was written out in detail in the script. The basic structure of their responses was the following: announcing their real name and status as a shareholder, indicating that they read about the resolution in the proxy statement, expressing approval of the resolution on the issue at hand, and asking the CEO to take a vote on the issue. As the CEO thanked each shareholder (*juju*), he called each resolution to a vote, at which time the other shareholders in the auditorium called out in unison that they supported the resolution, shouting "[We] second that!"[35] Following the vote, the CEO asked if there were any other opinions on the resolution, to which the members of the audience once again yelled out in unison, "There are no other opinions!"

In this way, the script plotted out the formal aspects of shareholder meetings (summary of financial results, announcement of company strategy, and so on). But its smoothness was not about presenting a clean corporate image—it was about anticipating possible interruptions, particularly by closely calibrating the call and response formats with natural and authentic interjections by audience members. In this way, the meeting adhered to the rules specified in parliamentary norms. This goes beyond just protection against threats to the company's face. If resolutions at shareholder meetings are delayed or not agreed on, this could cause problems for the (re-)election of new executives, directors, and auditors, not to mention major corporate decisions such as mergers, stock splits, or restructuring. All major governance-related decisions must pass through the bottleneck of the meeting's parliamentary process. In this light, it is not the case that extortionists necessarily break up scripted meetings; rather, scripted or formal meetings are created to interrupt extortionists who might not even be in attendance.

Shareholder meetings also involve physical or spatial barriers that make entrance into meetings more complicated. At the holding company's annual meeting, building security guards were rerouted to monitor the hallways leading up to the meeting on the fourth floor of the venue. This was not meant to prevent anyone from entering, but it likely slowed down potential *chonghoeggun* and tipped off managers. Other incidents, however, have highlighted how the entrance to a building can act as a site where norms of decorum abruptly end. A video from a reporter at the 2017 shareholder meeting of a POSCO company, South Korea's largest steel conglomerate, is a case in point. At the high-profile meeting, a video shows groups of men blocking the rotating doors as potential shareholders attempted to enter. The men blocking the doors stood silently, ignoring the legitimate shareholders' requests, but on occasion suggested to the potential shareholders to enter on another side of the building, where they encountered more human blockades. One shareholder interviewed by a journalist angrily labeled the CEO Kwon Oh-joon a dictator, depriving him of his shareholder rights and equating with him North Korean dictator Kim Jong-un. At that meeting, the CEO was up for reelection as director, which certain investors opposed, but the vote nevertheless passed handily. Those on the outside also included members of POSCO's metal unions who exclaimed their status as shareholders and affirmed their right to attend. In the video, these anonymous human barriers were referred to simply as "company side" (*hoesajeuk*) people, a vague reference to their general allegiance, though it is difficult to assess who, exactly, they are: deputized POSCO employees, contracted building security officers, or outsourced private security forces.[36] Spatial barriers such as these rely on para-procedural practices that are visibly unethical but hard to pin down as illegitimate; the meeting itself was being carried on smoothly inside. Furthermore, showing any intentional or observable form of suppression would constitute infringement of rights—a fact embodied in the silent human barriers who proclaimed no interest or intent in the POSCO shareholder meeting proceedings.[37]

Both the KLCA and individual companies maintain lists of known *chonghoe-ggun*. A finance manager at Sangdo told me he possessed a list for known extortionists. For him, it was originally used to ward people off at the door when their IDs were corroborated with the list. Recently, however, they could not use the list to turn people away due to a violation of shareholders' rights to attendance. He used the list instead to know whom to give money or goods to. In 2007, the KLCA established a support center specifically for extortionist issues, hoping to "end the tyranny" once and for all.[38] The center promised to create a database of the worst *chonghoe-ggun* offenders (with their full names, characteristics, and whereabouts) and circulate case studies on best practices and establish a telephone hotline for companies to call for consultation. The oft-repeated goal within these efforts by the KLCA was to create "law-abiding" and "rational" management methods for running meetings that companies could follow.[39]

The KLCA also issued a set of guidelines called "Tips for Running Shareholder Meetings." The document reiterated the basic principles of deliberative bodies like a shareholder meeting and outlined the general procedures for running a meeting. The document expends considerable attention specifying the proper role and authority of the meeting chairperson and how to deal with shareholder questions. While outlining these powers, the document makes clear that the chairperson is as equally vested in allowing deliberation as he or she is in controlling problematic shareholders. Only on a few occasions, such as stopping the meeting proceedings or presenting a false identity, for instance, can a member of the audience be removed. In this sense, meeting rules delimit the powers of corporate directors and other members as much as they outline what they are permitted to do. This is why a primary way of disrupting the disrupters, so to speak, is through meeting clustering via the Super Shareholder Meeting Day. By scheduling meetings at the same time and in different locations, coordination efforts prevent legitimate shareholders with stock in multiple companies from attending multiple meetings. This moment of cross-company collusion takes advantage of a body problem: shareholders, extortionists included, can only attend one meeting at a time. While this clustering of meetings is partly an outcome of shared fiscal calendars (such that companies generally plan to have their meeting at the same time of year), strict alignment to a specific time (and scattered locations) is no coincidence.[40] (American companies such as Walmart or Berkshire Hathaway do a variation of this by holding their shareholder meetings in hard-to-reach locations, replete with fanfare and entertainment as distractions.) Most South Korean corporate shareholder meetings nevertheless maintain highly formal meeting aesthetics centered in the metropole, Seoul. Coordination of this variety, while stemming the tide of potential *chonghoe-ggun*, minimizes the chances of extortionists entering, while hurting sincere (or at least non-extortive) shareholders who have interests in multiple companies.[41]

Shareholder meetings are ritualized events with specific roles, narrative sequences, and performance conditions. While this fact is meant to constrain actors and allow minority shareholders the right to speak, it also engenders a large production process that company actors are ultimately responsible for. This gives them particular control over how they manage the wider context of the meeting itself. Because these efforts are necessary to put on a legally recognized meeting, it grants leeway in how far company actors can go to restrict access to unwanted guests. It is one way of managing unwanted distinctions (and undesired payouts) from outsiders.

Institutional Challenges

A 2008 news piece titled "Where Have All the *chonghoe-ggun* Gone?" suggested that extortionists were disappearing from Korean shareholder meetings. One reason given was the effect of government crackdowns in the previous year. Another reason was that a stronger force had emerged: institutional investors (*gigwan juju*). These investors, such as the Korean National Pension

Service (NPS) or asset management firms, have different orientations to corporate performance from typical extortionists. They generally have larger stakes in a company, greater than 5 percent, with interest in the selection of directors, company mergers and sell-offs, and overall corporate strategy. For *chonghoe-ggun*, these issues are simply talking points to create the fiction of shareholder sincerity on the way to a payoff. For institutional investors, their payoff comes from the overall value of the investment itself. The NPS, for instance, has come to command significant sway in deciding corporate futures in South Korea with a value at roughly US$400 billion in 2014, making it the fourth largest in the world at the time. Their might became apparent in 2016 when it was revealed that South Korea's most powerful corporate group, Samsung Group, had attempted to influence the chief of the NPS to approve a merger between two Samsung subsidiaries, leading many in South Korea to see the NPS as simply a vassal of conglomerate family power. However, compared to many chaebol families, the NPS actually held a greater share in conglomerate affiliates than the sum of individual family members, which allowed it to demonstrate its power as an activist shareholder in certain key votes, even earning the rebuke of the Federation of Korean Industries (FKI), a conservative lobbying group.[42] Institutional investors have become a new disturbance in the investing landscape in South Korea, in part due to their financial stakes that manifest in the power of proportional voting in meetings.

Institutional investors are not the only ones to make corporate critiques through shareholder meetings. One highly publicized activist shareholder group in South Korea, People's Solidarity for Participant Democracy (PSPD, or *chamyeo yeondae*), has used shareholder meetings as a means to push for economic reform since 1994. After the Asian Financial Crisis raised significant concerns about internal corporate governance, members of PSPD became renowned for confronting the country's major conglomerates via vocal advocacy for minority shareholder rights and adherence to governance procedures. PSPD activists began asking questions at meetings that would expose management as incompetent. Unlike *chonghoe-ggun*, however, PSPD members sent questions ahead of time to management and even sued when companies tried to suppress their questions. In some cases, resolutions that they had submitted were voted on and approved by shareholders. Their targets were ultimately beyond the meetings themselves: they zeroed in on the country's largest groups such as Samsung and Hyundai to serve as a partial warning to other groups. They filed complaints with different agencies such as the Financial Supervisory Service over accounting discrepancies and the Fair Trade Commission over suspicious internal dealings.[43]

In 2016, Elliot Management, a large US-based hedge fund that held significant holdings in Samsung companies, combined strategies of both institutional investors and activists. Elliot, led by the US investor Peter Singer, began a public campaign to push for Samsung to adopt new resolutions, notably recommending that the company form a financial holding company and divest itself of direct family management. In advance of the annual meeting, Elliot created a website with a letter to the directors and a downloadable slide presentation outlining their recommendations to increase "value enhancement" of Samsung Electronics.[44] The documents argued along the same grounds as other activists that Samsung's corporate structure was hoarding value to the owning Lee family, away from shareholders, albeit couched in a language addressed not to South Korean citizens but to general, profit-minded investors. The gist of their criticism was that poor management meant Samsung was trading at a discount (or lower than it should be valued), a rate that would increase if Samsung improved its management practices based on Elliott's recommendations. A key outcome of the corporate restructuring would be a higher and variable dividend paid to shareholders based on quarterly earnings. Regular dividends are a staple of the shareholder-value movement that Singer had long advocated and one that South Korean conglomerates have been notably resistant to.[45] Up until 2015, South Korean companies paid only 15 percent of profits to shareholders compared with 46 percent in Hong Kong and 28 percent in Japan.[46]

Democratic Interruptions, New Distributions

Marx noted in Volume III of his *Capital* that the distribution of profit makes hostile brothers who must fight to decide over the surplus value that they did not labor for.[47] This chapter has focused on how shareholder meetings are sites where corporations are broken down into their financial and legal components, revealing a number of competing interests, while being mediated by a peculiar meeting event governing their interactions. In some ways, shareholder meetings are a model of democratic discursive practice precisely because they acknowledge each of these different interests, partly in the name of protecting the rights of minority shareholders and allowing even small parties to share their voices. This kind of radical parliamentary format, premised on difficult questions and answers with potentially real consequences, differs significantly from the vague calls for affective *sotong* (conversation) between employees, townhall meetings, or the psychometric collection of voices discussed in the previous chapter. Events such as those maintain a certain fiction of participation and communication without its more conflict-oriented connotations (that parliamentary discourse is meant to encourage). Many Sangdo managers seemed to loathe the burden of the meeting, in part because they had to carefully manage a public event outside of their normal work responsibilities. More importantly, the meetings were also a space that temporarily erased the existence of their own vision of a supercorporate ideal, casting them into new participatory roles entirely distinct from their workaday ranks and responsibilities; they became anonymous in the crowd, reduced to shareholders. One Sangdo manager, longing perhaps for an escape from his office role, did admit to me that he was envious of the *chonghoe-ggun* precisely because of the investment returns they got seemingly without working.

Shareholder meetings represent a useful foil for thinking about where the broader field of distinction and participation is shaped. This is precisely because they are imposed sites of distinction by the state wherein property, not tenure or managerial merit, becomes a key marker of claims to a supercorporate ideal. The complaints offered by the various institutional or activist actors point to their own criticisms of corporate management at specific companies or the corporate system. Moreover, they signal a commitment to a better functioning corporate system in which distinctions—in the form of monetary payout for some, a reduction in civil society inequalities for others—can be properly organized. (*Chonghoe-ggun* arguably do this too, as they can point out managerial improprieties corporate leaders might not want revealed.) The broader world that organizes shareholder meetings—auditors, financial regulators, financial markets, the KLCA, and the media—also points to the fact that the infrastructure of distinction is not solely controlled by internal corporate actors through formal ranks and organizational distinctions.

The meeting itself, then, is a kind of social fiction in which shareholders, activists, institutional investors, or even *chonghoe-ggun*, for a brief time each year, become privileged insiders, though they also turn to managing behind the scenes, to a degree. Elliot Management, despite its clout as a global shareholder activist, considerable financial holdings, and specially created website, still had to maneuver within the particularities of meetings: submitting a proposal, making a campaign, and garnering votes from other shareholders (including the NPS). Ultimately, Elliot did not get its resolution passed and later sold its shares in Samsung. (Elliott, for better or worse, was partially vindicated when Samsung was found later to have used presidential bribes and government coercion to force the NPS into publicly supporting a merger of two Samsung subsidiaries, even though it would incur a loss for the NPS and other shareholders.) PSPD and Elliot, despite their antithetical politics, both use meetings as sites for making injunctions into corporate restructuring in ways that are meant to threaten other companies as well. The moral claims differ considerably, however: NGO activists such as PSPD can frame their meeting crusades on behalf of civil society that is battling large corporations that are parasitizing off a working public and a distant state. Activity against one major group such as Samsung might reverberate across the economy to lead to wider social change for South Korea. And *chonghoe-ggun* must be relatively knowledgeable insiders to know what a corporation has or has not done in order to make a claim in public; they are, in some ways, shadow employees seeking a bonus by other means. In any case, meetings themselves are a reminder that the closed worlds of corporations and organizations—full of more banal meetings—always imbricate broader governance and control relationships, with many competing claims or interests. The meeting is the one site where these claims become recognized and protected by the state, but not necessarily by those with competing claims and points of distinction. Like the seeming inevitability of *chonghoe-ggun* interrupting meetings, the demise of which has long been predicted, competing aspirations will continue to converge on corporate forms. In the next chapter, I turn to another site that also appears difficult to purify from corporate life and where new kinds of distinction emerge: after-hours socializing.

6

Virtual Escapes

WHEN I FIRST VISITED SEOUL IN 2011, I went to a meeting at a prominent corporate tower on the island of Yeouido in the Han River, the site of some of the country's largest broadcasting, finance, and electronics companies. One particularly striking image from that visit was the scene of hundreds of men (and a few women) gathered in front of the tower on their smoking breaks. Gathered into small groups of two or three or alone looking at their phones, the smokers were easily identified with where they worked: replete in corporate suits, wearing company IDs around their necks, and standing closely around all sides of the company tower. The crowd operated as an obligatory passageway to enter or exit the tower. When I visited again three years later in 2014, the front plaza was conspicuously empty. I asked a friend who worked there what had happened to all the smokers. He told me that the smoking area had been relegated to a tiny garden area in an atrium within the basement of the tower. The space fit what seemed like nearly the same number of smokers but in a tenth of the space and out of sight of the rest of the workforce.

At around the same time, space around the Sangdo office was also becoming more and more delimited for smokers: only a small area behind a convenience store in front of the building was available. The sidewalks around the building and public areas in front of it had conspicuous "No Smoking" signs. Smoking was also being targeted in other parts of Seoul with posh areas such as Gangnam handing out hefty fines for smoking on main thoroughfares. Restaurants and coffee shops that once had smoking areas briefly transitioned to internal smoking rooms before finally getting rid of indoor smoking completely by 2016. Smoking within Sangdo had also become a stigmatized activity. Sangdo First, one of the largest subsidiaries in the group, had created their own antismoking campaign in 2014, encouraging workers to put their name on a list posted on the intranet with a commitment to quit. Factories, too, made commitments to be smoke-free zones. I had heard of one executive who had become tired of workers making the long trek to go to the designated smoking areas and inquired whether it would be possible to install cameras to see who was going and for how long. (It was not legally possible, it turned out). Secondary damage (*ganjeop heub-yeon*) from smoking also became a moral discourse, particularly the smell that lingered on smokers' clothing. One day when team manager Jang and I had emerged from an elevator after a smoking break, a more senior HR manager warned us about the smoke that lingers on our jackets—in particular the secondary harm that this might do to Ji-soon, our female coworker.

Regulating smoking was one area where South Korean companies, alongside municipalities and retail areas, had taken a hardline stance: public antismoking campaigns, higher taxes on cigarettes, outlawed spaces, and new moral discourses against smokers. The smoking rate among men during my fieldwork in 2014 was reported to be 43.1 percent but only 5.7 percent among women (according to data from www.nosmokeguide.go.kr).[1] For a longtime smoker like team manager Jang, the smoking bans and increased taxes were a misdirected attack on hardworking people who were trying to escape the doldrums of the workday. Moreover, many male office workers told me they started smoking during their obligatory military service because that was the only way that they could get an authorized break time. Jang did acknowledge that smoking could be a good way to kill time or at least putatively talk about work while getting some air. Smoking also afforded its own kind of sociality among men—it was a time during large group events when one could break off, decompress, and regroup. For me, it was an occasion to discover new locations—I once visited the roof of the Sangdo tower with a building manager on the basis of finding a new place to have a cigarette. Nevertheless, it was clear that antismoking had emerged as a strong object of control over individual behavior. Other stigmatized areas were more difficult to control, particularly drinking and after-hours socializing. Despite a number of actions taken to curb drinking (some of which had been directed at the illicit behaviors of older male managers described in Chapter 3), after-hours drinking remained a common social ritual. Where some company-sponsored drinking was curbed by cutting off funds or discouraging late-night ventures, employees were still free to go on their own time and money—and companies could do little to stop them. This point became evident when I spoke to members of Sangdo's auditing team. The auditing team was the closest thing to an internal police force within the group and had the authority to monitor and audit every branch in the entire Sangdo Group around the world. While they could, with some degree of impunity, ask for detailed information from any office about their business activities, recommend penalties or oversight, and investigate financial crimes, they had little ability to regulate after-hours behavior. Unless it was paid for by company money, they had no jurisdiction over private lives. They had helped to implement certain restrictions on the use of company credit cards: a program called "clean card" prevented cards from being used at white-listed business names associated with late-night hostess bars or bottle services. But they could not stop employees on their own money or time.

This chapter centers on the ambiguous boundary of after-hours socializing as a form of out-of-office distinction and participation at Sangdo, particularly in what it means to escape from work with coworkers and what kinds of distinctions can emerge in the shadow of corporate-centered social events. The chapter deals with a central genre of South Korean office social life—*hoesik* and some of its alternatives. *Hoesik* denotes a rather simple activity of eating or socializing with one's coworkers after work; its cultural connotation is much wider, hinting at the more nefarious elements of South Korean office life—secrecy, harassment, bribery, prostitution, wasted spending, and group punishment. As a generic event, however, *hoesik* can refer to a wide range of social activities that employees do after work together, sometimes subsidized by or promoted by their company or individual team, and sometimes not. It can refer to activities such as drinking *hoesik* (*suljari hoesik*), cultural *hoesik* (*munhwa hoesik*), mentoring *hoesik* (*mentoring hoesik*), and leisure *hoesik* (*rejeo hoesik*). Beyond formal, named activities, *hoesik* can also constitute spontaneous gatherings of employees after work when employees might share the cost or a team manager might pay for his or her team members. For many employees, however, defined distinctions between official or unofficial, sponsored or self-paid forms of *hoesik* are irrelevant: any time office relations are reconstituted after work implies a *hoesik* event.[2]

Hoesik comes under considerable public scrutiny every year in the South Korean news, as reports come out detailing just how much large conglomerates (as well as government offices and public corporations) spend on after-hours eating, drinking, and entertainment. In 2011, the *Kyung Hyang* newspaper noted that the country's reported "entertainment expenses" (*jeopdaebi*) topped eight trillion won (roughly US$8 billion) from more than 460,000 total legal entities reporting, with the largest companies reporting an average of US$3 million in expenses. The "uncomfortable fact" reported in the article was that although entertainment money was meant to be spent on guests, foreign business partners, and clients, most of the funds were largely spent by employees entertaining among themselves. It is for this reason that cultural critics such as Kang Jun-man have described the necessity of going to *hoesik* as a kind of structural violence. Events such as *hoesik* are part of efforts to increase absolute loyalty to organizations. In an opinion piece published in 2018, Kang goes so far as to call it a kind of mafia culture (*jopokmunhwa*) because of the way that employees will not betray their organizations, even when organizations have done them wrong.[3] At least the mafia, Kang notes, have no pretense for being hypocrites by claiming they are helping society. Kang draws a parallel between the slavish adoration of company prestige and over-identification with one's company in present-day South Korea with William Whyte's criticism of the soulless organization man of 1950s America.

One of the difficulties of analyzing something like *hoesik* and other alternatives is that such activities do not always operate in the name of bald corporate control. An ethnographic perspective from the Sangdo Group offers a window into a wide range of ways that employees socialized voluntarily and the different ways these contributed to or detracted from new visions of office social life. While many companies have looked to improve the quality of activities, such as shifting from drinking to dining and from late nights to early evenings, so as to minimize the social and financial harms caused by excessive drinking, this chapter addresses the kinds of social dynamics that emerge in the absence of company control. I suggest that tensions over distinction and participation present in workday activities also extend to after-hours socializing where signs of group participation become indirect forms of interpersonal distinction among team members and managers.

Descriptions of after-hours social life in East Asia have long oscillated between treating it as a site of social escape or of social obligation. In an early account by David Plath in *After Hours*, for instance, 1950s postwar Japan was a site of after-hours socializing in groups to recover a sense of *comunitas* from the alienation and individuation of modern, office-based work styles.[4] Leisure was not something to be enjoyed in the privacy of one's home but was to be experienced as part of a group. In *The Japanese Company*, Rodney Clark described the feeling of leisure with colleagues as like being a child again, enjoying hobbies such as mahjong, baseball, and hiking.[5] Anne Allison's *Nightwork* shattered some of these markedly male ideas of utopic after-hours leisure: in her account of a Japanese hostess bar, after-work drinking was about restoring a sense of self for male office workers through a reinvigoration of manliness and masculinity.[6] Late-night drinking encounters were not just about getting away but about recreating a highly gendered fantasy separate from work relations and home relations. This leisure escape for Japanese salarymen necessitated a particular kind of labor for women who worked at hostess bars.

Beyond the therapeutic aspects, there are also instrumental dimensions to participating in after-hours events such as developing *tsukiai* (associations), described by Reiko Atsumi, in which individuals strategically attend company dinners in Japan to build up their intracompany networks.[7] Overlaying informal events with instrumental purposes has been particularly thematized in the literature on Chinese *guanxi* (connections), long a focus of attention in studies of Chinese political and economic relations.[8] The focus on *guanxi*, which usually concerns complex networks of favors, has highlighted how affect and instrumentality are not opposed objects or entirely separate spheres of activities (as are imaginations of gifts and commodities in the West) but are deliberately overlaid on each other. In South Korea, the Act on Prohibition of Illegal Requests and Bribes that went into law in 2016 deliberately targeted the gift culture that was used to grant access (*juripcheo*) or curry favor across a range of institutional actors, including teachers, journalists, politicians, civil servants, and corporate actors. Prohibited items included cash gifts, gifted dinners, holiday packages, sexual entertainment, and free or discounted rounds of golf.[9] Leisure activities, precisely because they are ambiguous as both a commodity and event, can provide ideal frames for favor seeking.[10]

Alongside such politicized views of after-hours activities, *hoesik* also operates on smaller scales—and indeed many office workers experience *hoesik* as events organized around their teams. At Sangdo, individual teams had their own monthly *hoesik* budgets of around US$50 dollars per person that they could spend on group activities. While team managers were formally responsible for the credit cards and the spending, the youngest members of any team were often in charge of tracking the budget, picking restaurants, sending out invitations, or corralling members. Though *hoesik* itself is a type of event, any given event could engender its own forms of excitement or interest, such as choosing to go to a new activity or pairing up with a new team. The HR team, for example, periodically met with other HR teams as a way to build relationships across the group and to experience new sites of consumption. One special event, for instance, involved a large multiteam outing to a barbeque restaurant called Indian Forest Dining where we experienced American-style camping barbeque surrounded by mass-produced Native American paraphernalia (partaking of a South Korean trend toward retro-Americana). At such occasions, HR managers could chat personally and talk about recent company events such as new policies in effect or employees who had left. Which team would pay, how long to stay, who would keep or lose their composure, who had hidden storytelling or singing talents—these questions all added to the particular drama of any individual event. On one occasion, for instance, in a cross-team *hoesik* event with the legal department, the head of the legal department had employees pair up with someone from the opposite team and interview each other. Then going one by one, employees had to reveal something to the larger group that they had learned about the other person. In another event with a subsidiary HR team, one team manager framed it as a drinking contest in which we would try to "offer" so many shots of soju to the other team that they would give up early and go home (thereby proving our team as the stronger team and ending the event more quickly). At other *hoesik* events, the mood can be more sentimental: at a retirement event for the outgoing CEO of the Sangdo holding company, employees listened attentively around a large table as he recounted stories from his decades of working for the group. Some employees later went to a 7080 live music bar, where a band allowed members to sing classic Korean songs from the 1970s and 1980s.

Hoesik, while often associated with a heightened ritual of corporate sociality or even deal making, is often enacted as a form of college or friendship sociality, such as by enacting lighthearted drinking games, eating cheap food, singing in a private karaoke rooms, playing arcade games, or simply spending hours talking in a small group. Employees can reveal secret talents for creating special drinks or drink effects such as a tornado in a bottle or a unique way of pouring "bomb" drinks (a combination of beer and soju that often serves as the figurative icebreaker at many *hoesik* events). Team manager Jang had his own interactional style at *hoesik* events: he would often create mock quizzes with shy younger employees, asking them simple questions to put their conversational skills in the foreground—such as which of their bosses they liked more, whether they were dating anyone, which celebrity they thought they resembled, and how they would describe their own office fashion style. One particularly creative activity was *samhaengsi* (three-line poems). In this activity, one person names a word with three characters, usually a person's name (such as Hong Gil-dong), and another person must come up with a short limerick where each line begins with that character (Hong . . . , Gil . . . , Dong . . .), testing one's on-the-spot creativity. Short and punctual toasts at other events also tested one's creativity in front of a group, such as when the toast must always end with the phrase *wihayeo* (Here's to . . .)—the cue to raise a drink. At the last *hoesik* event I attended at Sangdo, the event served as a welcome for a number of new middle managers who had joined in the previous months. Each one had to get up in succession to offer a toast to the audience of about twenty. Each one had to creatively come up with a progressively more clever and intense toast that could top the previous one: while the first manager took just one shot of soju, the second took a glass, and the third drank an entire bottle.

Within even these small genres of creativity, however, lies an element of social pressure and individual evaluation, a seriousness and intensity to spontaneous acts of play, not of corporate loyalty in the abstract. This dual sense of after-hours events as both escape and obligation is felt across any typical office: many people will be eager to participate, others resistant. Take, for example, these two descriptions from a popular newspaper column called *Assistant Manager Kim and Assistant Manager Lee* that give contrasting accounts of this sentiment:

> Assistant Manager Kim is an aficionado of *hoesik*. He can have his favorite drink without paying his own money . . . There is a chance to loosen up tied things and break through blocked things. With a little drink, he can also explain his "poor performance," and sometimes he can get a thrill by standing up to his boss. The eternal charm of *hoesik* is that he can restore relationships with juniors and seniors that have been become alienated. Sometimes the boss breaks the subordinates and ruins the atmosphere, but Kim's experience is that there are many more benefits.
>
> Assistant Manager Lee is different. He drinks an adequate amount, but he hates the atmosphere. You have to drink and drink a glass that gets passed around without any meaning. You have to laugh at topics that don't have a speck of something called interest. It is difficult to endure a boss who unilaterally decides the alcohol, the topic, and the time to end.

For the Lees and Kims around the country, *hoesik* is literally the object of love/hate [*aejeung*].

Sociologist Minjae Kim has described how *hoesik* seems to go in the face of most sociological accounts of social conformity: given both love and hate for these kinds of events, why would a majority willfully engage in a collective activity that they perhaps do not like?[11] Part of the answer is that engaging in acts that are arduous reveals aspects of the self, commitment, and bonding in ways that conventional work contexts do not. It is not uncommon for male office workers (and men in general) to ask each other how many bottles of soju they can drink in one sitting (one's *juryang*, or drinking number), how many different bar "rounds" they make, or simply how often they go out to *hoesik*. These kinds of questions, in other words, operate as important social metrics of personal qualities.[12] While there is an element of radical leveling among employees at drinking events and the ability to release from work and participate in a kind of social undressing, there is also a sense of moving from one form of distinction to another, in which the metrics themselves can be highly emergent and the outcomes surprising.

Employees also sought out other after-hours activities that de-emphasized some of the performative pressures of these activities. For instance, one Sangdo office created its own intramural futsal team (5-on-5 soccer) called Sangdo FC. The players invested in high-quality custom uniforms modeled after the uniforms of a famous French Ligue 1 team with the Sangdo logo emblazoned on the front. When I played with them one day in July for their twice monthly game, I noticed that the players had added their own English names to the back, such as "J. J. Choi," "Ronaldo," and "Fermented Skate" (the last being a variety of fish famous in southeast South Korea). Comprising mid- and low-ranking men, the players organized themselves into impromptu teams without dividing according to company affiliations or roles. At one point they satirically organized into old and young teams, with the older players being those in their midthirties. The atmosphere was convivial as a few employees brought sandwiches and fruit for everyone to share. A photographer was on hand to create a segment in the Sangdo employee magazine about the group. He took pictures of the games and staged special action shots for the players to show off their skills. While the subsequent magazine article portrayed them as embodying one of the company values—"passion"—which they were able to demonstrate through their passion for soccer on the field, such an event was largely an oasis for young workers from some of the pressures of more official events, where they could ignore some of the intracompany hierarchies, adorn a different kind of uniform, and make fun of each other. Such escapes, however, can also become sites for new forms of distinction drawing, particularly around consumptive activities.

Virtual Escapes

It was about halfway through my time at Sangdo that I considered switching my research topic entirely—to virtual golf. I began to spend considerable amount of my time thinking about, talking about, and playing virtual golf with the HR team. Yet it was not an intentional decision, nor was it the proverbial ethnographic breakthrough that anthropologists have described as a particularly welcome moment in fieldwork when social patterns or unfamiliar norms start to make sense. In December, the team began to play virtual golf, or simply "screen" as it is known. At first, we played one day a week, soon followed by two days a week. By the time I left in June, one or all of us might play any free day a week, pending other social events. At one point, the team held a mock tournament on a Sunday that lasted from 10:00 a.m. to 5:00 p.m. when we played four rounds of simulated golf in one day. And we eventually made excursions to actual golf courses three times, including when I revisited the firm in 2016.

When we first began, I thought virtual golf was a virtual paradise that made the research process particularly fun. For the cost of about US$20, one could play golf in a private room, order beer and fried chicken, while playing within a high-tech surround. It was one way to avoid the normal *hoesik* activities that revolved around eating, drinking, and singing. However, by the end of my time at Sangdo in June 2015, playing golf had become a burden. It drained my limited stipend and research funding, it caused resentment among some team members, and it was almost worse than regular drinking given the amount of time it consumed. For my ethnographic research, it felt particularly damaging: the down time at the end of the day is cherished time when one takes what has been jotted down to do the ritual of a long-form write-up from interviews and observations during the day. After having interviews with IT managers and lawyers, building managers and marketers, I would be eager to return home to listen to interviews or write up what I had learned, when one member might tap me on the shoulder and ask, "What are your plans tonight?" Writing up notes was not a strong defense. (Since my time at Sangdo, the issue of veto power [*geobu-kwon haengsa*] over *hoesik* has become more prominent in recent years).[13]

Discussion of golf has often been framed as an issue around class, power, and access, such as when powerful corporations sought permits to build golf courses in the early 1990s, an era described as a "Golf Republic."[14]As both an activity and an analogy, virtual golf offers much to explore, however. If drinking together is primarily about forming or reinforcing social bonds through a symbolic descent from formality to informality, from clean to dirty, and from sobriety to inebriation, what could virtual golf possibly encapsulate as an activity? More than simply playing in front of a screen like a video game, it comprises practicing or playing eighteen holes of golf in a room set up with a screen, a projector, a tee with artificial grass, and a laser-guided tracking system attached to the ceiling or floor that detects the ball being hit. The key part of the simulated experience is that one plays with real golf clubs and golf balls. One can also choose to wear shoes, pants, shirts, and gloves made specifically for golf. In rooms painted green, there is a special platform where one stands with Astroturf that can mimic the grade and angle of a course. Physical and digital technologies capture one's swing and contact with the ball as a mat on the wall captures the ball safely. At the same moment, a simulated ball projected onto the screen flies through the air in near-instantaneous fashion. Unlike other kinds of simulated leisure games, such as baseball batting cages that dot amusement sections of neighborhoods around Seoul, virtual golf re-creates the experience of "real" golf.

Part of this experience is participation in commodified class making that has spread across South Korea in the past two decades, following the original boom of golf with the rise of middle-class consumption in the 1990s. There are virtual golf facilities all around Seoul and other metropolitan areas. Golfzon, the largest brand, began in the year 2000 and has to date almost one thousand domestic facilities, with expanding offices worldwide. Golfzon facilities usually occupy the area of a small office; they are built into office buildings themselves. Operated as franchises, some resemble karaoke-style facilities with a long row of separate rooms in otherwise unadorned hallways. More luxurious facilities replicate upscale golf clubs themselves, with wood paneling, member's welcome areas, and expensive clubs and bags on display. These facilities have exploded in popularity and are shifting from an after-hours gaming pastime to a multisited experiential marketing phenomenon that replicates the full simulation of a modern high-end leisure activity. There are Golfzon-branded academies where one can access lessons from golf pros, cosponsorships with golf clothing and equipment manufacturers, a robust mobile phone application for tracking one's progress in both virtual and real golf, a virtual golf tournament with virtual golf pros, and even real Golfzon courses, known as Golfzon County.

Within the virtual experience, there is a strong emphasis on verisimilitude: Golfzon has digitally re-created more than a hundred courses from South Korea and the world that one can play as exact replicas. The first time we played together I selected the famous Old Course at St. Andrews. While faithfully recreating the look and feel of the rolling dunes and open views of Scotland, it turned out to be one of the more boring courses to choose from—and it was particularly unrecognizable compared to the prestige courses of South Korea that my colleagues were interested in. The replications of courses in South Korea offered a glimpse into what wealthy South Koreans could experience on the field: mountainous terrain, large cliff drops, sweeping ocean vistas, elaborately designed holes. Playing a single round at courses like those would cost more than US$300. Virtual golf makes participating in that kind of experience slightly closer, providing one with the cultural literacy to know and talk about prestige real-world sites.

These kinds of consumer experiences appeal to male and female office workers in their thirties, forties, and fifties who are a key segment of the virtual golf market. They appeal to those who cannot afford to go to regular golf courses or who want to supplement their golf with a form of practice. Yet golf is no hobby; it is a new form of conspicuous consumption and financial investment, popular in South Korea since the late 1990s. Learning golf's somewhat arcane English terms such as bunker shot, sand wedge, handicap, and water hazard, along with embodied golf techniques, has become part of a new habitus for many middle-class urban office workers. For middle managers, basic knowledge of golf might be a professional necessity: for instance, knowing the difference between a pitching wedge and a 62-degree lob wedge or the difference between Japanese steel shafts and American graphite ones. These activities, in fact, have become well integrated into office life itself: one advertisement for Golfzon depicts office workers covertly watching golf videos on their phone while typing at their desks and practicing air swings and hip thrusts in front of the elevator. Golf has become a new site of class distinction, offering multiple ways to participate and consume, while demonstrating one's own individual discipline and measuring progress against others; on the surface, then, virtual golf represents a fusion of bourgeois techniques for individual self-development through technological literacy and familiarity.[15] To participate is to engage in a class-marked experience, but through a highly individuating series of performances that are both consumed by and evaluated by others, even friends—much like the way shots of soju individuate drinking skills and karaoke ballads individuate singing skills.

It is important to see virtual golf alongside a rise in other new kinds of entertainment in South Korea, given its combination of both physical and screen-based integration that creates the real feeling of being at a golf course. Players change their clothes, wear golf shoes indoors, wear real gloves and most importantly hit with real clubs and golf balls. In many ways, virtual golf is a multichannel media event: there are cameras, surround sound speakers, and an interactive computer screen for manipulating the weather, scenery, or course in real time. This kind of multimediated play experience resembles new changes to popular music consumption. In *K-pop Live*, Suk-young Kim notes that South Korean popular music (K-pop) cannot be understood only as a musical style or even a hybrid of multiple styles but as a multisite, multimodal experience that involves videos, projections, holograms, and diverse kinds of fan interactions with artists.[16] The K-pop industry, along with K-pop fans and consumers, are in the market for reproducing what she calls "liveness." Liveness is not about a bodily quality of experiencing something directly, like a concert, or authentically, such as an original version, but about the hyperpresence of multiple forms of experience at once. K-pop industries and fan coparticipation blend multiple modalities of experience in ways that defy more purist approaches to musical reception. Such hyperpresence is not about losing one's sense of self but about the simultaneous experience of both being in an experience and witnessing it, as well as sometimes coproducing it. For Kim, K-pop analysis represents a symbiosis of what we understand as art, technology, and consumption. The fact that these experiences happen in highly commercialized spaces such as concerts, experience centers, fan clubs, and branded merchandise is not incidental—K-pop is as heavily a marketed merchandising and brand experience as it is a musical one.

The virtue of virtual golf is not just that it has better technology than other forms of leisure. And it is not just that it allows one to partake in an elite sport that is largely inaccessible to middle-class participants. Rather, it lies partly in the fact that it allows an enhanced experience of the real thing. For every swing, the interface records videos to allow for viewing and analyzing afterward; occasionally, outstanding shots can be featured on the Golfzon home page, and bad shots can be ridiculed among friends. The virtual golf interface takes a visual or verbal evaluation and turns it into a quantitative one: it tells you your speed, rotation, distance—even the angle of the face on your club when you hit it. The Golfzon interface allows players to build profiles, exchange virtual gifts, and keep a record of every swing. Some players become so used to virtual golf that they never desire to go to the real course and instead became regular "club" members at their local Golfzon. Much like the burgeoning world of e-sports, there is also an emergent virtual golf league of semiprofessional golfers competing in Golfzon-sponsored tournaments and long-drive competitions to follow.

For average players like the members of the HR team, the various features that comprised liveness also allowed one to participate in the wider consumptive sphere of golf as a sport without being castigated as a discounted, or substitute, class experience. The mobile application, the website, and thousands of instructional videos and blog posts on the portal site Naver allowed one to learn the English terms, to invest in golf equipment, and to develop savoir faire. While these appear as ways of buying oneself into a higher social status through consumption, participation in this kind of consumption offers access to different forms of expertise that would once have been an exclusive domain of the wealthy. And it is important that these kinds of activities can be done in relative privacy, or at least through the quasi-anonymity of online interactions and closed golf rooms. The fun of playing golf is also part of what we might consider a way to develop a prestige skill while hiding the work involved in it.

Linguistic anthropologist Joseph Sung-yul Park has described how in contemporary South Korea fluent English language skills are highly valued, but demonstrating one's path to learning is not.[17] This, he suggests, has to do with the nature of individual skills in a neoliberal era: as language is meant to be a natural skill, English learners do much to mark themselves as natural as possible, that is, as close to native speakers as they can. In other words, it is enough just to know or speak English, but because English is the natural ability of those with class mobility, referencing one's educational pathways indexes the origins of one's (lack of) education in the first place. If English is the tangible skill that indexes a range of factors about one's class background for those early in their career, golf (and its various metrics) has become a requisite social skill necessary later in one's career. As team manager Jang wryly remarked one day, one presumably works for a long time to play golf in retirement; now, it seemed we were playing golf in order to improve our working status.

Anthropologist Karen Ho's ethnography of Wall Street bankers revealed that after-hours golf was an occasion when old social hierarchies were reinforced. That is, racial, gender, and class divisions that were so consciously denounced in company discourses of meritocracy reverted back to tropes of an old boy's club when it came to after-hours activities.[18] In the US context, such forms of leisure reflect a casualness (such as bringing one's gym bag to work) that is the exclusive privilege of the well-heeled as a reflection of their natural or inherited qualities (as opposed to others for whom such qualities must be learned). In South Korea, by contrast, there is a seriousness to playing golf. One might be expected to take lessons, invest in expensive equipment and clothing, and gradually improve so as to identify with one's handicap score.[19] This reflects in part what anthropologist William Kelly has described as the seriousness of leisure, particularly in karaoke practices in Japan.[20] Karaoke singers must exhibit some degree of earnestness toward their singing by memorizing the lyrics, attending to what others like, and avoiding mistakes in performance. Singing is highly individualized and must be performed for the enjoyment of others. Not taking it seriously, in other words, can ruin the fun. This explains, in part, the wider economy of karaoke lessons, schools, clubs, and guidebooks that pervade much of the karaoke culture that Kelly studied; they are as much about preparing for future performances as they are about enjoying the present.

Secret Leisure

One day, team manager Jang and assistant manager Min-sup disappeared for lunch together—and for a month we did not know where they went for one hour every day. Only later did the rest of us learn they were practicing golf with a trainer. Such was the first secret; when the rest of the team were informed and began to play, we kept the secret of where we were going from the rest of our coworkers. Sometimes it appeared that the five of us were simply going to dinner together. At other times, we exchanged text messages about coordinating a time to leave, agreeing to meet in the front plaza to catch a cab to the virtual golf facility; other times we took separate cabs. We chose a regular Golfzon facility that was further to reach than the one closer to our office to avoid running into coworkers. Even as we played for months, we never openly discussed golf with coworkers outside the team. To our boss, executive Cho, whose office was just a few yards from our team area, we never said a thing, even after we learned that he was an avid golfer himself. At one time, we heard the telltale app sound of Golfzon ring from someone's phone in the office and we chuckled as we realized that someone else was playing virtual golf and likely keeping it a secret from his or her coworkers as well. In one particularly complex arrangement, we told other workers that we were going out for HR training and left the office at lunch. We told executive Cho, however, that we were going hiking as a team-building exercise. That, too, was a partial fabrication. We actually went to a golf range outside of Seoul and spent the afternoon bonding as a team, playing our first round of golf together.[21] Why would such an activity be done in total secrecy?

Hiding things at work has often been framed as the simplest form of workplace resistance and the maintenance of other kinds of social bonds. Sociologist Michael Burawoy in his classic study of American factory workers noted how workers hid their own production by hiding completed pieces of machinework (that they called "kiddies") by their workstations which they could count for future work and avoid creating higher expectations for productivity.[22] At various times, team manager Jang narrativized our golf events as reciprocation for antipathy toward executive Cho who had imposed unreasonable demands on us for work. The most obvious way we leveraged this was to leave on time—around 6:00 p.m. rather than at the socially acceptable time for leaving work in South Korea, namely when executive Cho had left. In South Korean offices, leaving on time (without a good reason, such as attending to one's children) is one of the most conspicuous signs of antisociality or lack of awareness. The end of the day is the time at which a manager might receive some instructions from a higher executive who might ask for a quick turnaround on a report—it is the obligation of the manager's team to support such late-breaking requests. To leave on time, then, is to essentially abandon one's boss, particularly one who might be stuck with a late deadline.

There were other aspects to secrecy that were not just explained as a matter of resistance. Some of the team members did not tell their spouses about our secret trips. They would indicate they were working late or out at an actual *hoesik* event with coworkers, while instead we were in the comforts of the virtual golf studio. Participating in social events such as *hoesik* is not itself a secret thing; I have even heard of wives and mothers encouraging their spouses or children to stay late at work to build up social capital. In Anne Allison's account of Japanese salarymen going to late-night hostess bars, she describes the phenomenon as an open secret between husbands and wives: while what happens after hours may be taboo, it is at least serving an instrumental purpose of establishing oneself in a company or replenishing one's spirits so as to work better.

With team events around virtual golf, however, the politics seemed like a losing game, at least from the point of developing a social network within Sangdo. The HR team only played within the team, which had little ability to translate our temporal investment into a political one. Part of the virtue of going to *hoesik* with other teams is that one builds rapport where there was none, or one tests one's own abilities against new acquaintances. But the repetitive nature of virtual golf with the same people, under the same schedule, made the event seem like a waste. This dual sense of both fun and monotony represents what anthropologist Stephen Rea has captured about contemporary forms of digital play in South Korea such as e-sports. While e-sports represents new and virtual forms of play, which acts as an icon of South Korea's developmental speed via rest of the world, the gameplay can be monotonous and boring.[23] One must withstand such boring aspects of play to succeed and develop a digital character. This activity is labeled *nogada* (a word derived from the Japanese term for manual labor, *dokata*). In many ways, golf requires players to continuously work on swings, technique, scenarios, and other forms of know-how in order to achieve a cultivated skill. The social investment can come at a cost, however. For me, I came to resent golf precisely for this reason—it seemed to detract from the ethnographic research process itself, even as it was an escape from regular work. I went to practice on my own, had to invest in new clothing, and otherwise felt compelled to keep up with the others. For assistant manager Ji-soon, it seemed like a wise investment: she and her husband both worked in corporate circles, and she soon invested in a full set of golf clubs and took golf lessons.

For Ki-ho, the junior member on the team, however, the stakes were different. As the youngest member on the team, he was responsible for much of the low-level labor required on the team, from managing the complex requests with other subsidiaries and departments to participating in all the team's social outings. At karaoke bars, Ki-ho took it upon himself to create a positive atmosphere by being lively and energetic. He visibly sacrificed much to be a dutiful employee: he lived an hour away from the Sangdo office and stayed out late at night but still caught early morning buses to arrive at the office by

8:oo a.m. The efforts, however, were not without a cost: not a strong drinker, he nevertheless was the target of many *beolju* (punishment shots) from others. He also made minor mistakes on forms and data entry that earned him rebukes from the senior male members of the team. Dating someone at the time, he told me he broke up with her shortly after we began to play golf. I suspected this was due to the burden of committing his time exclusively to after-hours events; he was discouraged from answering the phone while we were at play. (He was also an honorary member of the Sangdo FC futsal team but rarely had the time to attend.) When I returned to Sangdo for a visit one year after I had left, I found out that Ki-ho had left the company and moved on to another steel company, though not one as prestigious as the holding company and located in a satellite city—a constellation of markers that indicated he had dropped down a step. Team manager Jang noted the reason he left was that his mistakes had mounted too high, but I also suspected that he sought to escape the difficult conditions of distinguishing himself, not in the corporate sector in general, but on that particular team, across so many forms of burdensome participation.

Embedded in Others' Distinctions

The myriad pressures of virtual golf followed what organizational thinkers have described as what happens when hierarchies are flattened and formal organizational rules abandoned in organizations: more difficult forms of control emerge. In his book *Discipline of Teamwork,* James Barker has described what happened after formal hierarchies and workplace rules were abolished in an American factory. Without a designated time to come to work, for instance, workers eventually adopted their own sense of what was appropriate. However, they became more rigid about who showed up on time, creating their own norms in place of rules. Barker labeled this phenomenon "concertive control," referring to the way group pressures could be in fact more difficult than formal bureaucratic rules because there was no mechanism to refute them— they existed in an absence of formal control.[24]

Questions of bureaucracy in Western organizations often revolve around poles of verticality and horizontality, hierarchy or the absence of hierarchy. As discussed in Chapter 2, these framings also shaped South Korean ideas about organizational change and organizational ideals as a point of distinction vis-à-vis the West. However, as I have discussed throughout the book, other forms of distinction do not necessarily disappear amid such discourses; in many cases, flat organizations are simply just another form of distinction, even as they might explicitly reject hierarchical or bureaucratic forms of organization. *Hoesik* and other after-hours activities are often framed as a reimposition of hierarchy in the face of otherwise formal office reform. It is more useful to think of it a site where distinction and participation become entangled in one's immediate team relations, where new distinctions, normally individualized in formal settings, can become collective activities. Moreover, distinctions also become partly transitive: what one manager or executive likes may also be good for his or her team members. Workers at Sangdo often associated after-hours events with individual people—that is, as styles of events that emanate from managers' tastes. On the surface, events may be coded as company events, small group events, or even fun sporting events, but they took on the qualities or character of specific bosses. As the beneficiaries of corporate-sponsored meals and the personal gifts of their superiors, junior employees were often in difficult positions to refuse such after-hours offers.

Whatever virtual golf meant in the context of South Korea generally, to our team it was the preferred pastime of the team manager and it was to his preferred decisions that we generally adhered. Jang could generally dictate when, where, and for how long we would stay out, even when such things were framed as friendly invitations. As Ki-ho noted one night when team manager Jang was about to relieve us for the night, but he instead asked us to go to karaoke for another hour, *eojjeol su eopda*—"there's nothing [we can] do about it." While the specifics of managerial styles differed, the pattern was prominent elsewhere. One manager at Sangdo First whom I came to know liked to take his team out to hip new restaurants and then invite his team members back to his family's apartment where his wife would prepare late-night snacks. Such events were more intimate and less commodified but brought employees into spaces that were more difficult to leave or decline. Another HR manager encouraged all of his team members to participate in their office's bowling league. One member of the ownership group at Sangdo would often hand-select individuals to enjoy fancy Italian lunches in an upscale chain restaurant below the Sangdo tower; such events were well-sponsored treats, but well-mannered accountants were forcibly encouraged to drink wine during the middle of the day while being careful not to make a career-ending mistake in front of a member of ownership. Some tastes were more low-brow: a short-tenured team manager in HR preferred McDonald's when working late; his team, too, had to spend their *hoesik* funds at a McDonald's below the Sangdo tower before coming back to the office to work late.

Even within more traditional *hoesik* drinking events, which often appear to be marked by conventional or generic norms of workplace culture such as exchanging shots of soju, more careful attention suggests that managers or executives often recalibrate the rules of dining in their own styles. One HR team manager mandated that at the conventional point when a group might take a shot of soju together, no one should turn their head out of respect. Rather, he adamantly forced everyone to keep their heads looking straight, a surprisingly awkward immobile gesture for those accustomed to averting their glances. (He was not opposed to excessive drinking, just that one particular marker of deference). Another manager who had spent a number of years as an overseas representative in the US preferred to avoid soju all together; instead, he preferred to bring bottles from his personal wine collection to small barbeque restaurants as a way to demonstrate his knowledge of wine and avoid the frequent shot-taking afforded by small soju shot glasses. Some managers simply made their mark by wrapping events up early so employees could decide their own evenings together.[25] Many of these modified events and styles were personal forms of resistance against typical *hoesik* events, new riffs on a conventional type. Yet they nevertheless necessitated the cooperation and in some cases coercion of others. For many aspirational corporate workers, such obligations appear part of the bargain of earning one's form of individual distinction within a team environment. The irony here, however, is that as certain forms of leisure explicitly reject models of socializing associated with older forms of after-hours leisure, in many cases they generate new forms of obligation in less conventional and less visible formats, such as virtual golf, that model a different form of class aspiration (which may not be everyone's aspiration). These suggest the way that leisure itself, unlike health hazards like smoking, is never just a matter of pure individual choice (and hence easier to regulate) but one entangled in the choices and preferences of others. It is in *hoesik* that the very categories of distinction and participation become curiously entangled in ways that seem to properly achieve neither.

For some, these new activities redouble older habits and tendencies. Jaehang Park, an advertising veteran and opinion writer, as well as a personal acquaintance, wrote for the *Dong-a* newspaper in 2017 that screen golf was getting out of hand.[26] Park suggested that virtual golf had become like other virtual pastimes in South Korea such as the computer game Second Life. In

2007 and 2008, Second Life turned from a pleasurable game into a large racket of the game's currency, Linden Dollars. Similarly, Park notes, the anonymity and freedom once afforded by virtual golf was leading to the return of reality: "One can get peripheral services for a price even cheaper than a room salon." Referencing the existence of expensive private room-based bars that are associated with sexual services, Park observes that one who now goes to virtual golf gets a few "strange side-eye looks" (*myohan nunchori*). What was meant to be an escape and the virtualization of privileged outdoor sport was now reverting to other associated late-night pastimes and those associated with a less clean past. Park instead advocates that people go outside to play real golf, where they can observe the dew on the grass, build up a sweat, and hum the tunes of old songs as they enjoy nature.

As described in Chapter 3, many companies have reframed the terms of *hoesik* to make it more wholesome, accommodating, and inclusive of diverse activities, reframing them away from drinking, staying out late, and putting employees (and company reputations) in compromised positions. Removing stigmatizing and damaging activities where employees might be distinguished by how much they drink is, of course, important, even if it might move after-hours activities into sites of clearer class-consumer distinctions (McDonald's versus an Italian restaurant, screen golf versus real golf) that employees may or may not feel invested in. The broader issue is not necessarily which category employees become invested in but rather how they might feel that their own distinctions must map onto the tastes of those around them, particularly their team managers.

The team manager remains a key nodal point in South Korean organizational structures. He or she is the head of the basic unit of work and the one who gives out individual evaluations, nurtures careers, and resolves minor workplace issues. In this sense, team members might feel particularly obligated to attending to a manager's tastes and sentiments. What becomes an act of distinction for a boss, for example, might well become an act of distinction for the employee as well by proxy. Conversely, a manager who might not obligate his or her employees to meet up after work may be seen as one who puts them at some disadvantage organizationally. At one company where I briefly did some early fieldwork in 2012, I worked with team manager Hwang. Though in his late forties or fifties, Hwang eventually left the company, seeming to retire early. His team members were fond of him because he was a particularly kind and gentle person and never made them go to extensive *hoesik* events. He also had his own hobbies such as photography, TV writing, and coffee making that he did not impose on others. After he left the company, his former team members would still call him by an honorary title (*gukjangnim* or chief) as a matter of personal respect. In private, however, one of the team members told me that the fact that he was so nice might not have portended well for the team in the long run. By not going drinking or going to *hoesik,* she surmised, he put the team at a disadvantage since he might not be playing organizational politics, making their team a dead end for their own individual aspirations.

Conclusion

THIS BOOK HAS PRESENTED an ethnography exploring what I have described as a supercorporate ideal in a post-hierarchy South Korean work culture. The supercorporate ideal focuses on a tension around what post-hierarchical office work should look like. As corporations and professional work remain key endpoints of educational trajectories and sites for narrating and locating middle-class mobility, one question that sits uncomfortably at the heart of such aspirations is whether corporate work should minimize distinctions and differences between people to create positive sites of cooperation, distinct from the harsh trade-offs of a hierarchical past and open to all, or whether corporate work should more accurately and fairly evaluate and reward people in a fair and meritocratic system. This book has focused on how this tension emerged in the context of the Sangdo conglomerate where executives and managers in the holding company saw their role as one of improving systems of distinction making and the experience of teamwork across a conglomerate. Such new ideas coincided with the growth of the Sangdo holding company that was ambiguously positioned as an expert guide vis-à-vis the rest of the conglomerate atop the Sangdo tower.

Hierarchy, distinction, and participation are three concepts that have come to define the parallax of South Korea's recent developmental trajectory. Seen from one angle, South Korean development is marked by its measurable and visible distinctions in annual GDP growth beginning in the 1960s and continuing to today as part of the grand narrative of economic growth. This history

157

of distinctions has been marked by different kinds of notches in recognized accomplishments legible both inside and outside the country: export achievements, international certifications and standards, per capita income numbers, global award wins, and perhaps most recently, the rise of venture capital firms. These national distinctions shift in tone and quality, but the emphasis on them as ways of recognizing South Korea's developmental path seems to show no sign of abating. The same history could also be viewed from the point of view of hierarchy. Looking at almost the same set of facts, one can see a history of labor suppression, government corruption, wealth concentration through chaebols, the dominance of large firms over small ones, and, more recently, increasingly standard versus nonstandard labor categories. Each of these issues (and surely many others) points to unwelcome hierarchies across different sets of relationships: men to women, state to citizens, chaebol owners to laborers, big unions to nonunion workers, domestic workers to migrant ones, big groups to small companies. Finally, participation and its connected ideas, such as solidarity, teamwork, and democracy, appear to capture the many social and labor movements that have marked large-scale protests in urban centers where South Koreans visibly reject the authority of the powerful through mass demonstrations—precisely by denying forms of individual distinction on a large scale. Depending on one's perspective, then, South Korea might appear to be in the process of becoming more distinguished, ever more hierarchical or ever more democratic.

Grand explanations can play a role in how these concepts relate. During my fieldwork in 2014, for instance, the terms *gap* and *eul* were all over the news. The two terms refer to a basic distinction akin to alpha and beta, used primarily in Korean legal contracts to neutrally refer to two different parties. Through circulation in the news, the terms came to refer to a dyadic framing of the power of one (the *gap*) over one weak person (the *eul*). It was effective in calling attention to the ways that service and retail workers, in particular, were subject to verbal debasement by angry customers and the ways that those of distinction (in high class or organizational positions), depending on the affective or emotional labor of those below them, made their distinctions in part dependent on respectful treatment from subordinates. The *gap-eul* model was also applied to the ways that subcontractor firms were ruled over by larger firms or even how powerful departments could lord over other departments. Thus *gap-eul* was and is a powerful framing device because seemingly anyone in a subordinate position can become a beta relative to an alpha. *Gap-eul* can apply to any two-part participant structure of hierarchy from the present to the past, linking the legacies of master-slave relations in nineteenth century Korea (Joseon) to interpersonal relations in an Emart department store in the twenty-first century. For popular historian and cultural critic Kang Jun-man, author of the 2013 book *The Country of* Gap *and* Eul, the historical persistence and widespread appearance of *gap-eul* relations date to the subordinate position of the Korean peninsula at the end of the nineteenth century in which the nation's modernity was brokered by higher powers—first by Japan and then by the United States.[1] According to Kang, this led to South Korea perennially seeking its modernity through the compromised *eul* position. More than just a perennially subordinate position, however, the *eul* is both within the fold of the *gap* and dependent on him or her for success and access to modernity. For Kang, a psychosocial tension at the heart of South Korean society is that the *eul* secretly wants to be or be like a *gap,* an alpha, and might use various techniques such as willful subordination to reach that status. Here, *gap-eul* not only presents a model or diagram of all South Korean relations but it also evinces the tension between hierarchy (as a form of unwanted subordination) and its pathway to distinction (as a form of desired difference).

The appeal of *gap-eul* comes from the fact that it provides a universal structure into which all kinds of relations can fit, both organizational and interpersonal, that seem to diagram broader national narratives. One can certainly locate *gap-eul* relations in office life, as Chapter 3 demonstrated. In concluding this book, however, I emphasize that locating forms of hierarchy and distinction are more complex than a reduction to a dyadic (two-part) model of superior-subordinate or master-slave might suggest. Rather, it is useful to think of the complex intersections that values like distinction and participation generate on the ground in the strange topography of modern office life. Where a supercorporate ideal might provide a general kind of formula for an individual's relationship to the promise of modern corporate life, these facts never exist in the abstract; actors must always draw their own associations through the particular company contexts, coworkers, and events that make up their working life.

There are several reasons why this way of approaching issues in South Korean capitalism might be more useful than thinking through grand narratives. First, the fact that there are multiple sites of distinction making, from *hoesik* to annual evaluations to shareholder meetings, reflects that institutional life has no core or center with one singular set of distinctions or hierarchical relationship. In many ways, the sheer number of sites where relations to organizational groups and relations to other people are cast reflects the complexity of locating a single principle or model to link it all together. My coworker Ki-ho, for instance, the junior member of the HR team, found himself at a contradictory site: from one perspective, he had social distinction working for a large corporate group and may have found himself above others by virtue of working in a holding company. From another perspective, he faced the pressure of working within a difficult team environment premised on frequent bodily commitment to drinking and leisure—an experience from which it seemed he ultimately sought employment elsewhere.

Second, corporate life is complicated by the fact that there are sites of different efforts over many years to both purify and manage their own forms of workplace distinction while eradicating negative aspects of hierarchy. This has created its own archaeology of corporate reforms within organizations. For instance, the number of titles, roles, responsibilities, and forms of address (*jikchaek, jigwi, jikgeup, yeokhal, myeongching*) reflects the ways that efforts to purify and manage forms of distinction and participation can themselves add to the ever-growing stratigraphy of office life. Third, marks of distinction are also emergent within interconnected ties of work where marking off one's kind of work from another is complex (as discussed in Chapter 1 and Chapter 6). For managers on the performance management team, for instance, though they were seemingly at the top of a chain of information, they nevertheless struggled to distinguish data from information in a way that would make them be distinguished as managers. This, in many ways, led to them imposing certain kinds of demands on others so that they might become properly recognized as expert managers. Finally, how people—employees, CEOs, social critics, or even researchers—draw or locate models of distinction and hierarchy is itself a creative act, such as assistant manager Baik's account in the introduction to this book. Baik saw Sangdo's fragile position in the market being threatened by global and domestic shifts in the steel industry, which, if Sangdo did not act on quickly, would lead to catastrophic results. Baik did not necessarily locate Sangdo's prestige in its forms of internal distinction (such as ranks or titles), but he connected those distinctions to Sangdo's broader position in the market. If Sangdo were to fall, it would dramatically change the equation for thousands of Sangdo workers.

Locating Hidden Distinctions

Acts of locating problematic hierarchies or new ideals reflect not the fact that such things are social constructions or misunderstandings by employees about how things really work, but that there are so many intersecting forms that interpreting all of them together is a kind of narrative skill in and of itself. John Weeks has described this as a kind of "lay ethnography" in which employees or managers offer their own accounts of how things work.[2] In part, this is a way that some people reveal that they are organizational insiders, distinguishing themselves from outsiders or new hires. On one of my last nights as a worker at Sangdo in 2015, I went out to a fried chicken restaurant around the corner from the Sangdo tower. I ended up speaking with manager Choi who had recently joined the holding company and the strategy team from a large financial company. As he was new to the company and had heard that I was doing research inside the company, he was eager to offer me his own first impressions of Sangdo. A few beers in and drawing on his English, he said "Sangdo is so *Christian*? Haven't you noticed it?" In a quasi-confessional manner, he indicated that he picked up on this fact quickly as he started to observe different facets of the office. He intuited that the owning family itself was Christian and he could see covert signs of their elite Christian manners throughout the office, including the emphasis on humility (*gyeomsonseong*) in different company writings, their philanthropic support of classical music, and their minimal levels of corporate debt.

This was a shock to me since, for over a year, I had not once seen or heard of any overt religious talk by anyone in or from the company. Some individual employees I knew to be Catholic or Christian based on where they held their weddings, but I had little idea even of the religious beliefs of any of my coworkers, let alone the ownership. No one ever discussed religious practice, so I avoided inquiring. This is in stark contrast to the account given by the anthropologist Choong Soon Kim of the Poongsan Corporation in the 1980s where certain religious aspects were integrated into corporate culture. The chairman led employees up a mountain near the Confucian village of Andong to perform a ceremony for one of his (and by extension, the company's) ancestors, linking through ritual the company, Korean history, and ancestor worship.[3] Hearing manager Choi's words, however, I also realized that I had somehow missed, for over twelve months, subtle cues that might be self-evident to others.[4]

Christianity was not the only overt institution embedded in Sangdo that I had somehow missed. One day, when an overseas manager (*jujaewon*), assistant manager Dong-min, came back to the office for a short reunion, he came over to say hello to his friend Ki-ho who sat next to me in HR. The two had been friends and they immediately embraced in a jocular, tight-gripped handshake while using their left hands to grab the other's elbow, extending the gesture just long enough to turn it into a miniperformance. Dong-min turned to me, seated, and said, "See, this is military culture!" Both men had served in the more heavily militarized divisions for their military service, albeit at different times and places (Dong-min was a graduate of the national military academy and Ki-ho had trained on heavy artillery in the army). Dong-min said that I would never understand South Korean office culture without understanding the subtle references to military culture embedded in office life. Dong-min, however, was not referring to the brash masculinity that often defines pictures of being a "real man" (*sanai*). He was referring to the presence of field manuals that dictate exactly how to operate. He said the holding company did not have any field manuals (*yajeon gyobeom*) to run the business and was thus an imperfect model of what good operations should be—in which every employee has a clear task.[5] Though he was saying that South Korean office life was like the military, he was also attesting that Sangdo itself was not achieving the model of efficiency he came to expect of the military.

Signs of the military could be found elsewhere in the Sangdo office and in other offices I visited: the Sangdo corporate song (*saga*), imprinted in every notebook given out by the company, goes to the tune of a military march from the 1970s. The roof of the Sangdo tower itself, like other tall office buildings in Seoul, had been fitted specifically to allow soldiers to store weapons and defend in the case of an attack from the North. It was not uncommon for workers to say that other people or companies were more like the military than others such as Sangdo South, which was purported to have a stronger military culture than the other Sangdo offices because of its proximity to a large Korean military base in the southern part of the country. Some on the engagement survey decried the "vertical military culture" they saw in their office. It was only in the final days of my fieldwork that I found that there was even a particular military-associated and rule-governed register of honorifics known as *apjonbeop* that some office workers personally used that is distinct from what is generally regarded as the more conventional honorific register.[6]

The historical connections between South Korean corporations and the
military are being newly reevaluated. Historian Peter Banseok Kwon has investigated how the "miracle on the Han River," which for a long time has been
framed as a story of the role of government in driving South Korea's fast industrialization in developmental narratives, was really a story of military-
driven industrialization, a topic that remained largely taboo in developmental narratives because of the complicated legacy of authoritarian President
Park Chung-hee (1961–79) as well as purer narratives focused around markets and industrial growth.[7] Many of the country's largest extant conglomerates all had their start in or were encouraged to start producing for military industries; Samsung, Hanwha, Hanjin (Korean Air), Daewoo, Hyundai,
and others began or greatly expanded with Park's industrial-militarization
drive. Today, many of the largest conglomerates maintain subsidiaries with
considerable defense portfolios, though their exact purpose is not clear to the
public (such as the ambiguously named Hyundai Wia, LIG Nex1, or Hanwha
Techwin). Such military links are still lying just beneath the surface of many
conglomerates.

As comparisons, Christian relations and military relations draw on not
only different institutional sites but different explanations for hierarchy across
aspects of the corporate ecosystem. First, both relations link one institution
that is embedded within the public face of another, in ways that are not immediately visible to outsiders and require some investigation by insiders. These
crypto-distinctions give the illusion, especially to insiders, of being the true
underlying model, value, driver, or cause of an institution, much in the same
way that the stereotype of older managers was seen as a hidden figure in Chapter 3. By virtue of this, such institutional (under)currents or value structures
appear to mediate what at the surface is merely corporate or businesslike.
South Korean corporations, in this view, can really just be understood as military operations; or Sangdo really is at heart a Christian firm. The fact that
two wildly divergent models as Christianity and militarism can so easily fit
makes locating ultimate forms of hierarchy (as power relations) or distinction
(as class markers or social distinctions) all the more difficult.

Second, these kinds of comparisons do not operate in the same way merely
by virtue of being underlying. Protestant Christianity in twentieth century
South Korea has been closely tied to modernist distinctions and pursuits,
such as art, music, and academia—marking itself off, in other words, from

features, rituals, and practices most commonly associated with tradition however defined. It operates within a cultural binary of enlightened forms of self-
cultivation, distancing itself from what came to be described as backward elements of Korean society, such as ancestor worship, traditional music genres,
and vices such as drinking or smoking (not to say that such things do not per-
sist in practice). In manager Choi's fleeting remark at the chicken restaurant,
the owners of Sangdo were not just wealthy owners, but their refined and civilized collection of art and interest in the opera distinguished them from the
rest of their largely industrial and regional workforce. Here, the ownership
presumably embodies this cultural form of distinction and is embedded subtly in the fabric of the company in ways that are not ritually foregrounded
or directly referenced. The military model works differently: as alluded to by
Dong-min, the military stood as a model of an idealized, perfectly bureaucratic organization where everything operates efficiently and smoothly. This,
too, reflects a tension at the heart of ongoing historical debates about South
Korea's period of domestic military rule that generally revolve around the
idea that such rule was cruel, but effective. Such debates are often historically
misguided, but they nevertheless present a different kind of hidden distinction: one in which an older organizational model was more effective for getting through difficult challenges. Having a dysfunctional organization without clear lines of control or elaborated rules may explain why Sangdo might
fail where other corporate groups succeed.

Office-Level Ethics Between Distinction and Participation

I chose the name Sangdo as a pseudonym for the conglomerate at the heart of
this study in part because the word *sangdo* in Korean refers literally to a market ethic (Sino-Korean, 商道). Most commonly, it refers to the ethics among
the merchant class for fair dealings in terms of price, delivery, and promises
made, even among merchants of different orders (and there is a 2001 historical drama of the same name). The Sangdo Group was not necessarily any
more ethical than were other groups, whatever that might mean in the age of
corporate social responsibility and public image campaigns. The group did,
of course, engage in particular forms of corporate philanthropy, volunteer-
ism, and donations to communities in Seoul and its regional headquarters in
ways that are common among large corporate groups. There was also an ethics

pledge that employees had to sign every year promising that they would not give out company secrets or support coworkers who engaged in illegal activity, which was more about compliance than ethics per se.

By ethics, I am referring instead to the shopfloor ethical dilemmas that come from navigating distinction and participation in the workplace. In each of this book's chapters has been a particular ethical conflict about the tensions between distinction and participation. In Chapter 1, managers on the performance management team had to weigh how they might mark out their own distinction in relation to those of the subsidiaries, which were tied to the monthly report that subsidiaries had to submit. What was a distinction for them (appearing as an expert) would have created a new hierarchical imposition for those in subsidiaries (by making them working on the weekend). This kind of dilemma also happened elsewhere: when Ki-ho on the HR team had to call to collect information from subsidiaries, it was often from employees who ranked higher than he did. At one particular *hoesik*, one manager from a subsidiary pleaded with Ki-ho, asking for consideration when calling them to send data because the subsidiary, too, had its own difficulties in everyday work. In Chapter 2, what to HR workers might have been a more ethical way to reward employees through individual bonuses based on their own performances was to others a potential sign of disruption, creating unwanted forms of distinction within teams. Likewise, flat name policies such as that at Minjong, while seeming to motivate young workers by rendering them as managers, also potentially wiped out the distinctions of those who actually had been managers. In Chapter 3, ethical considerations also converged over the castigation of older male managers. While those managers might have been seen as problematic forces, they were also the targets of labor-related policies, including new evaluation systems and early retirement schemes. As an ethical matter, HR managers had to create a system that could in theory apply the same evaluation policies to all executives and team managers while collecting 360-degree feedback. In Chapter 4, what might have been an attempt to fix problems with workers at the subsidiaries by channeling their voices through a survey was a roundabout way of curtailing the expertise of others' local knowledge, such as that of other HR managers. In Chapter 5, what might be considered a zone of protected democratic participation, the shareholder meeting, also devolved into concerns over manipulation by both extortionists and activists. In Chapter 6, what was a fun environment on the HR team in the holding company, distinct from normal office routines by holding meetings in coffee shops and learning golf together, also verged close to a site of intense normative compliance and bullying. Golf was an escape from conventional forms of coercive participation, but it came to be a burden precisely through its monopolization of other areas of participation in (personal) life.

In organizational researcher Robert Jackall's ethnography of workplace ethical trade-offs, *Moral Mazes*, he wrote about how the higher that one went up in managerial hierarchies in US industrial companies, the worse the moral trade-offs became.[8] In South Korea, workplace ladders become complicated for another reason: workers are often in charge of determining the distinction and participation of others, thrusting the ethical burden of one person's advancement or satisfaction onto another person. A commonly narrated ethical dilemma I had heard about regarded how team managers had to give evaluation grades to their employees and in some cases create forced distributions among them, such as by having to rank their team members in order. I had heard of cases where team managers would give rankings out in order of seniority; this was done to avoid the biblical dilemma of choosing among their team members to determine who was best. As much as employees might feel normative pressure from their team managers, so, too, did team managers have complex moral burdens about handling the time at which their employees were promoted. The DRIVE system, discussed in Chapter 1, was one way of working around this problem. It attempted to create an objective system that might remove the ethical dilemma from team managers (while also ruling out some of their biases or favoritisms). In this sense, a new kind of technocratic system was one frontier for solving the ethical dilemma of having some people be responsible for the working relationships of others.

Distinction making, especially when done by or within corporations, has often been treated as an artifice imposed for the sake of corporate rationality, disciplining the workforce, or creating artificial points of differentiation between workers, particularly along qualities that are arbitrary and immeasurable, such as passion, insight, or impact. At the same time, participation has also been critiqued for either radical efforts at flattening or staged forms of face-to-face interaction to conceal other forms of hidden inequality. This ethnographic portrait of Sangdo has shown that, aside from such criticisms, distinction and participation remain part of a supercorporate ideal, shaped by ideas about corporations in broader society and what kinds of promises they hold in a South Korea that has gradually abandoned kin and clan distinctions for university, professional, consumer, and corporate credentials. As participation for many comes through hours spent with coworkers and distinctions come from these very same interactions, the workplace will undoubtedly continue to be a site where these tensions play out with and through others.

Methodological Appendix

In this appendix, I discuss aspects of the ethnographic research process and how it was significantly shaped by many of the concerns around organizational distinction and participation that I have described. As much as anthropological ethnography can bring clarity to the way things look on the ground, it is always a partial science. This is due to the unevenness of access and the equivalence that anthropologists attempt to provide between their own forms of social examination and those they research (or research alongside with). As a method premised on a researcher's direct physical presence, anthropological ethnography actively embraces the complicated logics and values of the researcher being connected with a community, a space, or a set of practices rather than a logic of scientific purity, impersonal bias, or distanced ideological critique. This can create interesting dynamics in the context of expert communities like managers, scientists, or bureaucrats, whose own work aspires to or models that of formal scientific research.

This research project focused on the afterlife of hierarchy in South Korea by looking at competing tensions between distinction and participation within big organizational life. In any field situation, researchers have to accommodate themselves to norms, social etiquette, and patterns of life. However, there are other ways that forms of distinction intersect at or emanate from sites of research that shape both research and researcher. Most typically, this kind of concern reflects the prestige that Westerners, universities, and Western science can intentionally or unwittingly bring to a field site, which creates its own kinds of implicit dynamics within a research encounter.

My own research was strongly shaped by a strange contrast in categories of distinction. On one hand, American universities, American management thinking, and English speaking have been lionized in South Korea since at least the American occupation after World War II. English itself is a measure of managerial skill at most major corporations and many managers I met aspired to send their children to American universities, or perhaps to receive an MBA degree themselves. These forms of distinction granted me a certain degree of access to meeting or speaking with people in the South Korean corporate world. On the other hand, I found myself as an intern in a tower of high-corporate expertise marked by elite South Korean class distinctions. On my first day at Sangdo, I noticed one employee wearing a Rolex received as a wedding present while another was reported to be wearing suits acquired from a recent business trip to Italy. (Part of my early research budget was spent on improving my wardrobe so I did not stick out too much from the crowd.) These contrasts in forms of distinction are useful as an act of reflection, for instance, thinking how my own demographic categories (linguistic, racial, educational, and class) were situated vis-à-vis South Korean prestige categories.

Other kinds of distinctions shaped the nature of research within Sangdo significantly—in particular, how anthropology as a field was positioned vis-à-vis other kinds of expert knowledge such as strategy, marketing, or organizational behavior (it turns out, comparatively much lower). In this sense, the anthropology and the anthropologist of South Korean office life does not simply bring back unique perspectives that reveal the inner lives or voices of those in a corporate system. Rather, the discipline, the researcher, and the actors come to interact with and influence one another in particular ways. In what follows, I discuss how the encounter with these distinctions (as well as some unexpected ones) shaped my research and also allowed me to understand how my own understandings of difference shaped themes in my research and were shaped by them. I focus on how I selected a research site, how I interacted with other experts, how I came to appreciate seemingly low-level corporate knowledge projects, and how I eventually came to rethink some of my more ingrained judgments about hierarchy, democracy, and corporate control.

Finding the Field: A Pure Research Setting

My doctoral research in 2013 had proposed to explore how techniques of democratic organization were being translated into different aspects of South Korean office life through new ideas such as *uisasotong* (mutual communication) between workers and experimentation with flat organizational structures. To do so, my initial research plans had proposed to work alongside South Korean workers inside a company.

I made this choice for a number of reasons. First, from very early on in my studies, I became aware of just how fragile access to corporate spaces was as a researcher in South Korea. Speaking to other anthropologists I met through Seoul National University, I learned there were many hazards that an outsider must navigate. Framing a question too critically might spoil an interview if one appears to be posing as an undercover intellectual (*wijang chwieop*); such a question might set off red flags across an organization or a team and close off access.[1] I had heard an anecdote of a South Korean graduate student doing research where the employees who had permitted the research were later fired based on what the student had written in her dissertation. Aware of this pitfall, I thought that working quasi-naturalistically (as a ratified insider) might skirt some practical issues around gathering information solely via interviews. Second, I was inspired by Roger Janelli's ethnography of the pseudonymous Taesŏng group, but I was aware of one limitation that he mentioned to me personally when I was an early graduate student: in his ethnography, he was only able to dip into and out of certain work contexts as a fly on the wall. I was interested in focusing on work and materiality of work to understand South Korean office work not as a completely generic space made up of generic norms and social ranks but of distinct areas of managerial practice and organizational politics that animate much of office life for employees themselves.[2] I decided that HR would be the professional discipline to conduct ethnography alongside since they are the main managerial area that has its own eye cast onto the workforce itself. Third, I was intrigued to combine approaches to the analysis of formal institutional language emerging from scholars in linguistic anthropology with approaches to the multigenre workplace that had been developed by organization studies scholars. This combination would capture, in theory, the ideological dynamics of actual institutional communication while considering the explosion in the diversity of genres, materialities, and techniques.[3]

In 2014, after finishing an intensive language course in Seoul and months of initial interviews with contacts from friends, university connections, and former colleagues, I was searching for a company that might allow me to work as an intern for six to twelve months. Through various contacts, I sought out businesspeople with whom I only had limited personal connection. In part, this was to have a pure window of research via strangers and avoid any concern I was a *nakhasan* (someone who arrives by parachute)—that is, as a personal favor to an executive. At the time, I believed that a nationalistic interest in contemporary research on South Korean office culture might be motivation enough for a company to host me. (In the anglophone social sciences, at least, ethnographies of South Korean office life had not been done since Janelli's and Kim's research in the late 1980s). In retrospect, this was rather naive on my part, since I should not have expected a stranger-executive to go out on a limb to a bring in an American researcher for what can only be (from a corporation's viewpoint and a personal viewpoint) a total risk with little payoff, especially without formal institutional ties between the university and the corporation. (In contrast to business-school research, anthropology doctoral students usually do not have formal institutional connections from professors or advisors, which can compound problems of access but allows certain degrees of freedom.) Attempts at doing para-ethnography around corporate sites was intriguing, but also difficult: observations made during interviews, visits to company lobbies, and things overheard in coffee shops turned out to be not particularly good methods for collecting the office-level encounters I sought.[4]

With no luck after six months, I had thought of shifting my project completely. Through a series of phone calls, meetings, and favors (some of which I do not know of myself), I was fortunate to receive an offer from an owner-executive at the Sangdo Group whom I had met through an alumni connection. The owner-executive granted me an opportunity to work at Sangdo for an initial period of six months as an intern; this was later extended another six months as a contract worker (*gyeyakjik*), marking a full year at Sangdo. I asked the owner-executive if I could work in the HR department and he set up an interview for me with the team manager at the holding company. Team manager Jang was initially confused about what exactly I would do with the team. I was not put there as a researcher with an explicit plan that we had agreed on, nor was I particularly well qualified to do HR work. I was technically an intern, but not the typical university student studying business or economics with corporate aspirations. (In this sense, I am sure I was likely seen as a pure "parachute" by coworkers.) Nevertheless, on my first day, I explained to my coworkers in HR that I was an ethnographer who did research largely through observation and note-taking; everyone agreed to the basic informed consent protocol. Likewise, I explained to everyone I met that I was also working on my PhD loosely around changes in office relations, technology, and communication in large companies.

To make my research speak to concerns around a representative site of South Korean office work, I had requested to work in a generic HR team at a Sangdo subsidiary. I was even willing to move to a regional office out of Seoul if necessary. As I came to discover, no personal favor can ever result in truly generic placement. Any space is shaped by its relationship to the personal relationships that preceded it and that already compose it. The owner-executive placed me in the HR department of the holding company, down the floor from his office and where workers with more Western experience were located (that is, where more people spoke English). I suspected this had to do with the limit of the owner-executive's power at the time (he could not necessarily make personal directives to place people in other companies); I also assumed that he did not want to create political interference by making one subsidiary an experiment for hosting a partially unvetted American (especially when many subsidiaries were in uncertain economic conditions at the time). It may also have been due to my lack of comprehension of the highly specialized steel-related and management registers they used that would be too obscure for someone generically interested in office culture. Finally, I suspected there was a sense of propriety in not wanting to expose a young foreigner to certain aspects of office life known to occur within the steel industry such as heavy drinking or demanding bosses at some subsidiary offices. Figures in the South Korean steel industry at the time showed that the workforce at most major companies was 90 percent male. The steel industry was particularly known for after-hours socializing.

So it was that I ended up working in the more effete holding company. This created its own difficulties, in part, for its uniqueness and the strange contrasts of distinctions: the holding company was a relatively new organizational form, and the workforce was a mix of legacy employees and midcareer hires, with many having only begun working there a few years ahead of me. Most importantly, it was an office of high confidentiality, dealing with many executive-level tasks and serious concerns around the countless operations of a multinational conglomerate. Because of these high-level concerns, my initial interest in the role of low-level genres and technologies of office work , such as styles of writing email or the role of the company intranet, must have struck my coworkers as missing the forest for the trees.

During the course of my research at Sangdo, I gradually turned my focus more toward what my coworkers were interested in, which was the holding company's role and the relationship with communication (see below). Socially speaking, I attempted to chart my own course within Sangdo the conglomerate, making friendships with different people in the holding company and subsidiaries through activities such as briefly joining the futsal club, going to the company gym, and meeting people at the company café. I became good friends with an experienced IT manager who knew more about Sangdo's history than most other managers at the holding company; I visited a midlevel manager at his home in the southwest part of the country after he had been transferred; I went to every wedding or *hoesik* event I was invited to; and I was also able to visit a number of extramural sites—visits to two different factories, the shareholder meeting, a steel industry expo in Incheon, a classical musical concert put on by the ownership, and 16th annual Iron & Steel industry half-marathon/5k.

Such freedoms were subtly shaped by the fact that I was tied to the owner-executive, even if our paths did not cross frequently. The owner-executive personally recruited many of the new managers and executives in the holding company and helped shape many of the new projects (as discussed in Chapter 1). To those elsewhere in the tower or group, bringing on a foreigner as part of a new expert group at Sangdo was perhaps not all that unusual, given how many other Western-linked executives and managers came in. But my strange status as an intern-PhD student connected to an owner-executive shaped how I interacted with other managers within the holding company. When I met with them individually, some managers thought that my research was for the owner about their (the managers') working style. Even when I flatly denied it, I suspected that they suspected that I was providing the owner-executive with answers or at least indirect evaluations of their participation. Likewise, I imagine that many of the freedoms I had to attend different events and even shadow different teams was premised on the fact that if someone had turned me down, it might have had some adverse impact on their reputations. One team manager, after I spent a day with his team, told me (with a wink) to let the owner-executive know that his team had been supportive of my research.

In this sense, more than an outsider mixing with insiders, my presence became entangled precisely because of the contrast of distinctions and associations: I was at the lowest rung of the holding company but personally linked to its highest rung, all the while engaged in an ambiguous form of knowledge collection (anthropology) that was rather unknown in the professional contexts of corporate work. (I also had become associated as a member of the HR team, which may not have helped people consider me as a neutral researcher.) In sum, it is difficult to know how such contrasting positions affected my own work or the work of those around me or if I would have heard different kinds of accounts had I been positioned differently. It is clear that distinctions—both brought to a field and emergent within it—are not just something that affect a researcher's point of view but things that partially change the field site encounter at the same time.

In the Field: Distinctions of Expertise

At the same time that I might have unwittingly been positioned in particular ways within the workplace, my own research interests were also being reshaped by the context around me, as I began to see my research in light of the projects of the other managers. One day a few months into my work at Sangdo, assistant manager Sang-jin from the strategy team took me aside and inquired about the exact nature of my research plan. Even though I had been on the HR team and was making passive observations mostly through note-taking, Sang-jin was still curious. I suspected he must have been acting on behalf of someone higher up who was curious as well—or possibly worried that I had no concrete plan at all. When I told him that I was interested in the topic of the holding company and its relationship vis-à-vis subsidiaries, he told me that I should focus more concretely on a comparative study between two subsidiaries or talk about Sangdo as a representative of the steel industry. He steered me away from talking about Sangdo as representative of South Korea—in part because he believed the company was too unique to generalize.

More than being suspicious of whether I was being subversive, I had a hunch it was my own research identity and methods (largely participatory, observational, and inquisitive) as well as the way anthropology tends to scale from microinteractions to national contexts that were causing some confusion. Sang-jin himself was a former consultant preparing to do an MBA overseas, so he was literate in the dynamics of business-school case studies where businesses are treated as representative of an industry and where they become studied for a discrete change in strategy or policy making. In this sense, the fact that I likely looked like a business researcher but sounded like an anthropologist probably appeared rather contradictory.

Practically speaking, anthropologists do not often adopt formally marked research identities in situ to better enable building personal relationships (no clipboard or separate research office, for instance). An ethnographic approach, as I came to understand, was also highly unusual for those who were steeped in and socialized to working in discrete "project forms," particularly those socialized in consulting backgrounds. By the project form, I refer to the basic unit of work that has shaped much work around the world, from learning projects to consulting projects.[5] Project work is defined not by fixed roles with tasks and responsibilities (as an organizational role) but by bounded activities that create roles for individuals or groups to achieve some goal, usually some change or effect that can be rendered measurable or visible. Despite the diversity of their respective departments, Sangdo holding company teams were largely engaged in project work, such as a project to assess brand image internally, a project around possible new markets in China, and even a project to develop new methods for tracking projects. As an intern simultaneously trying to learn about as well as learn from those much more experienced, I gradually started to see my own research as a "project" in the light of how experts saw theirs.

The project to track projects, DRIVE, discussed in Chapter 1, had a particular impact on me. DRIVE was a work-tracking and recording system built on ERP software that categorized the work done by all employees in terms of discrete projects. Some of the first meetings I attended were about the finalization and launch of the system in the holding company to test it before it launched. DRIVE was unique in that as a new software interface, it divided work into discrete tasks, goals, and resources that could each be evaluated by a manager with a grade and given a weight in terms of its importance to an employee's job. It was also covertly meant to be a tool for breaking negative influences from bosses by subtly nudging managers to give oral feedback more frequently to their team members.

If anthropology is about epistemic relativity—or treating other ways of knowing about the world as equal to one's own—and a reflexive orientation to adapting within the field, I began to be more sympathetic to the projects that the HR team was constructing. This was partly because I was impressed by the sincerity and effort from HR members, especially from my coworker assistant manager Ji-soon who was my age and allowed me to sit in on her initial meetings with other teams. She was sincerely invested in solving what seemed like a tricky workplace problem around the bias of managers and the legibility of work.

Nevertheless, working on, hearing about, and seeing the logic behind a project such as DRIVE began to shape how I thought about my own research on office work and my own value to the team. I became aware that my own skills as an anthropologist were not particularly useful for the kinds of applied organizational behavior projects that my coworkers were involved in.[6] As an intern, I was also on the hook to produce these. Executive Cho asked me early in my time at Sangdo to produce a report on "HR Strategy During Mergers and Acquisitions (M&A)." Despite my best efforts to learn various principles of M&A and how they affect HR practices (such as how HR systems should be combined during a merger), the PowerPoint slide deck I produced for him barely passed his muster, even when he let me write it in English to avoid translation issues. For him, it failed the basic principle of MECE (mutually exclusive, comprehensively exhaustive). MECE is a principle for making sure categories of analysis are clearly distinct and that all categories are included. It is also a principle associated with McKinsey & Company, which was widely known in South Korean corporate circles. I tirelessly attempted to work on the PowerPoint to produce some expert object that would meet Cho's approval. But my lack of training in HR consulting left me with little to show in terms of a report that would satisfy what he wanted. Team manager Jang suggested that I just stop working on it, as executive Cho might eventually forget about it. Yet the experience of failing at a project as a worker also made me realize that I was part of the field of distinctions around knowledge and expertise. I began to fear what performance grade I might receive were I a full-time employee.

A concern around wanting my research to be recognized by those I worked with shaped how I approached the rest of my fieldwork. I adjusted my research focus to something that might be palatable and recognizable to those around me. In the spring, about eight months into my time at Sangdo, I created a formalized research plan. I identified a topic that seemed organizationally relevant but not too critical: what were the relationships between the holding company and the subsidiaries in terms of communication links. I developed a list of people I wanted to interview, requests for team shadowing, methods descriptions, and goals that I submitted to the owner-executive. I created sample interview questions and submitted them to executives ahead of time. This was a way of coming to agreement on what my actual formal research was; but in my own mind it was also an attempt to fit my research into their epistemic worlds. In the end, the owner-executive did agree to the plan I made, which allowed me to spend time with various departments, learning the different communicative patterns and relationships that they constructed with the subsidiaries.

In framing my research to them, I followed (subconsciously or not) the MECE logic and the ways that HR managers thought about cultural (that is, behavioral) differences: I tried to account for all the teams in the holding company and sought to understand how they were distributed across different styles or types of communication based on their unique domains of work. At one point, I even attempted to create an Excel table that could categorize the full variety of genres in the office and classify teams according to which genres they used more often to communicate with other teams. That effort did not go very far, as I only had access to teams for a few days at a time and I did not construct any mechanism beyond observations of meetings, one-on-one interviews, a few hours of shadowing, and perusal of team files.[7] In retrospect, I could have done what many of the teams themselves did to gather information: make particular demands of other teams to produce knowledge via a survey or a form about their communication patterns. However, I also had internalized another company distinction: that I was an intern in the presence of senior managers and I could not demand of their time beyond what was gifted to me. In this sense, I felt lucky at least to do fly-on-the-wall observations, given my low rank.

After the Field: Appreciating the Value of Low-Level Projects

One company project I was able to work on extensively was the employee survey (the subject of Chapter 4). The survey was itself a rather low-level project for the HR team and one I suspected they gave me to occupy my work without exposing me to more sensitive personnel information. At the time, work within the team was staggered by a division of labor overseen by team manager Jang: Min-sup, the highest assistant manager, worked on complex issues around salary and executive promotions; Ji-soon, the next highest, worked on new programs such as DRIVE; and Ki-ho, the junior-most employee, worked on an assortment of small projects and tasks as part of a wider training in areas of HR management.

I was initially excited about the possibility of working on the survey. It felt at times to be an odd synthesis of pseudo-anthropological ideas around culture mapping paired with the HR team's prerogatives that might generate interesting results. After the initial excitement, however, much of my fieldwork time was occupied by spending weeks in front of an Excel spreadsheet, organizing and analyzing survey data. The problem with the survey was that the data had irregularities as did the question structures and analysis, prolonging the final analysis into April. My own interest in the diversity of office genres began to feel constrained by the fact that I had become anchored to two office genres, the spreadsheet and the PowerPoint file, that in the scheme of work projects seemed insignificant compared to the other genres coworkers in HR were working on that involved more complex conglomerate-level policies, such as the creation of a new bonus system, the digitization of employee records, team manager evaluations, and overseas worker policies. Indeed, in my final month at Sangdo I had requested to talk with other members of HR about certain policies and documentation around these policies, but it seemed I had missed my window to access more advanced documents that composed the infrastructures of distinction as I was coming to understand them. In retrospect, it certainly would not make sense to grant an intern access to more advanced files on his way out! At the time, however, it seemed as if I had missed out on a golden opportunity.

Nevertheless, as I analyzed my materials, the role of the survey turned out to be a useful one for understanding the dynamics around certain conglomerate politics as well as basic ideas about representations of others. The survey was one of the few venues in which the relations between holding company and subsidiary did not go through representatives or CEOs but went straight to the employees while preventing executives and team managers from participating. In that light, I realized that surveys enacted their own participant structure of exclusion by leaving out team managers, which would in theory allow the holding company to speak for the employees, albeit through numbers. Higher-level projects, to the extent they might have directly affected employees' salaries, benefits, or even job statuses, were much more sensitive within the conglomerate and demanded particular care and attention in how they were presented to employees or subsidiaries. The survey is interesting in this regard because it was one genre that could circumvent many (if not all) of those concerns.

Likewise, as the analysis of the survey broke down and the HR team struggled to find new ways of analyzing or slicing the data, the survey was dramatically reframed in terms of what it could promise. At the time as an employee, this was particularly stressful; I even found myself going in to work on a Sunday to try to make sense of the data. I was disappointed that the results were not what we had planned. As I was analyzing my notes much later from a much different position, I found it useful for understanding the malleability, evidentiality, and fragility of managerial promises. In one sense, the team was able to effectively erase many of the high-level managerial categories for which they had promised to present a different kind of analysis in the final reports. This suggested that what seemed like grand promises could in theory be changed without significant consequences. In another sense, as much as managers drew contrasts between themselves and subsidiary management, the numbers, facts, and evidential logic were of utmost importance. Even the distinction of using advanced models or the help of an American-based statistician would not have sufficed the kind of hard logic that they felt they needed to present. It also suggested that what was at stake was the position of the HR team, and by proxy the holding company, as experts distinct by their very projects. If even simple projects could not be shown to work, then that might reflect poorly on trust in their other more ambitious projects.

Writing this Book: Moving Beyond Hierarchical Assumptions

As part of my original research proposal and even after I left Sangdo in 2015, I considered terms such as democracy and hierarchy to be somewhat abstract ideological poles that might describe different work cultures, opinions on how work should be, or genres of communication. My thought was that these forms might clash in the office, either between different generations and work environments and become manifest in particularities of linguistic form, like the dropping of honorifics, turn-taking, or as politeness strategies. Implicit in this initial proposal was a deeply held value distinction: that hierarchy was part of an older, conservative approach to organizational or social order and that concern for interpersonal distinctions reflected inherent inequalities, control, or manipulation on behalf of management or at some late stage of capitalism. In short, the abstract concept of hierarchy itself existed within a hierarchy of values in the West, where democracy, flatness, or nondistinction are supreme values associated with liberal ideas of progress and equality. Coming to awareness around those embedded distinctions was a longer process.

Being embedded at Sangdo for one year, I developed close relationships with employees and their work. I also heard many of their own explanations for office-level or corporate dynamics. I realized quickly that democracy and hierarchy were not particularly strong (or even contrasting) ideological poles in everyday work life, though they can occasionally be useful interactional threats or motivations for new kinds of public relations discourses or qualities that are emphasized on surveys as imagined types. Much office work rarely falls into these broader poles which is more often concerned with technocratic procedures and bureaucratic principles. Nevertheless, even as I shifted my interest toward the relationship between the holding company and its subsidiaries, as discussed in Chapter 1, I maintained a basic distinction that office places operated within a dialectic of control and resistance. Even if some form appears to be more enlightened or accommodating, it might just be another tactic of control.

Wary of admitting that there was no core struggle embedded in the Sangdo workplace, during the publishing of my dissertation I focused on the imposition of new forms of control. I described what I considered the creation of a new control tower at the top of the Sangdo Group that was being imposed on the previously autonomous Sangdo subsidiaries through new centralized management techniques distributed across many projects. This view was partly confirmed by South Korean friends and close informants from outside of Sangdo who interpreted any superficial shifts in managerial policy as a political realignment, such as a new generation of ownership or an up-and-coming executive.[8] In their view, any change to a new promotional system or creation of a new brand was in effect the repositioning of someone trying to make a name for themselves within the group. Implicit in this was a notion that corporations are, at their core, sites of political contest that must necessarily limit the freedom of those who are caught up in such status contests. I considered hierarchy in the form of asymmetric relationships to be an inevitable ethical tradeoff for employees, who might have had to choose to align with one boss over another, as a means of ensuring their own sustained existence as an employee within the group.

Framing what was happening at Sangdo in this way was not entirely incorrect, but it fell into a common trope of (Western) capitalist expansion and its assault on "paradise," where paradise is understood as the local, traditional, or qualitative. In this case, I had rescaled the relationships to those within Sangdo: elite (Western-trained) holding company managers attempting to impose a new order onto (local) subsidiaries. It was only when approaching the writing of this book that I began to focus more on the degree to which corporate spaces are also aspirational zones for distinction for everyone involved. In this sense, looking at vertical rankings, for instance, as an aspirational form of labor or class mobility is much different from treating them as necessary objects of control from one group over another or something that employees are otherwise opposed to. Prestige labor structures are part of much longer trajectories of mobility and corporations a wider institutional site for articulating South Korea's changes in a complex twentieth century than I had previously considered. I had to consider that office workers themselves were combating certain negative views of hierarchy through their new systems or projects. In this sense, it was important to separate out local understandings of hierarchy from forms of distinction that to an outsider might look like the same thing ("South Korean corporate culture").[9]

Acknowledging that employees might want to invest in certain forms of distinction created or managed by corporations (marked by salaries, prestige, fulfilling work, meaningful collaborations with others, and recognition for their work and accomplishments) was a new development in my approach and led me to focus on the broader notion of the supercorporate ideal. If one underlying notion of the supercorporate ideal is that corporations should be sites of personal distinction and mobility, then I reevaluated what both hierarchy and democracy (and their associated forms) did within corporate life. In regard to hierarchy, I turned to approaching hierarchy as not an inveterate problem in corporate life (whose opposite is naturally democracy) but as a culturally described force from the past, embodied into particular styles or worker types, that was impeding sincere forms of distinction and participation in corporate life. The tension, apparent right in the results of a survey I had long worked on, was one of how to reconcile two different ideals of posthierarchical office work in South Korea.

Distinction and participation are ideals that are often imagined in discrete forms (for instance, commands versus conversations, ranks versus teams). However, as ideals they intersect in complex ways in the realities of office life when workers of different ranks and responsibilities interact on teams, teams work together, and organizations direct other organizations. Moreover, as much as certain kinds of infrastructures of distinction posit that distinctions can be reduced to discrete signs linked to single individuals, like performance grades, they invariably become entangled relationally with others:

team managers depend on junior members to perform, and junior members might seek to appease their team managers for support. This is why the role of the manager (such as a *timjang* or *bujang*) so often appears as a kind of problematic locus in resolving problems of office life. Manager-employee relations can also be a site of affective asymmetry, a form which is fondly looked on in other South Korean institutional relationships, such as senior and junior relationships at school.

Participation is also more complex than simply the freedom from control or the absence of distinction. It is mediated in particular kinds of encounters or sets of interactions, the outcome of which can never be known in advance. Much like in the West, where democracy is itself a higher-order ideal vis-à-vis other forms of government, participation in South Korea fits into ideas about interorganizational value distinction: new forms of corporate-level policies like title-flattening were meant to make corporate work more appealing and attractive vis-à-vis other workplaces. The goal of such forms of participation is not always harmonious or flat communication, but to act as a higher-order sign of enlightenment. It turned out that more genuine spaces of democratic participation were quite rare, namely shareholder meetings discussed in Chapter 5. Shareholder meetings were not particularly well liked by employees, in part because they are premised on being agonistic encounters among parties with different interests.

Post-hierarchical notions of distinction and participation do not mean that there are no other forms of negative hierarchy to locate across the South Korean economic landscape, either domestically or further afield. Indeed, with the continued global expansion of South Korean companies, brands, and operations, not to mention the continuous development and expansion of aspects of the corporate sector in South Korea, there are many new sites from which to understand how hierarchy, distinction, and participation intersect in complex ways. This book has suggested that what might appear to be clear instances of corporate hierarchies (in the negative or devalued sense) can also be seen simultaneously as sites of attainment for many on the outside and on the inside of such system. Scholars would be remiss to only see vertical, stratified, or gradated arrangements as necessarily negative, regressive, or outdated. To do so would reflect a Western methodological blind spot. It is worth considering the sincere work that the men and women at places like Sangdo and elsewhere do to make both distinction and participation realizable ideals within organizational life, however imperfect a task.

Notes

Introduction

1. Kelty (2019, 1) writes, "The power of participation, at its best, is to reveal ethical intuitions, make sense of different collective forms of life, and produce an experience beyond that of individual opinion, interest, or responsibility. But in the twenty-first century, participation is more often a formatted procedure by which autonomous individuals attempt to reach calculated consensus, or one in which they experience an attenuated, temporary feeling of personal contribution that ends almost as soon as it begins." See also Kelty (2017).

2. One particular focus of critique has centered on forms of rank, evaluation, and grading on the grounds that such systems treat people like things and render people into the very objects that capitalism produces—the universal commodity. For well-known critiques of corporate ranking systems, see Foucault (1977), Burawoy (1979, 95–122), Townley (1993), Acker (1990), Bourdieu (1991, 238), Klikauer (2014), and Hoskin and Macve (1986) for different perspectives. The invention of hierarchical distinctions within Western organizations has been well documented historically, such as the adoption of measures of individual evaluation and ranking, which moved from the military to early managerial organizations in the nineteenth century (Hoskin and Macve 1986). As Miller and O'Leary (1989) described, debates around workplace hierarchy have also shifted over time, such as serving prosocial functions in American organizational life across different eras in the twentieth century. For an extensive description of South Korean personnel management in the 1980s, see Janelli and Yim (1993, 134–153).

3. Kunda (1992); Weeks (2004); Krause-Jensen (2010); Koo (2001).

4. See Lee (2011), Chun (2011), and Yi and Chun (2020) for sociological accounts of issues around solidarity within informal labor categories, as well as Schober (2018) for an anthropological account of women's labor protests in South Korea. While hierarchical distinctions within labor groups have long been a focus of attention and solidarity across labor categories is hard-earned, the question of labor success often does not concern whether workers or unions overcome a corporate hierarchy *tout court* but whether they become included in formal workplace structures—a point from which

they could make claims as employees vis-à-vis their employers (see Chun 2011, chapt. 5 and chap. 6). The tension between enterprise unionism and cross-labor (solidarity-driven) unionism has long been a point of tension within South Korean labor movements. See also Doucette and Kang (2018).

5. This does not mean that superficial corporate ethics should *not* be critiqued; a growing number of anthropologists have tackled these issues precisely, especially in encounters between Western corporations and managers and non-Western actors (Kirsch 2014; Rajak 2011a ; Welker 2014).

6. Hegel and Knox (1967, 225); see also Klikauer (2016, 73–98).

7. Hegel and Knox (1967, 226).

8. South Korean firms have long experimented with different work structures, including the advent of team-based working units in the 1990s (Park 2006). However, the cultural and political impetus to locate hierarchy as a problem has been most evident in the wake of the Asian Financial Crisis (or IMF Crisis) of 1997. As Bae and Rowley (2003) have noted, at that time changes were seen to be needed across all levels of HRM as workers themselves came to be seen as problems (*insamangsa*). A host of reforms were pursued across all levels of HR practices with the assumption that they were seen to be linked to an IMF way (Bae and Rowley 2003, 96). Likewise, anthropologists Song (2009) and Kim (2018 [2001]) have also noted how the financial crisis portended new divisions among types of working men.

9. See Davis (2009, 39–40). For the original articulation of "the society of organizations" notion, see Drucker (1992).

10. See LeBlanc (2012) and Dasgupta (2013).

11. See Matanle (2003), Miyazaki (2013), and Allison (2013, chap. 2).

12. Kim (1997) has made an important intervention to show that the conglomerates, while continuously involved in South Korea's economic "miracle" that has unfolded since the late 1960s, have nevertheless had a shifting and at times antagonistic relationship with the state. Clifford (1994) in *Troubled Tiger* also provides a journalistic account of shifting and antagonistic relationships among bureaucrats, businessmen, and politicians. See also Kim and Park (2011) for a historical account of the antagonism between Park Chung-hee and corporate chairmen in the early 1960s.

13. As Doucette (2015) has described, despite the seemingly strong differences of opinion around the concept of economic democratization (*gyeongje minjuhwa*) in South Korea, most commentators still take large corporate organizations to be the modal object for channeling social and economic reform.

14. See Cho (2001); see also Moon (2001) in the same volume.

15. This is not actually that much different from certain Western innovations or aspirations to create better kinds of corporate organizations—those that differentiate from more canonical corporate-managerial forms, such as cooperatives (Paranque and Willmott 2014), employee stock-owning companies (Souleles 2019), or activist shareholding (as one kind of ownership) (Welker and Wood 2011).

16. See Iteanu (2013) and Hickel and Haynes (2018) for recent anthropological thought reevaluating hierarchy as an analytical concept. Peacock (2015) suggests

that in the *longue durée* the emphasis on the radical commensurability of all things through exchange value brought on by capitalism has also devalued other forms of value, namely social hierarchy. She suggests that this is why both popular movements and social scientists alike since the 1960s have been so receptive to new ideas around different kinds of notions for flatness (networks, rhizomes, actors, fields, and so on) that radically presume there are no presumed hierarchies. This ideological effect is particularly felt in recent ethnographies of organizations that, according to her, have not adequately accounted for the forms of hierarchy that animate organizations; see also Peacock and Kao (2013).

17. This was the case for sociologist Yuko Ogasawara who documented her own concerns describing the seemingly paradoxical power commanded by secretarial "office ladies" in mid-1990s Japanese workplaces. Ogasawara (1998, 1–2) candidly wrote that "[In the US,] I spoke of the intense sex discrimination in Japan. I described the severe obstacles women faced in establishing a professional career in a male-dominated society and how many women who had graduated from top universities ended up typing documents and serving tea in the office . . . . Many people I talked to had a preconception of Japanese women as gentle, shy, and obedient. My account seemed to tally with this image and confirm that Japanese women, submissive and deferential, were the victims of society."

18. See Dunn (2004), Ho (2009), Welker (2014), Cohen (2015), Chong (2018), and Wilf (2019). If much of the trend by anthropologists toward corporations has been to focus on effects on communities as exogenous forces (particularly in extractive industries), scholars have also focused on the internal transformation of corporations by outsider forces (such as finance or innovation experts). The general thrust of this body of research reflects a broader anthropological concern of what happens in the context when "incommensurate ontologies" clash (Kockelman 2016), either across national spaces or within institutional spaces. See also Hull (2010) on the export and imposition of democratic technologies of speech after World War II from the US to India.

19. This tradition stems from the impact of Foucault's work on the study of organizations in British and North American scholarship. In a seminal paper, Townley (1993) brought the breadth of Foucault's insights to the field of HR management, showing how practices of both subjectification (through things such as job interviews) and objectification (through things such as ranking matrixes) operate together. See also seminal papers by Burrell (1988) and Rose (1988); see Mennicken and Miller (2014) for an overview of the "Foucault effect" in organization studies. Where some Foucauldian scholarship has turned more recently to narratives around the management of the self, flexibilization, and precarity as a reflection of processes of individuation, including in the South Korean labor market (see, for instance, Seo 2011), an organizational focus nevertheless underscores that institutional processes of selecting, sorting, and ranking across arrays of people are still important.

20. Amid narratives of delayering of formal middle-management ranks, there has been an assumption that other signs of legible hierarchy have also disappeared from labor markets. Anthropologist Ilana Gershon has shown that, at least in the US,

job seekers are closely attuned to tracking their employability on their résumés and LinkedIn profiles as markers of their temporal progression through a career. While this is not tracked by a single corporate employer or through a fixed set of legible ranks, workers are keenly aware of how time and responsibility are correlated and what this says about an implicit hierarchy of normative career progression and work stability. See Gershon (2017; 2018; 2019).

21. See Chong (2018) for an ethnographic account of the way management consultants attempt to embed financial distinctions into personnel categories in China.

Chapter 1: A New Tower

1. A visit I made to the headquarters of Naver Corporation, one of South Korea's largest technology companies, in Bundang on the outskirts of Seoul, revealed the way that corporate office towers integrated multiple sites of architectural distinction: The Naver building was entirely encased in green glass, with tropes of high-end design and spaces designated for public traffic. The Naver building featured a library, a reading room, and a café and gift shop as quasi civic spaces.

2. Welker (2014, 4). For anthropological discussions of the give-and-take of corporate identity, see Urban and Koh (2013, 2015) and Rogers (2012).

3. Koo (2001, 193). Krause-Jensen (2017, 117) writes that "present-day organisations, in that they are officially and symbolically denying hierarchy . . . , the incessant restructurings reaffirm and are a constant reminder of the reality of such power-relationships." Inoue (2007) similarly notes the way that female Japanese office workers were welcomed into the workforce in the 1990s through an emphasis on equality and liberal values. However, any office problems, such as inveterate sexism, were framed as issues of individual psychology that women workers should overcome on their own. See also Fleming (2014).

4. Holding companies are not unprecedented in East Asia. The pre-World War II Japanese conglomerates or *zaibatsu* were also organized into holding companies, which allowed founding families to maintain central control. In contrast to today's holding companies, however, subsidiaries and affiliates in *zaibatsu* also owned each other, maintaining ownership within the group (Clark 1979, 42–3). American postwar policy both dismantled holding company structures and promoted foreign investment to weaken Japanese ownership concentration. See Hadley's (1970) *Antitrust in Japan*.

5. The newspaper *Hankyoreh* has noted the irony that after the year 2000, many chaebol families have actually concentrated ownership rights despite the shift to holding companies. The holding company structure was supposed to promote corporate transparency in part by making it easier to see internal shareholding relationships; however, by cutting off intersubsidiary relations and directing all shareholding relationships through holding companies, chaebol ownership has in some ways been cemented in place. "Behind Holding Companies, the Chaebol Laugh," *Hankyoreh*, May 4, 2013, http://h21.hani.co.kr/arti/cover/cover_general/34447.html.

6. Legal scholar Iwai (1999) has observed that corporations largely oscillate between conceptions of themselves as persons (that act, contract, etc.) or as things (that can be bought or sold). He notes that traditionally, Japanese conglomerate groups subverted the thing-ness of corporations by using cross-shareholding links among affiliated companies to prevent foreign corporate takeovers, such as through leveraged buyouts. In this case, owning another corporation as a subsidiary was in part a defense mechanism.

7. Perhaps the most infamous of these strategic planning offices was by the Samsung Group, a site of both central planning and secretive politics. One peculiar feature of strategy offices at the time was that they often did not exist as corporate legal entities (*beobin*) but were simply organizationally recognized as constituting an office affiliated with the chairman, instructions or commands from which needed to be followed. Samsung's office did come under particular scrutiny in 2017 as a possible site of the political scandal involving Park Geun-hye, South Korea's former president, and Samsung vowed to disband it. See, for instance, "Samsung's 'Control Tower' Completely Disbanded," *Hankyung*, February 28, 2017, https://www.hankyung.com/news/article/2017022851021.

8. At Sangdo, a special issue of the company magazine focused on crises. A motivational quote introducing the issue encouraged employees to remember an older Korean industrial mantra of "it can be done" (*hamyeon dwenda*), while encouraging employees to "shine ever more even within a crisis" (*wigi sogeseo deo-uk binnaneun saram*). A four-page photo spread and profile of a product development team from a Sangdo subsidiary described how each member possessed an iron will (*bulgul-ui uiji*) to overcome crises in their jobs. Crisis management can be a cover term for simply imposing new rules: one informant at a large conglomerate reported that crisis management within her group led to the rigidization of rules, including having crisis hours (work beginning at 8:30 a.m. instead of 9:00 a.m.) and concentrated work time so that important issues could not be interrupted by meetings or socializing.

9. Despite the prominence of certain conglomerates that have been continuous since the 1960s, many others have failed or bought and sold subsidiaries frequently over many years. Mergers and acquisitions of subsidiaries also have political relations: One example is the Kukje Group, one of the largest conglomerates in the 1980s that quickly disappeared off the map when political bribes from corporate groups were normatively enforced. In 1984, the chairman of the Kukje Group, Yang Chung-mo, refused to make a political donation to President Chun Doo-hwan's new philanthropic foundation. As a sign of revenge, the Korean Bank refused loans to Kukje in 1985 and the group quickly was declared bankrupt. Tellingly, its subsidiaries were simply absorbed into other conglomerate organizations (Janelli and Yim 1993, 64–5; Kim 1997, 200–201).

10. While kinship tropes are often rightly criticized for their use in or as corporate propaganda (CEO as father), Jang's comment reflects other ways that kinship idioms can be creatively used or provide analytic models. Riles (2004, 400–401) reported

that Japanese bankers referred metaphorically to the Japanese central bank, The Bank of Japan, as "our mother." In the Japanese case, the private banks and central bank had such a close relationship that it was difficult to ethnographically identify the relationship at all, in much the same way, she argues, that Japanese mothers and sons have unspoken, intimate relations.

11. This is not to say that no forms of collective representation were present prior to my time there or to the advent of the holding company. I found archives of the Sangdo Group magazine from the 1990s that exhibited a group-wide athletics day with images of the chairman intermingling with employees from different companies. All companies largely shared the same logo system prior to the new branding. However, there were many sites that revealed the limits of a cohesive identity: for instance, at the annual Iron & Steel industry half-marathon/5k, which is sponsored by the large companies in the industry, two Sangdo subsidiaries sponsored separate tents and took out separate advertisements in the promotional magazine, both using their own in-house advertising.

12. See Park (2006, 12).

13. Hochschild (2012 [1983], 147).

Chapter 2: Infrastructures of Distinction

1. Haggard, Lim, and Kim (2003, 1). See also Son (2002); Haggard, Lim, and Kim (2003); and Chang (2006).

2. Chang and Shin (2003, 56). See also Kalinowski (2009).

3. Sociological research on global movements toward eroding middle management or delayering have pointed out how both promanager and antimanager stances proliferate, with attacks and scrutiny on individual middle managers along with greater management oversight (which, in theory, does not require managers) (McCann, Hassard, and Morris 2004; Hassard, Morris, and McCann 2012). These kinds of approaches—supportive of managerialism as a technique or technology but hostile toward individual (costly) labor—reflect a comment by anthropologist Alfred Gell on Westerners' "enchantment of technology" and the mystique surrounding what he described as "costless production" (Gell 1992, 62ff.).

4. As Bae and Rowley (2003, 96) have noted, the "'IMF factor' was always incorporated into the formula of all activities and programmes of government, firms, and all of society." Moreover, "all thinking, ways, methods, and activities different from the traditional ones were accepted if the password of 'It's an IMF way' was uttered."

5. Person naming is ripe for social commentary and political attention. Social and political movements regularly seek to make names and titles the objects of reform. Van Luong (1988) has described how pronouns and kin terms in communist Vietnam become ideologically revalued, coming to demarcate different sociopolitical orders: Marxist revolutionaries adopted flat kin terms, reflecting a new vision of society, while kin terms that stressed hierarchy became negatively associated with elites. Harkness (2015) has similarly described how a Protestant Christian mode of religious kinship in South Korea based on equal sibling terms *hyeongje* (universal brother) and

jamae (universal sister) came into conflict with an organizational hierarchy of the church, which organized members through hierarchical roles. Naming systems rely on contrasts between them and others: vertical versus horizontal or hierarchical versus democratic. Koyama (2004) has critiqued how differences between Japanese society and Western societies have long been explained through the comparison of systems of address and honorifics, with Japan standing for formal and hierarchical and the West standing for informal and nonhierarchical, despite the fact that honorifics were not historically important in most dialects in Japan. The continued salience of naming systems within such societies has led to the perception that they also are the main objects of such systems or at least their "root" signs. When Minjong and other South Korean companies sought to debureaucratize their workforces by changing titles, they were following a long tradition of using language (and certain features of linguistic systems) to remodel social and political relations.

6. This is the thrust of the popular (but also highly disputed) account by Gladwell (2008) in his description of Korean Air crashes in the 1990s in *Outliers*. For Gladwell, a series of three plane crashes of Korean Air flights was due to social norms against confronting elders, even, it appears, in matters of life and death. Assistant pilots were so committed to this norm, which Gladwell borrowed from intercultural psychologist Geert Hofstede, that they were willing to not alert their pilots to impending dangers. Alongside other criticisms of Gladwell's account, it is not hard to notice Gladwell's linguistic and cultural bias when South Korean pilots were said to finally succeed when they were forced to switch to communicating in English and be trained by American pilots.

7. "KT Introduces Unified Manager System," *Money Today*, February 20, 2012, http://www.mt.co.kr/view/mtview.php?type=1&no=2012022008221371083.

8. This is not to confirm a myth that there was no such thing as employee evaluation prior to the Asian Financial Crisis; on the contrary, Janelli and Yim report in their 1980s ethnography that managers were regularly evaluated using performance metrics to determine promotions. The difference was that someone of a lower rank, in theory, could not outstrip someone of a higher rank.

9. Star (1999, 380) notes, "For a railroad engineer, the rails are not infrastructure, but topic. For the person in a wheelchair, the stairs and doorjamb are not seamless subtenders of use, but barriers (citation omitted). One person's infrastructure is another's topic, or difficulty." See also Larkin (2013).

10. Fenster (2017); Levine (2004).

11. Simmel (2004). Anthropologists and sociologists have long expressed concern about commensuration processes in local communities, such as when noncapitalist societies are made with (or against) global standards (Espeland and Stevens 1998; Hankins and Yeh 2016). See also Kockelman (2016).

12. "Evaluation Season: The Active Role of the 'Cigarette Crowd' . . . . Instead of Promotion, Earnest Team Members Transfer," *Hankyung*, December 7, 2013, https://www.hankyung.com/society/article/2015120764101.

13. I have altered the real figures here in an illustrative example: in the previous system, the bonuses, based on a percentage of a single month's salary, were the same rate for every employee, such as 150 percent (1.5 times one month's salary). Both Kim (S) and Lee (B) would receive 150 percent of their respective one-month base salaries. In the new system, Kim's would be 300 percent based on his team and individual grade, while Lee's would stay at 150 percent.

14. See Park (2006, 18).

15. Goffman (1956, 486–7).

16. This is the difference between organizational terms *jikgeup, jikchaek, jigwi,* and *jingmyeong,* each of which loosely translates to rank or title in English. Each may be different for the same person in a South Korean office. It is worth observing another of Goffman's famous observations on the risk of *losing* one's job or even title, a process he equated with death itself. Focusing on failures, he noted, leads us to see how "we can go or be sent to our death in each of our social capacities, the ways, in other words, of handling the passage from the role that we had to a state of having it no longer. One might consider the social processes of firing and laying off; of resigning and being asked to resign," (Goffman 1952, 462–3).

17. "If We Get Rid of Titles, Will Organizational Culture Change?," April 16, 2018, https://ppss.kr/archives/108981.

Chapter 3: Old Spirits of Capitalism

1. "'Old men have got to go': Corporations' rank diet" [*Gocham dduigehara: gieop-deul jikgeup daieoteu*"], April 10, 2015, http://news.donga.com/3/01/20150410/70623742/1.

2. Locating generations such as the "386" generation—those born in the sixties, who went to university in the 1980s and were in their thirties in the 1990s—can be useful devices for locating classes of actors, those who might be shaped by particular historical events or forces, who also come into clashes with others.

3. Wilf (2015, 21).

4. Boltanski and Chiapello (2018, 240).

5. Vogel (1963).

6. LeBlanc (2012, 867); see also Dasgupta (2013).

7. Chang (1999).

8. For general literature on how mobility is a narrativized object among the middle classes (and not just a statistical reference point) in South Korea, see the extensive work of anthropologist Nancy Abelmann (1997, 2003). For background on sensitivities around distinction and what consumer objects distinction is mapped onto, see Lett (1998) and Nelson (2000).

9. Ogasawara (1998, 89–90).

10. Allison (1994, 98).

11. See, for instance, Drucker (1992).

12. Ho (2009, 252, cited in Wilf 2015).

13. Whyte's dark vision of organizational life in the 1950s United States was premised on precisely the loss of a certain kind of distinction (individuality) in an evident fear of the homogeneity assumed by collectivization, an outlook no doubt shaped by incipient Cold War fears: "The corporation man is the most conspicuous example, but he is only one, for the collectivization so visible in the corporation has affected almost every field of work . . . . The word *collective* most of them can't bring themselves to use except to describe foreign countries or organizations they don't work for—but they are keenly aware of how much more deeply beholden they are to organization than were their elders" (Whyte 1956, 3–4). For a discussion on the relationship between California hippie culture and new cyber cultures of Silicon Valley, see Turner (2006).

14. Goffman (1974); Hastings and Manning (2004, 304); see also Hall (2014).

15. Choi (2018 [2016]) has described the emergence and circulation of a typified humor genre known as *ajae* (middle-aged man) gags. More than a narrative genre, such gags are cited by young people and women to mark middle-aged men as particularly *not* funny.

16. Sahlins (1972, 195–6). "'Negative reciprocity' is the attempt to get something for nothing with impunity, the several forms of appropriation, transactions opened and conducted toward net utilitarian advantage." While Sahlins had in mind acts of haggling in one-to-one market-like exchanges, asymmetrical relations (such as boss-subordinate) can also involve positive and negative reciprocity (that being, work with no longer term payoff to the subordinate). See Yan (1996).

17. Thus, it is not just a hierarchical relationship itself but the abuse of the privileges of an intimate hierarchy. Most dyadic (two-person) social relations in South Korea rely on dyadic relationships of superiority and subordination, occurring even among young children (Ahn 2016).

18. Kendall (1985); Harkness (2011).

19. Kim (2018 [2001]); Song (2009).

20. Harkness (2013b).

21. These speech elements were overheard at lunch where I was not able to write down notes. They were partially reconstructed from my memory and with the help of another intern who was also present who I had asked to confirm executive Kang's comments.

22. See Inoue (2003) for a discussion of the transduction of Japanese women's language via American white women's language.

23. See Weeks (2004) and Wästerfors (2008) for ethnographic work that explores complaint in the context of lay ethnography (insiders' accounts of their own organizations).

24. The well-known South Korean movie "Oldboy" (2003) by Park Chan-wook hinges on forgotten acquaintances from high school.

25. In the nationalist accounts of industrial history, South Korea has often been categorized as managerial style in which managers are circulated and trained in a wide variety of disciplines such as accounting, HR, strategy, and operations. See Vogel (1991).

26. The normative judgment against people who leave on the clock is the premise of the 2013 television drama "Queen of the Office" (*Jikjangui sin*) starring the actress Kim Hye-su as a contract worker (*gyeyakjik*) who leaves precisely at quitting time no matter the circumstance, to the shock of her coworkers.

27. The social pressures might appear so strong that extreme measures are needed. One informant from a different conglomerate reported that they cut the power and turned off the lights so that employees could literally not even work. These problems seem directly rooted in the physical presence of a boss. When a boss is on vacation, employees mention that they, too, are on a vacation. One employee once described days without the boss as *eorinui nal* (kid's day). And these pressures are related to one's direct boss(es), not necessarily bosses from other departments.

28. Lutz (1989); Benson and Kirsch (2010).

29. "President Roh-created Bureaucrat's 'Multi-Rater Feedback' Disappears," *Oh My News*, January 10, 2008, http://www.ohmynews.com/NWS_Web/View/at_pg.aspx ?CNTN_CD=A0001297738.

30. Elsewhere in discussion with executive Kang, he warned of the problem of *balbonsaegwon* (the rooting out of a problem). He saw this as a potential problem with 360-degree feedback where bosses would interpret it as a kind of reversal of the boss-subordinate relationship and seek out the team member (even anonymized) who wronged him. I had heard indirectly of cases where a manager sought to find out supposedly anonymous responses via HR managers. Ogasawara's (1998) account of Japanese office ladies reflects how putatively low-level gossip can in fact sink the careers of managers who treat staff badly. However, the participant structure of gossip (passing among office ladies to higher level managers whose source is never directly revealed) shields individuals from retribution in ways better than the quasi-scientific obsession with individualized anonymity does.

31. Foucault (1973); see also Hacking (2002 [1986]) on the ways that people are made through institutional categories and Rhodes (2004) on the way that sorting prisoners into categories of "mad" and "bad" fundamentally shapes treatment in American maximum security prisons.

32. Bourdieu (1984).

Chapter 4: Surveying Sangdo

1. Briggs (2007, 553) has discussed a parallel account of the "interview society" in which varieties of interviewing, polling, surveying, and talk shows are all premised on a notion of extracting thoughts from the minds of rational, thinking individuals. Such presumptions enact a Lockean view of rational individuals who must communicate their inner thoughts in clear ways to others, a process often mediated by experts in the media or the academy. See also Bauman and Briggs (2003, 5–10).

2. Bourdieu (1979, 128).

3. As Bourdieu notes, "The politician who yesterday said 'God is on our side,' today says 'Public Opinion is on our side'," (Bourdieu 1979, 125). Elsewhere De Santos

(2009) has described the way that survey data and statistical numbers circulate as "fact-totems" to underscore public belief.

4. Surveys are also involved in a politics of representation that has a complicated history in South Korea, such as when intellectuals in the 1980s sought to represent the voices of blue-collar workers as the oppressed proletariat. As historian Lee (2005, 924) has described, this reflected a discourse of moral privilege where intellectuals, by virtue of appointing themselves as representatives, created their own implicit hierarchy: "The epistemological logic of the intellectuals' representation of themselves as socially conscious and responsible hinged on the workers as the object and beneficiary of their act of conscience" (p. 924).

5. Distinguishing white-collar and blue-collar work in South Korea is complicated as the categories themselves overlap and exclude part-time work and certain kinds of professional or technical categories such as IT. The basic term for white-collar work is *samu(gisul)jik* (lit., office[-technology] work, akin to clerk) and blue-collar is *saengsanjik* (production work).

6. See Silverstein (2003) for a theoretical account of how such orders operate semiotically and ideologically. For examples of second-order phenomena in work settings, see Cristea and Leonardi (2019); Bourgoin and Muniesa (2016); Gershon (2017); and Prentice (2019).

7. A colleague once described this to me in the following way: if a superior offers to buy his subordinates coffee, it is always wise to buy the default option, a black Americano. This is read not as a sign of concern for the superior's wallet but as a sign of repression of one's own personal desires (for a latte, cappuccino, etc.) as a public act. More generally, drinking of a shot of strong liquor (like Korean *soju*) can be taken as a sign of loyalty precisely because it is something that one would not want to do.

8. Conflicts between different second-order values are most visible in cross-cultural encounters, such as between American and Russian ideas of good managerial communication (Cohen 2015), competing American and Chinese ideas about quality (*suzhi*) (Chong 2018), and Italian and Chinese notions of good governance in family companies (Yanagisako 2012). These sites, which may appear as an encounter with the hard world of transnational commodity production (a seemingly first-order zone) are nevertheless wrapped up in implicit cultural notions of prestige and value, which are shaped by particular contexts and histories (second-order phenomena).

9. HR in South Korea is conventionally divided into management (or planning) (*insa gihwoek*) and development (or education) (*injae gaebal*) (with some larger groups having a third area, culture (*jojik munhwa*). Sangdo had the two—planning and development—with no separate culture team. While these appear to be a simple division of labor within a more general HR program, there were strong differences between the two: the planning team had a broader authority to evaluate employees and see their relative strengths and weaknesses, whereas development was focused on employee potential and education-as-benefit. Because of the reputation of education programs to be areas of empty accomplishment with little tangible impact on the business, people

on the planning side saw their work as closer to the holding company's broader vision of making significant changes across the conglomerate and not just administering programs.

10. This structure, visualized in the form of a spider chart, also drew on another consultant's analytic skill: MECE or mutually exclusive, collectively exhaustive. MECE was a preferred technique of executive Cho and itself comes from McKinsey Consulting's playbook of analytic methods. The idea of the method is to ensure that whatever phenomenon one is modeling includes categories that do not overlap, and they make sure to include all possible categories. See Minto (2009, 102).

11. The castigation of impersonal bureaucracy is also found in Boltanski and Chiapello's account of the new spirit of capitalism in France in the 1990s and discussed in Chapter 3. The "discrediting of bureaucracy and its project of eliminating everything that is not 'rational'—that is, formalizable and calculable should . . . facilitate a return to a 'more human' *modus operandi*, in which people can give full vent to their emotions, intuition and creativity" (Boltanski and Chiapello 2018, 98). In Western contexts, the opposite of bureaucracy is imagined not necessarily as greater insight into work, but greater human freedom, creativity, and passion away from work. See, for instance, Strathern (2008), Fleming (2014), and Reed (2017).

12. See Knoblauch (2008) on the way PowerPoint is used to perform expertise in work settings. Expertise has also become a function of institutional narratives where it might be promoted as a quality or feature of an institution or profession; see Ho (2009), Chong (2018), and Wilf (2019). In her work on the culture of genius surrounding Stephen Hawking, Mialet (2012) describes how genius is as much a cultural category that fascinates Western publics as it is an inherent property of certain individuals. While imagined as the property of the pure mind, acts of expressing and witnessing genius rely on a number of technical artifacts and conventional narratives in order for genius to be made apparent (and more often than not, genius is revealed to be more conventional under inspection).

13. Notions of "non-genericness" are connected to themes in anthropological discussions of commodification and brandedness, discussed by Moore (2003), Manning (2010), Agha (2011), and Nakassis (2016). These accounts describe how marketing professionals and others invested in brands do repeated work to emphasize the brandedness (nongenericness) of a product or style.

14. ERP software is a generic term for large-scale networked database programs that are highly customizable and used for all aspects of modern management, from supply chain logistics to personnel management. The issue here is not that the headquarters and subsidiaries were separated by a form of materiality (i.e., paper vs. digital)—in fact, both had ERP platforms—but that the scale of investment, implementation, and elaboration was quite different. Chong (2018, 18–20) has suggested that ERP systems are tied to broader financialization logics within corporations, as ERP systems allow every function of an organization to be considered measurable, adding to the general idea of thinking about the office as a kind of inventory. Here, the Sangdo

holding company's HR team felt at a disadvantage because they were too small as a team to merit investment in such large-scale systems.

15. Chumley (2013) has observed that evaluation techniques often include both quantitative and qualitative elements (e.g., tests and interviews, certifications and cover letters) to measure two aspects of personhood. Most satisfaction surveys include qualitative sections to give a fiction of this duality by including an open-response section at the end.

16. A scene in the graphic novel turned television drama *Misaeng* depicts a young employee concerned about how to rate her boss in an upcoming evaluation—whether to be favorable or honest. A colleague advises her that "if an evaluation is weird [*eongddunghage*], the evaluator also gets judged." Manager Choi from Minjong noted in a personal conversation that South Korean employees will never give negative responses because of what he described as the psychological contract (*simnijeok gyeyak*) between a team manager and a team member; any honest or negative review might be considered a form of blasphemy (*modok*). Rakova and Fedorenko (2021) also report how South Korean employees exhibit concern around the indexical links to their judgments even on anonymous sticky notes created during group brainstorming meetings when their bosses are present.

17. Law (2009, 242) writes, "In general . . . in scientific practice sustainable knowledge rests in and reproduces more or less stable networks or hinterlands of relevant instruments, representations—and the realities that these describe. And this is why realities . . . generally feel solid and reliable." Oppenheim (2008) also draws on the concept of hinterlands in his analysis of South Korean regional politics, where local authorities drew on different local objects and the history of specific practices to justify their resistance to the development of a new train line.

18. Kelty (2017, S88) notes, "Contemporary participation is resolutely focused on the individual participant; the 'wisdom of crowds' presumes an emergent collectivity but no necessary sense of belonging. Even the focus on 'teams' is simply a way to make individual characteristics complementary with each other rather than some attempt at solidarity of a cointerested collective. Today participation is no longer about the participation of groups but rather about the participation of individuals." See also Kelty (2019).

19. See Weeks (2004, 114–19).

20. That subsidiary was not above using a certain kind of league table to rank employees publicly: Chun's HR team instituted an antismoking campaign in which employees nominated themselves to quit smoking, with the threat of having to take a urine test to prove they had stopped smoking after a period of two months. When the campaign ended, participants' names were shared on the company intranet to indicate who had succeeded or failed.

21. This point reflects a wide set of literature in anthropology on how expertise (as both an individual performance and an institutional one) must continually be performed or be adapted for its claims to be maintained across different sites. See Boyer

(2008); Carr (2010); Mitchell (2002); Wilf (2021); Goodwin (1994); Jacobs-Huey (2003); Redfield (2006); and Choy (2005).

22. See Harkness (2013b, 201–25) on the notion of *maeum* (sharing of heart-mind).

23. A variety of new subgenres dedicated to promoting flatness through talk have emerged. The company Hunet, for instance, in its recruiting promotions, touted the following programs that were part of its "open flat culture" (*yeollin supyeong munhwa*): "space for barrier-free communication," "Hunet-family [online] chat-room," "real-time talk with the CEO via messenger," "'value day' for talking with employees from other departments," "CEO 'took&talk' hotline," and "Imagination Park for submitting innovative ideas."

24. Turco (2016).

25. Habermas (1989); Fraser (1992); Warner (2002); Cody (2011).

Chapter 5: Interrupting Democracy

1. Rajak (2011b); Nyqvist (2015). For other ethnographic accounts of corporate shareholder meetings, see Schneider (1998); Hodges, Macniven, and Mellett (2004); and Foster (2008). While both are forms of organizational governance, shareholder meetings should be considered as slightly different from annual general meetings in the United Kingdom and Europe that are not necessarily sites of wide institutional conflict among financially interested strangers. Clark (1979) and Janelli and Yim (1993) both give vivid accounts of shareholder meetings in Japan and South Korea.

2. Schneider (1998, 296).

3. Schneider (1998).

4. For accounts of ethical activism, see Welker and Wood (2011); for accounts of T. Boone Pickens (and other corporate raiders) in Japan, see McGill (2021).

5. "Another Chaebol Squabble: Family Infighting a Part of South Korea's Corporate Landscape," *Hankyoreh*, July 30, 2015. These scenes can also be replicated on television programs: a scene in the drama *The Heirs* (*sangsokjadeul*) depicts the elder chairman of the Jeguk Group taking revenge on his executive-level son for going behind his back. He does this precisely by putting a resolution to fire his son as president (*sajang*) up for a shareholder vote. While the son is dramatically not fired in the end, the meeting and vote serve as a staging of power to remind the son that his father can manipulate the wills of shareholders behind the scenes if needed.

6. Dunlavy (2006, 1352).

7. The dynamics of the Japanese situation are much different in part because of the size and strength of the yakuza groups and spin-off *sokaiya* groups as well as the emergence of the bubble economy in the 1980s. While, in this chapter, I am discussing issues that largely happened over debates within actual shareholder meetings, in Japan in the 1980s and 1990s the relationship was partly mediated by the notion of protection as corporations were not merely victims but also used *sokaiya* as forms of mafia-like protection (often from other extortionists). See Szymkowiak (2002, 176–8).

8. See Freeland and Zuckerman (2018) for a conceptualization of voice hierarchies in the firm.

9. See Power (1997, 1–14).

10. On the relationship between meeting and civilization, see Van Vree (1999). See also Hirschman (1977) on accounts of Western economic philosophy's early worry about economic activity leading to too much unbridled passion.

11. Minority shareholders are guaranteed other rights such as the right to call extraordinary meetings, the right to open accounting books, and the right to demand dismissal of directors, among others, which vary depending on percentage of a company owned. See Lee (2001) for a description of minority shareholder rights in South Korea.

12. Robert's Rules of Order, 10th edition, 1996.

13. See Reed (1990) for a discussion of how Robert's Rules were seen to be a counterrevolutionary form in Portugal because of the way they constrain freedom of interaction.

14. See Kwon (1995, 2003, 2004). In some cases, South Korean corporate law is stricter than others, as Kwon notes that the role of outside auditors in South Korea is seen as adversarial to directors in the eyes of the law, whereas in US law the auditor is seen to assist the board in preparing documents for accountability (2003, 330–31). See also Kalinowski (2008) on the role of minority shareholders in South Korea.

15. See Black, Cheffins, and Klausner (2011); Kim (2000).

16. See G.-c. Kim (2005) on parliamentary procedures in South Korea.

17. The American Bar Association recommends other parliamentary rules and not Robert's Rules for shareholder meetings. The reason is that they are too complicated for a shareholder meeting and would require hiring an official parliamentarian. The KLCA, however, has directly cited Robert's Rules as an appropriate parliamentary procedure given that the rules are part of the Korean Parliamentary Association and that they are part of the Standard Shareholder Meeting Management Regulations established in 1991; see http://www.klca.or.kr/KLCADownload/eBook/P8352.pdf.

18. Habermas (1994, 52) specifies the bourgeois public sphere as "the sphere of private individuals assembled into a public body, which almost immediately laid claim to the officially regulated 'intellectual newspapers' for use against the public authority itself." Grice (1975, 45) defined his "cooperative principle" of basic interactional norms as follows: "Make your conversational contribution such as is required, at the stage which it occurs, by the accepted purpose or direction of the talk exchange in which you are engaged."

19. One of the most well-known examples of disrupters is the American Evelyn Davis who became known as a "corporate gadfly" in the latter half of the twentieth century. A *Vanity Fair* article once described her as a "ticking time bomb" willing to do anything to disrupt a meeting, even, the articles notes, if "she must resort to whipping off her coat to reveal nothing but a bathing suit underneath" (Bennets, 2002). Though Davis used the register of a well-intentioned shareholder by submitting resolutions to companies she owned stock in, she used it largely as an extortionary ring for her newsletter *Highlights and Lowlights*, to which companies subscribed for US$500 a year.

20. The term "meeting extortionist" is an approximate translation; the first two characters (*chonghoe*) refer to shareholder meeting, while the last character, *ggun*, is a productive morpheme to denote a person marked in relation to the noun attached. It denotes someone who is good at a kind of work and depends on it for sustenance. It can take on negative meeting if the noun it combines with is not a typical work category. Meeting extortionists can also be referred to as *juchong-ggun* or *hwoebang-ggun* (disrupters).

21. "The Rights of Minority Shareholders During Meeting Season, Legally it Seems Secure but . . . ," February 25, 1981, *Joongang Ilbo*, https://news.joins.com/article /1560096.

22. "The Real Reason *chonghoe-ggun* Don't Disappear," May 2, 2016, *Ohmynews*, http://www.ohmynews.com/NWS_Web/view/at_pg.aspx?CNTN_CD=A0000237720.

23. Post, "Do you know *chonghoe-ggun*?" September 9, 2014, *PGR21*, https://pgr21 .com/freedom/73761.

24. "Request for the Government to Strongly Deal with the Shareholder Meeting Disrupters Known as *juchong-ggun* or *chonghoe-ggun*," created March 16, 2018, Citizens Petitions (in Korean), https://www1.president.go.kr/petitions/167399?page=13.

25. "The Coming Shareholder Meeting Season . . . How to Deal with *chong-hoeggun*," February 8, 2007, *Edaily* (in Korean), http://www.edaily.co.kr/news/news _detail.asp?newsId=01935206583028552.

26. "Approaching Shareholder Meeting Season . . . Tricks to Deal with *chonghoe-ggun*," February 16, 2016, *The L*, http://thel.mt.co.kr/newsView.html?no =2016021610558233944.

27. Scott (1989, 54–55).

28. "Is it a Humble Shareholder or an Extortionist . . . the Best Make $100K," February 25, 2007, *The Korean Securities Daily News* (in Korean), http://www.ksdaily.co.kr /news/articleView.html?idxno=17186.

29. "KLCA Strategy: *Chonghoe-ggun*, Disrupters, Firm Counter-Measures," January 25, 2001, *Maeil Gyeongje*, https://www.mk.co.kr/news/home/view/2001/02/44892/.

30. "Listed Companies 'grrrrr' as *chonghoe-ggun* Evolve," March 16, 2014, *SBS Biz*, https://biz.sbs.co.kr/article/10000637546.

31. There are two Korean words to frame the illicitness of the payment being made: first, *ddeok-gab*, which originally referred to the bonus money a company might give so that workers could pay for gifts on return visits to their home towns. *Ddeok-gab* has come to connote more widely a designation for corporate bribes, though in the case of extortionists it is they who requested such a bonus from companies. The second word is *bbojji*, which refers to the pity money a winner of a bet might pay to the loser.

32. Post, "Do you Know *chonghoe-ggun*?" September 9, 2014, *PGR21*, https://pgr21 .com/freedom/73761.

33. *"Chonghoe-ggun* as a Job? It's Even a Family Business," March 25, 2016, *Maeil Gyeonje*, https://www.mk.co.kr/news/stock/view/2016/03/224133/. In Szymkowiak's account of Japanese *sokaiya* and their relationship to corporations, he notes that the

ethical positioning around *sokaiya* depends on what one considers corporate (lack of) ethics in the first place (Szymkowiak 2002).

34. See Janelli in Janelli and Yim (1993) for an almost identical account in his field-work in the 1980s.

35. Because Korean is what is known in linguistics as a pro-drop language, pro-nouns such as I or you are not obligatory and are typically used only for marked pur-poses. In this case, when audience members shout "I/we second that" (*jaechongham-nida*), person is ambiguous because of individuals speaking in unison to create a collective voice, much like a vote.

36. Such use of private security forces that seem to have no affiliation with the hir-ing party is not uncommon in contemporary South Korea where violent enforcement can be and is outsourced. See Porteux and Kim (2016).

37. The POSCO chairman Kwon was caught up in another racket in 2018 that he could not escape: he was wrapped up in a philanthropic donations scandal tied to for-mer President Park Geun-hye and her confidant Choi Soon-sil. POSCO made dona-tions to false-front philanthropic groups (such as a fencing team). Whether he was forced to comply or whether POSCO received corporate benefits as a result of the do-nation was unclear at the time.

38. "KLCA Sets Up *'chonghoe-ggun* Counseling Support Center'," February 8, 2007, *Meoni Tudei*, http://news.mt.co.kr/mtview.php?no=2007020810463074706.

39. "Question and Answer," *KLCA Bulletin*, 2007, issue 3, http://www.klca.or.kr /KLCADownload/eBook/P5773.pdf.

40. Clustering is not unique to South Korea: public companies in Japan, Taiwan, and Singapore also experience the phenomenon. This is, in part, related to shared commercial codes and fiscal calendars across these countries, but there are few ac-counts as to why meeting times are clustered across Asia.

41. Only one account I found argued that *chonghoe-ggun* collaborated with com-panies. It recounted a story of a shareholder lamenting the seeming coordination of shareholders whom he called *yong-yeok* (or "for hire" chonghoe-ggun). "Listed Com-panies and *Chonghoe-ggun* Collaboration," March 29, 2016, *Maeil Gyeongje*, https:// www.mk.co.kr/opinion/journalist/view/2016/03/232955/.

42. "NPS Poised to Flex Shareholder Muscles," March 2, 2015, *The Korea Herald*, http://www.koreaherald.com/view.php?ud=20150302001112.

43. For an account of PSPD, see Kim and Kim (2001).

44. "Samsung Electronics Value Enhancement Proposals," October 5, 2016, https://sevalueproposals.com/.

45. In the investing world, there is a common phenomenon known as the "Korea Discount," which is believed to be the discount under which the real value of equity capital is trading, reflecting dislike of the majority-ownership by families and their conglomerate structures. See Choi, Lee, and Pae (2012) for discussion.

46. "Higher South Korea Dividends Fuel Hopes for Kospi Re-Rating," *Financial Times*, February 10, 2015, https://www.ft.com/content/1cbb1276-aab4-11e4-91d2-00144 feab7de. See Clark's (1979, 86) and Gerlach's (1992, 56, 234) accounts of shareholding in

Japan. Because large companies in Japan traditionally shared close institutional histories and structures with affiliate companies and banks, institutional investing was less a connection between profit-driven strangers seeking a dividend and more a sign of good faith between already connected institutions.

47. Moseley (2002) offers a treatment of Volume III of *Capital* that sees it as dealing with the problem of profit distribution rather than the falling rate of profit.

Chapter 6: Virtual Escapes

1. Anthropologist Kim Kwan-wook (2018) has observed that smoking is a gender-marked topic in South Korea because the *oyeom* (pollution) or stigma of smoking is related to the view of women as childbearers who may be potentially damaging future children. Even in a call center where smoking by women was accepted, such activities were screened and hidden from outsiders because of worry about smoking affecting the company's reputation.

2. The question of whether *hoesik* constitutes a work event has had to be decided in court. In 2013, a worker leaving a company launch party event in the city of Changwon slipped and fell, fracturing his spine. Initially the Worker's Compensation and Welfare Service denied his claim for medical bills, citing that it occurred after *hoesik* on his way home. After a lawsuit, courts deemed that *hoesik* was an extension (*yeon-gwan*) of work because it was seen as compulsory for the worker to go to the event. It was deemed a "work-related accident" (*eommusang jaehae*). "'Work-Related, Attendance Forced' *Hoesik* is an Extension of Work," reported in *Gyeong-nam Il-bo*, December 15, 2015.

3. "Organizations are Violence," *Hankyoreh*, February 11, 2018, https://www.hani.co.kr/arti/opinion/column/831816.html.

4. Plath (1969 [1964]).

5. Clark (1979).

6. Allison (1994). Today, these gendered after-work encounters in Japan can be ascribed as a form of healing (*iyashi*) labor that female sex workers can do on behalf of male salarymen. See Koch (2016).

7. Atsumi (1979, 64) defines *tsukiai* "as personal relationships cultivated as a result of social necessity or feelings of obligation. It is sometimes referred to by Japanese employees as their 'official' or work relationships. In contrast, there are 'private' friendships which develop out of mutual liking, attractions, interests, and likemindedness." See Nozawa (2015) for more contemporary discussion of Japanese sociality.

8. See Yang (1994), Kipnis (1996), and Yan (1996) for anthropological accounts of *guanxi* and gift giving in China.

9. The act is generally referred to as the Kim Young-ran Act after the former Supreme Court justice and National Human Rights Commission head who proposed it. The act aimed to circumvent a large loophole in corruption law that required a price relationship between what was given or received, and even plain-faced gifts of luxury items between officials could be easily disclaimed.

10. Gifted events can also be traps for people in corporate settings. The head of the PR team at Sangdo told me that much of her job entailed interacting with trade journalists who covered the company. It was common, she said, for these journalists to request to meet at night over dinner, where they might aim to curry favor by buying dinner; she said she avoided this kind of interactional trap by scheduling her meetings during the day.

11. Kim (2017).

12. Answering such questions also requires some social awareness about how to properly answer them. To answer accurately with a high number can be taken as a challenge for an older employee to test that number in practice. To answer too low may indicate that one is intentionally lying. While men often discussed how much they could drink, it was rare that anything like an actual competition took place or anyone regularly kept count. The questions were, in effect, part of the banter that preceded or added drama to any individual *hoesik* event. They were also a way to figure out who might be fun to go out with. Assistant manager So-yeon, who sat to my right for an entire year, rarely went out after work. When asked, she would say she reacted negatively to alcohol. She created her own metric to explain: her maximum was one drop (*han bang-ul*) of alcohol.

13. The job site Saramin, for instance, ran an infographic in 2019 describing the rise of employees who feel comfortable exercising veto power over *hoesik* invitations and requests. This has shifted the problem of *hoesik* from the activity itself (such as drinking alcohol) to the nature of how employees are implicitly or explicitly coerced to attend. See "6 out 10 Office Workers "Exercise Veto Power . . . up 9.4% from Last Year," *Dong-a*, October 22, 2019, http://www.donga.com/news/article/all/20191022/98003285/1.

14. Cotton and van Leest (1992).

15. Much of the discourse around work life in the US has been described as the blending or blurring of work and personal lives, particularly by integrating lifestyle aesthetics and communicative styles (Fleming 2014; Turco 2016), reminiscent of others kinds of casual stylizing or register-downshifting popular in the American political sphere (see, for instance, Reyes [2015]). In contrast, a view of South Korean white-collar workers and workplaces suggests that style choices veer toward alignment with upper or upper-middle class markers of distinction.

16. Kim (2018).

17. See Park (2009, 2010).

18. Ho (2009).

19. Forms of scoring may seem like part of new shifts toward quantification, but they also fit within a larger idea of organizing group activities around skill levels so as to elevate the seriousness of play. When I visited a Sangdo factory in the south, the team members took me out to a game of billiards (*dang-gu*) where they organized themselves into small groups based on their average scores, with some players at near professional levels. Similarly, as team manager Jang and assistant manager Min-sup

improved at golf through hours of investment, they decided to play among themselves, even incorporating in-game money bets at one point. Ji-soon and I were relegated to what was described as a "kid's game."

20. Kelly (2005).

21. There is a parallel literature in organization studies on the utility of "away days" and what purpose they serve for organizations (Hodgkinson et al. 2006; Healey et al. 2015), as they are in theory meant to be a temporal and spatial escape from typical workday routines to ritually focus on higher order goals such as strategy making or employee (re)training. However, they often serve as a kind of in-house paid vacation. In South Korea, a similar genre exists—known as *emti* (MT or membership training) where cohorts of students, club members, or company teams go to a remote location to build up relations, primarily through eating together, sleeping in a large room, and drinking until late.

22. See Burawoy (1979). In a more contemporary example, Whitelaw (2014) has described the practice of convenience store owners in Japan who use food that management dictated was expired but was otherwise still edible as a means to nourish bonds among temp workers, deliverymen, and local homeless populations. Such gifting practices had to be done in secret, however, as all expired food was meant to be disposed of and not repurposed.

23. See Rea (2018).

24. See Barker (1999). The contemporary example of this is described in new workplace movements in the US where workers are "encouraged to be themselves" (Fleming 2014). This is why some such as Turco's *The Conversational Firm* (2016) have observed occasions when employees now want *more* hierarchy, bureaucracy, or rules rather than less.

25. Of course, it can be a manager's style to not go out drinking with employees or employees to eschew after-work events entirely; one informant suggested that managers who did not mandate any after-work gatherings were nice but politically impotent within the organization. That is, they would not be good managers to work for because they lacked the willingness to go to *hoesik* with other managers, essentially locking themselves out of inside knowledge and personal connections with higher level executives.

26. "Screen golf and virtual reality," *Dong-a*, September 7, 2017, http://www.donga .com/news/article/all/20170907/86215783/1.

Conclusion

1. Kang (2013).

2. Weeks (2004, 6).

3. See Kim (1992). This description of an implicit Christianity was also in stark contrast to another company I visited while searching for a field site. Albeit a company on a much smaller scale, the "GG Cable Company" (a pseudonym) was overtly Christian. The logo of the company, which was a small-scale custom cable assembly operation, had an ichthys symbol prominently embedded in it and a picture of Jesus hung

on the wall along with a few other crosses; the small assembly office resounded with a mix of Christian hymns and sermons over the radio throughout the day. The head of that company of around six people told me that he recruited his employees from his church and that "GG" itself was short for "God's Grace." (I've altered the acronym to fit the pseudonym).

4. The embedded dimension of a Christian ethic within secular South Korean institutions is not uncommon. Harkness (2012) has described how classical music, particularly vocal music (*seongak*), is interlaced with elite forms of Christianity. This is done at ostensibly public concerts by capping secular Italian and German art songs with an obviously recognizable Christian hymn as the encore—allowing the singer to "characterize the secular content of the recital as a form of music that is ultimately in the service of Christianity, while presenting a group of Christians to itself as the general public for this secular music" (2012, 356).

5. In fact, the HR team in years prior to my beginning had established clear process guidelines (*eobmu peuroseseu*) for every team in the holding company, describing the scope and flow of work, with detailed charts in PowerPoint breaking down in precision each step of their tasks and who was responsible for each task. I rarely saw these referenced in actual work, however.

6. *Apjonbeop* (literally, "a rule for pressured respect") is a social convention for the use of honorific discourse in which honorifics are extended only to the highest-ranking person mentioned and not to others who may be higher than a speaker. For instance, if a low-ranking office worker were talking to a CEO about a middle manager, the low-ranking officer worker would not extend honorifics when referring to the middle manager, even though such a person is technically above him or her. It is common in everyday honorific register to extend honorific markers to multiple addressees. The military was one of the last institutions to encourage *apjonbeop*, but it was formally discontinued in 2016.

7. See Kwon (2019).

8. See Jackall (2010).

Methodological Appendix

1. Direct factory-level work (*hyeonjang chwieop*) was a tactic used by university students trying to raise consciousness among the South Korean working classes during the 1980s. Lee (2005, 915ff) has described how the government and media depicted this as disguised employment (*wijang chwieop*) "to impute criminality to working in a factory with a forged identity card" to malign the student and broader civil society (*minjung*) movement.

2. This reflects what is known as the practice turn in studies of organizations. Vaara and Whittington (2012, 4) describe the practice turn as a focus on "the embedded nature of human agency, the importance of macrosocial institutions, emergence as well as design, the role of materiality, and the critical examination of the otherwise taken-for-granted." In the context of South Korean workplaces, this meant taking their organizational spaces seriously as sites of complex practice, rather than as

merely microcosms of broader macroeconomic dynamics or as set behavioral models. See also Barley and Kunda (2001) and Whittington (2006).

3. For inspirations from linguistic anthropology, I developed theoretical ideas and methodological choices from works by Duranti (1994), Philips (1998), and Cameron (2000). Regarding work on communication by organization studies, I drew ideas from Orlikowski and Yates (1994), Yates and Orlikowski (1992), and Spinuzzi and Zachry (2000).

4. Glorifying insider spaces has lost some of its appeal as substantive research by anthropologists has come in and around corporate sites among people trying to get in or even contemplating their escape (Allison, [1994]; Wilf [2019]; Rogers [2012]; Dasgupta [2013]; Miyazaki [2013]; Whitelaw [2014]; Ho [2009]; Orta [2013]; Gershon [2017]). Allison's *Nightwork* is an ethnography on the important role that hostess bars play in corporate identity making in after-hours Japan. In South Korea, there are many sites that would be useful for doing para-ethnography of the corporate world, including final-year university students, job training centers, consulting businesses, alumni associations, retiree communities, training institutes (*hakwon*), hobby groups, franchise operators, and invitation-only internet groups for professionals. Early on, I had attempted to create my own English-language study group for business people with the help of a café owner I met; and we met a few times to discuss office life in English, but it did not lead to any larger developments. I also played on an amateur basketball team with a number of professionals, but we rarely broached talking about their professional lives. A year after my research and on a return visit, I was invited to an HR professionals study group by a former coworker at Sangdo who thought it would be good for me to observe. Such small group meetings, where practitioners spoke candidly of their company and professional challenges and discussed academic writings on HR in English and Korean, would have been ideal as a site of para-ethnography, precisely because it was free from workplace norms and politics.

5. For critical discussion of projects and the spread of the project form, see Hodgson (2004). Arguably, academic projects, even those in anthropology, have fallen under the logic of the project form, with fixed budgets, goals, and documentation to mark beginnings and endings, but it is possible to mark very different institutional expectations for what projects look like.

6. Anthropology as a field had little recognition at Sangdo. Where known at all among corporate office workers, anthropology was more commonly associated with studies of small-scale tribes and islands, not the study of modern office life. The field also had none of the residual romance or prestige accorded in North America and Europe where it is associated, albeit misguidedly, with corporate culture movements and kitsch ideas of office tribes. The South Korean managerial viewpoint might have deemed an anthropological method as imprecise compared to the field of organizational behavior.

7. Shadowing worked well on some occasions and poorly on others. The disjointed nature of work sometimes left me sitting in a team area while workers quietly did work on their computers. The open-floor plan also made it awkward for employees

to narrate their work in front of others. One incident occurred with the assistant manager in the strategy department as he allowed me to shadow him as he wrote an email in English to a consultant advisor in the United States. As I looked over his shoulder, the encounter grew increasingly uncomfortable for both him and me as I watched him compose an email with the invisible preoccupation over English skills making it awkward.

8. This narrative was partially confirmed, at least in the liberal-leaning newspaper *Hankyoreh*, which has reported over the years on the relationship between holding companies and chaebol families. For instance, in an article from 2013 titled, "Behind the Holding Company, the Chaebol Laugh," the newspaper reports that holding companies, created to effect a transparent governance structure, have actually enabled more concentration in family ownership rather than create the conditions in which transparency will lead to economic democratization, in part because the holding company minimizes how much subsidiaries can own of each other. May 4, 2013, http://h21 .hani.co.kr/arti/cover/cover_general/34447.html.

9. My views on the point of attending to issues of distinction (as an aspirational quality) alongside a focus on negative hierarchy in the South Korean context have been shaped in part by the concept of mass dictatorship put forth by the German-based Korean philosopher Jie-Hyun Lim (2010). Lim wrote on the difficult questions in modern South Korean history around the popularity of Park Chung-hee in what is otherwise framed as a period of authoritarianism and social dissent. Likewise, the work of historian Namhee Lee (2007) on the status distinctions and hierarchies that shaped student protest movements in the 1970s and 1980s was formative for thinking of the ways that elite students can both participate with and distinguish from those they believe to be below them in the economic pyramid. Finally, anthropologist Nancy Abelmann's (1997) turn to the class mobility narratives of middle-class South Koreans was also crucial for thinking about how the individual (and family) experience of economic transformation provides unique and often competing perspectives against dominant narratives of national development.

References

Abelmann, Nancy. 1997. "Narrating Selfhood and Personality in South Korea: Women and Social Mobility." *American Ethnologist* 24 (4): 786–811.

Abelmann, Nancy. 2003. *The Melodrama of Mobility: Women, Talk, and Class in Contemporary South Korea.* Honolulu: University of Hawai'i Press.

Acker, Joan. 1990. "Hierarchies, Jobs, Bodies: A Theory of Gendered Organizations." *Gender and Society* 4 (2): 139–58.

Agha, Asif. 2011. "Commodity Registers." *Journal of Linguistic Anthropology* 21 (1): 22–53.

Ahn, Junehui. 2016. "'Don't Cry, You're Not a Baby!': Emotion, Role and Hierarchy in Korean Language Socialisation Practice." *Children and Society* 30 (1): 12–24.

Allison, Anne. 1994. *Nightwork: Sexuality, Pleasure, and Corporate Masculinity in a Tokyo Hostess Club.* Chicago: University of Chicago Press.

Allison, Anne. 2013. *Precarious Japan.* Durham, NC: Duke University Press.

Atsumi, Reiko. 1979. "Tsukiai—Obligatory Personal Relationships of Japanese White-Collar Company Employees." *Human Organization* 38 (1): 63–70.

Bae, Johngseok, and Chris Rowley. 2003. "Changes and Continuities in South Korean HRM." *Asia Pacific Business Review* 9 (4): 76–105.

Barker, James R. 1999. *The Discipline of Teamwork: Participation and Concertive Control.* Thousand Oaks, CA: Sage Publications.

Barley, Stephen R., and Gideon Kunda. 2001. "Bringing Work Back In." *Organization Science* 12 (1): 76–95.

Bauman, Richard, and Charles Briggs. 2003. *Voices of Modernity: Language Ideologies and the Politics of Inequality.* Cambridge: Cambridge University Press.

Bennets, Leslie. 2002. "The C.E.O.'S Worst Nightmare." *Vanity Fair*, July.

Benson, Peter, and Stuart Kirsch. 2010. "Corporate Oxymorons." *Dialectical Anthropology* 34 (1): 45–48.

Black, Bernard, Brian Cheffins, and Michael Klausner. 2011. "Shareholder Suits and Outside Director Liability: The Case of Korea." *Journal of Korean Law* 10 (2): 325–61.

Boltanski, Luc, and Eve Chiapello. 2018. *The New Spirit of Capitalism.* Translated by Gregory Elliott. London: Verso. Original edition, 1999.

Bourdieu, Pierre. 1979. "Public Opinion Does Not Exist." *Communication and Class Struggle* 1:124–30.

Bourdieu, Pierre. 1984. *Distinction: A Social Critique of the Judgement of Taste*. Cambridge, MA: Harvard University Press.

Bourdieu, Pierre. 1991. *Language and Symbolic Power*. Edited by John B. Thompson. Cambridge, MA: Harvard University Press.

Bourgoin, Alaric, and Fabian Muniesa. 2016. "Building a Rock-Solid Slide: Management Consulting, PowerPoint, and the Craft of Signification." *Management Communication Quarterly* 30 (3): 390–410.

Boyer, Dominic. 2008. "Thinking Through the Anthropology of Experts." *Anthropology in Action* 15 (2): 38–46.

Briggs, Charles. 2007. "Anthropology, Interviewing, and Communicability in Contemporary Society." *Current Anthropology* 48 (4): 551–80.

Burawoy, Michael. 1979. *Manufacturing Consent: Changes in the Labor Process Under Monopoly Capitalism*. Chicago: University of Chicago Press.

Burrell, Gibson. 1988. "Modernism, Post Modernism and Organizational Analysis 2: The Contribution of Michel Foucault." *Organization Studies* 9 (2): 221–35.

Cameron, Deborah. 2000. *Good to Talk?: Living and Working in a Communication Culture*. Thousand Oaks, CA: SAGE Publications.

Carr, E. Summerson. 2010. "Enactments of Expertise." *Annual Review of Anthropology* 39 (1): 17–32.

Chang, Ha Joon, and Jang-Sup Shin. 2003. *Restructuring "Korea Inc.": Financial Crisis, Corporate Reform, and Institutional Transition*. London: Routledge.

Chang, Kyung Sup. 1999. "Compressed Modernity and its Discontents: South Korean Society in Transtion." *Economy and Society* 28 (1): 30–55.

Chang, Sea Jin. 2006. *Financial Crisis and Transformation of Korean Business Groups: The Rise and Fall of Chaebols*. Seoul: Cambridge University Press.

Cho, Haejoang. 2001. "Living with Conflicting Subjectivities: Mother, Motherly Wife, and Sexy Woman in the Transition From Colonial-Modern to Postmodern Korea." In *Under Construction: The Gendering of Modernity, Class, and Consumption in the Republic of Korea*, edited by Laurel Kendall, 165–95. Honolulu: University of Hawai'i Press.

Choi, Jinsook. 2018 [2016]. "A Linguistic Anthropological Study of the Typification of Middle-Aged Men in Korea: An Examination of Ajae Joke Data." *Korean Anthropology Review* 2:109–39.

Choi, Tae H., Eunchul Lee, and Jinhan Pae. 2012. "The Equity Premium Puzzle: Empirical Evidence for the 'Korea Discount'." *Asia-Pacific Journal of Accounting and Economics* 19 (2): 143–66.

Chong, Kimberly. 2018. *Best Practice: Management Consulting and the Ethics of Financialization*. Durham, NC: Duke University Press.

Choy, Timothy K. 2005. "Articulated Knowledges: Environmental Forms After Universality's Demise." *American Anthropologist* 107 (1): 5–18.

Chumley, Lily Hope. 2013. "Evaluation Regimes and the Qualia of Quality." *Anthropological Theory* 13 (1–2): 169–183.

Chun, Jennifer Jihye. 2011. *Organizing at the Margins.* Ithaca, NY: Cornell University Press.

Clark, Rodney. 1979. *The Japanese Company.* New Haven: Yale University Press.

Clifford, Mark. 1994. *Troubled Tiger: Businessmen, Bureaucrats, and Generals in South Korea.* Armonk, NY: ME Sharpe.

Cody, Francis. 2011. "Publics and Politics." *Annual Review of Anthropology* 40 (1): 37–52.

Cohen, Susanne. 2015. "The New Communication Order: Management, Language, and Morality in a Multinational Corporation." *American Ethnologist* 42 (2): 324–39.

Cotton, James, and Kim Hyung-a van Leest. 1992. "Korea: Dilemmas for the 'Golf Republic'." *The Pacific Review* 5 (4): 360–69.

Cristea, Ioana C., and Paul M. Leonardi. 2019. "Get Noticed and Die Trying: Signals, Sacrifice, and the Production of Face Time in Distributed Work." *Organization Science* 30 (3): 552–72.

Dasgupta, Romit. 2013. *Re-Reading the Salaryman in Japan: Crafting Masculinities.* New York: Routledge.

Davis, Gerald F. 2009. "The Rise and Fall of Finance and the End of the Society of Organizations." *Academy of Management Perspectives* 23 (3): 27–44.

De Santos, Martin. 2009. "Fact-Totems and the Statistical Imagination: The Public Life of a Statistic in Argentina 2001." *Sociological Theory* 27 (4): 466–89.

Doucette, Jamie. 2015. "Debating Economic Democracy in South Korea: The Costs of Commensurability." *Critical Asian Studies* 47 (3): 388–413.

Doucette, Jamie, and Susan Kang. 2018. "Legal Geographies of Labour and Post-democracy: Reinforcing Non-Standard Work in South Korea." *Transactions of the Institute of British Geographers* 43 (2): 200–214.

Drucker, Peter F. 1992. "The New Society of Organizations." *Harvard Business Review* (September–October): 95–104.

Dunlavy, Colleen A. 2006. "Social Conceptions of the Corporation: Insights from the History of Shareholder Voting Rights." *Washington and Lee Law Review* 63: 1347–88.

Dunn, Elizabeth C. 2004. *Privatizing Poland: Baby Food, Big Business, and the Remaking of Labor.* Ithaca, NY: Cornell University Press.

Duranti, Alessandro. 1994. *From Grammar to Politics: Linguistic Anthropology in a Western Samoan Village.* Berkeley: University of California Press.

Espeland, Wendy Nelson, and Mitchell L. Stevens. 1998. "Commensuration as a Social Process." *Annual Review of Sociology* 24 (1): 313–43.

Fenster, Mark. 2017. *The Transparency Fix: Secrets, Leaks, and Uncontrollable Government Information.* Stanford, CA: Stanford University Press.

Fleming, Peter. 2014. *Resisting Work: The Corporatization of Life and its Discontents.* Philadelphia: Temple University Press.

Foster, Robert J. 2008. *Coca-Globalization: Following Soft Drinks from New York to New Guinea*. New York: Palgrave Macmillan.

Foucault, Michel. 1973. *Madness and Civilization: a History of Insanity in the Age of Reason*. New York: Vintage Books.

Foucault, Michel. 1977. *Discipline and Punish: The Birth of the Prison*. New York: Vintage.

Fraser, Nancy. 1992. "Rethinking the Public Sphere: A Contribution to the Critique of Actually Existing Democracy." In *Habermas and the Public Sphere*, edited by Craig Calhoun, 56–80. Cambridge, MA: MIT Press.

Freeland, Robert F., and Ezra W. Zuckerman. 2018. "The Problems and Promise of Hierarchy: Voice Rights and the Firm." *Sociological Science* 5 (7): 143–81.

Gell, Alfred. 1992. "The Technology of Enchantment and the Enchantment of Technology." In *Anthropology, Art and Aesthetics*, edited by Jeremy Coote and Anthony Shelton, 40–63. Oxford: Clarendon Press.

Gerlach, Michael. 1992. *Alliance Capitalism: The Social Organization of Japanese Business*. Berkeley: University of California Press.

Gershon, Ilana. 2017. *Down and Out in the New Economy: How People Find (or Don't Find) Work Today*. Chicago: University of Chicago Press.

Gershon, Ilana. 2018. "Employing the CEO of Me, Inc.: US Corporate Hiring in a Neoliberal Age." *American Ethnologist* 45 (2): 173–85.

Gershon, Ilana. 2019. "Hailing the US Job-Seeker: Origins and Neoliberal Uses of Job Applications." *Culture, Theory and Critique* 60 (1): 84–97.

Gladwell, Malcolm. 2008. *Outliers: The Story of Success*. New York: Little, Brown and Co.

Goffman, Erving. 1952. "On Cooling the Mark Out: Some Aspects of Adaptation to Failure." *Psychiatry* 15 (4): 451–63.

Goffman, Erving. 1956. "The Nature of Deference and Demeanor." *American Anthropologist* 58 (3): 473–502.

Goffman, Erving. 1974. *Frame Analysis: An Essay on the Organization of Experience*. New York: Harper & Row.

Goodwin, Charles. 1994. "Professional Vision." *American Anthropologist* 96 (3): 606–33.

Grice, H. Paul. 1975. "Logic and Conversation." In *Syntax and Semantics 3: Speech Acts*, edited by Peter Cole and Jerry Morgan, 45–58. New York: Academic Press.

Habermas, Jürgen. 1974 [1964]. "The Public Sphere: An Encyclopedia Article." *New German Critique* 3:49–55.

Habermas, Jürgen. 1989. *The Structural Transformation of the Public Sphere: An Inquiry into a Category of Bourgeois Society*. Translated by Thomas Burger. Cambridge, MA: MIT Press.

Hacking, Ian. 2002 [1986]. "Making Up People." In *Historical Ontology*, edited by Ian Hacking, 99–120. Cambridge, MA: Harvard University Press.

Hadley, Eleanor M. 1970. *Antitrust in Japan*. Princeton Legacy Library. Princeton, NJ: Princeton University Press.

Haggard, Stephan, Wonhyuk Lim, and Euysung Kim. 2003. *Economic Crisis and Corporate Restructuring in Korea: Reforming the Chaebol*. Cambridge Asia-Pacific Studies. New York: Cambridge University Press.

Hall, Kira. 2014. "Exceptional Speakers: Contested and Problematized Gender Identities." In *The Handbook of Language, Gender, and Sexuality*, edited by Susan Ehrlich, Miriam Meyerhoff, and Janet Holmes, 220–39. Hoboken, NJ: Wiley-Blackwell.

Hankins, Joseph, and Rihan Yeh. 2016. "To Bind and To Bound: Commensuration Across Boundaries." *Anthropological Quarterly* 89 (1): 5–30.

Harkness, Nicholas. 2011. "Culture and Interdiscursivity in Korean Fricative Voice Gestures." *Journal of Linguistic Anthropology* 21 (1): 99–123.

Harkness, Nicholas. 2012. "Encore!: Homecoming Recitals in Christian South Korea." *Journal of Korean Studies* 17 (2): 351–81.

Harkness, Nicholas. 2013a. "Softer Soju in South Korea." *Anthropological Theory* 13 (1–2): 12–30.

Harkness, Nicholas. 2013b. *Songs of Seoul: An Ethnography of Voice and Voicing in Christian South Korea*. Berkeley: University of California Press.

Harkness, Nicholas. 2015. "Basic Kinship Terms: Christian Relations, Chronotopic Formulations, and a Korean Confrontation of Language." *Anthropological Quarterly* 88 (2): 305–36.

Hassard, John, Jonathan Morris, and Leo McCann. 2012. "'My brilliant career'? New Organizational Forms and Changing Managerial Careers in Japan, the UK, and USA." *Journal of Management Studies* 49 (3): 571–99.

Hastings, Adi, and Paul Manning. 2004. "Introduction: Acts of Alterity." *Language and Communication* 24 (4): 291–311.

Healey, Mark P., Gerard P. Hodgkinson, Richard Whittington, and Gerry Johnson. 2015. "Off to Plan or Out to Lunch? Relationships Between Design Characteristics and Outcomes of Strategy Workshops." *British Journal of Management* 26 (3): 507–28.

Hegel, Georg Wilhelm Friedrich, and T. M. Knox. 1967. *Hegel's Philosophy of Right*. London: Oxford at the Clarendon Press.

Hickel, Jason, and Naomi Haynes. 2018. *Hierarchy and Value: Comparative Perspectives on Moral Order*. New York: Berghahn Books.

Hirschman, Albert O. 1977. *The Passions and the Interests: Political Arguments for Capitalism Before its Triumph*. Princeton, NJ: Princeton University Press.

Ho, Karen Z. 2009. *Liquidated: An Ethnography of Wall Street*. Durham, NC: Duke University Press.

Hochschild, Arlie Russell. 2012 [1983]. *The Managed Heart: Commercialization of Human Feeling*. Berkeley: University of California Press.

Hodges, Ron, Louise Macniven, and Howard Mellett. 2004. "Annual General Meetings of NHS Trusts: Devolving Power or Ritualising Accountability?" *Financial Accountability and Management* 20 (4): 377–99.

Hodgkinson, Gerard P., Richard Whittington, Gerry Johnson, and Mirela Schwarz. 2006. "The Role of Strategy Workshops in Strategy Development Processes:

Formality, Communication, Co-ordination and Inclusion." *Long Range Planning* 39 (5): 479–96.

Hodgson, Damian E. 2004. "Project Work: The Legacy of Bureaucratic Control in the Post-Bureaucratic Organization." *Organization* 11 (1): 81–100.

Hoskin, Keith W., and Richard H. Macve. 1986. "Accounting and the Examination: a Genealogy of Disciplinary Power." *Accounting, Organizations and Society* 11 (2): 105–36.

Hull, Matthew. 2010. "Democratic Technologies of Speech: From WWII America to Postcolonial Delhi." *Journal of Linguistic Anthropology* 20 (2): 257–82.

Inoue, Miyako. 2003. "Speech Without a Speaking Body: 'Japanese women's language' in translation." *Language and Communication* 23 (3): 315–30.

Inoue, Miyako. 2007. "Language and Gender in an Age of Neoliberalism." *Gender and Language* 1 (1): 79.

Iteanu, André. 2013. "The Two Conceptions of Value." *HAU: Journal of Ethnographic Theory* 3 (1): 155–71.

Iwai, Katsuhito. 1999. "Persons, Things and Corporations: The Corporate Personality Controversy and Comparative Corporate Governance." *American Journal of Comparative Law* 47 (4): 583–632.

Jackall, Robert. 2010. *Moral Mazes: The World of Corporate Managers.* Oxford: Oxford University Press.

Jacobs-Huey, Lanita. 2003. "Ladies Are Seen, Not Heard: Language Socialization in a Southern, African American Cosmetology School." *Anthropology and Education Quarterly* 34 (3): 277–99.

Janelli, Roger L., and Dawnhee Yim. 1993. *Making Capitalism: The Social and Cultural Construction of a South Korean Conglomerate.* Stanford, CA: Stanford University Press.

Kalinowski, Thomas. 2008. "State-Civil Society Synergy and Cooptation: The Case of the Minority Shareholder Movement in Korea." *Korea Observer* 39 (3): 339–67.

Kalinowski, Thomas. 2009. "The Politics of Market Reforms: Korea's Path from Chaebol Republic to Market Democracy and Back." *Contemporary Politics* 15 (3): 287–304.

Kang, Jun-man. 2013. *Gabgwa eului nara: Gabeulgwangyeneun daehanmingugeul eotteohge jibaehaewassneunga [The Country of Gap and Eul: How Gap-Eul Relations Came to Rule the Republic of Korea].* Seoul: Ilmunkwa Sasangsa.

Kelly, William H. 2005. "Training for Leisure: Karaoke and the Seriousness of Play in Japan." In *Japan at Play*, edited by Joy Hendry, 170–86. London: Routledge.

Kelty, Christopher M. 2017. "Too Much Democracy in All the Wrong Places: Toward a Grammar of Participation." *Current Anthropology* 58 (S15): S77–S90.

Kelty, Christopher M. 2019. *The Participant: A Century of Participation in Four Stories.* Chicago: University of Chicago Press.

Kendall, Laurel. 1985. *Shamans, Housewives, and Other Restless Spirits: Women in Korean Ritual Life.* Studies of the East Asian Institute. Honolulu: University of Hawai'i Press.

Kim, Choong Soon. 1992. *The Culture of Korean Industry: An Ethnography of Poongsan Corporation*. Tucson: University of Arizona Press.

Kim, Eun Mee. 1997. *Big Business, Strong State: Collusion and Conflict in South Korean Development, 1960–1990*. Albany: State University of New York Press.

Kim, Eun Mee, and Gil-Sung Park. 2011. "The Chaebol." In *The Park Chung Hee Era: The Transformation of South Korea*, edited by Byung-kook Kim and Ezra F. Vogel, 265–94. Cambridge, MA: Harvard University Press.

Kim, Gyo-chang. 2005. "Meeting Procedures for Annual Meetings for Corporate Bodies (in Korean)." *Journal of Korea Parliamentary Law Institute* 3:6–87.

Kim, Hyun Mee. 2018 [2001]. "Work Experience and Identity of Skilled Male Workers Following the Economic Crisis." *Korean Anthropology Review* 2:141–63.

Kim, Joongi. 2000. "Recent Amendments to the Korean Commercial Code and Their Effects on International Competition." *University of Pennsylvania Journal of International Economic Law* 21 (2): 273–330.

Kim, Jooyoung, and Joongi Kim. 2001. "Shareholder Activism in Korea: A Review of How PSPD Has Used Legal Measures to Strengthen Korean Corporate Governance." *Journal of Korean Law* 1 (1): 51–76.

Kim, Kwanwook. 2018. "Creating Polluted Spaces and Bodies: Labor Control in a Call Center and the Stigma of Female Smoking." *Korean Anthropology Review* 2:73–108.

Kim, Minjae. 2017. "A Man Is Known by His Cup: Signaling Commitment via Costly Conformity." *Academy of Management Proceedings* 2017 (1): 11239.

Kim, Suk-Young. 2018 *K-pop Live: Fans, Idols, and Multimedia Performance*. Stanford, CA: Stanford University Press.

Kipnis, Andrew B. 1996. "The Language of Gifts: Managing Guanxi in a North China Village." *Modern China* 22 (3): 285–314.

Kirsch, Stuart. 2014. *Mining Capitalism: The Relationship Between Corporations and Their Critics*. Berkeley: University of California Press.

Klikauer, Thomas. 2014. *Seven Moralities of Human Resource Management*. London: Palgrave Macmillan.

Klikauer, Thomas. 2016. *Hegel's Moral Corporation*. London: Palgrave Macmillan.

Knoblauch, Hubert. 2008. "The Performance of Knowledge: Pointing and Knowledge in Powerpoint Presentations." *Cultural Sociology* 2 (1): 75–97.

Koch, Gabriele. 2016. "Producing Iyashi: Healing and Labor in Tokyo's Sex Industry." *American Ethnologist* 43 (4): 704–16.

Kockelman, Paul. 2016. *The Chicken and the Quetzal: Incommensurate Ontologies and Portable Values in Guatemala's Cloud Forest*. Durham, NC: Duke University Press.

Koo, Hagen. 2001. *Korean Workers: The Culture and Politics of Class Formation*. Ithaca, NY: Cornell University Press.

Koyama, Wataru. 2004. "The Linguistic Ideologies of Modern Japanese Honorifics and the Historic Reality of Modernity." *Language and Communication* 24 (4): 413–35.

Krause-Jensen, Jakob. 2010. *Flexible Firm: The Design of Culture at Bang & Olufsen*. New York: Berghahn Books.

Krause-Jensen, Jakob. 2017. "Fieldwork in a Hall of Mirrors: An Anthropology of Anthropology in Business." *Journal of Business Anthropology* 6 (1): 102–20.

Kunda, Gideon. 1992. *Engineering Culture: Control and Commitment in a High-Tech Corporation*. Philadelphia: Temple University Press.

Kwon, Jae Yeol. 1995. "An Isolation in Systems of Law: Differences Between the Commerical Codes of the United States and Korea." *Loyola of Los Angeles Law Review* 29:1095–1106.

Kwon, Jae Yeol. 2003. "The Internal Division of Powers in Corporate Governance: A Comparative Approach to the South Korean Statutory Scheme." *Minnesota Journal of Global Trade* 12 (2): 299–336.

Kwon, Jae Yeol. 2004. "Corporate Governance from a Comparative Perspective: Specific Applications of the Duty of Loyalty in Korea." *UCLA Pacific Basin Law Journal* 22:1–28.

Kwon, Peter Banseok. 2019. "Building Bombs, Building a Nation: The State, Chaebŏl, and the Militarized Industrialization of South Korea, 1973–1979." *Journal of Asian Studies*. 79 (1): 1–25.

Larkin, Brian. 2013. "The Politics and Poetics of Infrastructure." *Annual Review of Anthropology* 42:327–43.

Law, John. 2009. "Seeing like a Survey." *Cultural Sociology* 3 (2): 239–56.

LeBlanc, Robin M. 2012. "Lessons from the Ghost of Salaryman Past: The Global Costs of the Breadwinner Imaginary." *Journal of Asian Studies* 71 (4): 857–71.

Lee, Boong-Kyu. 2001. "Don Quixote or Robin Hood: Minority Shareholder Rights and Corporate Governance in Korea." *Columbia Journal of Asian Law* 15 (2): 345–72.

Lee, Byoung-Hoon. 2011. "Labor Solidarity in the Era of Neoliberal Globalization." *Development and Society* 40 (2): 319–34.

Lee, Namhee. 2005. "Representing the Worker: The Worker-Intellectual Alliance of the 1980s in South Korea." *Journal of Asian Studies* 64 (4): 911–37.

Lee, Namhee. 2007. *The Making of Minjung: Democracy and The Politics of Representation in South Korea*. Ithaca, NY: Cornell University Press.

Lett, Denise Potrzeba. 1998. *In Pursuit of Status: The Making of South Korea's "New" Urban Middle Class*. Cambridge, MA: Harvard University Asia Center.

Levine, Amy. 2004. "The Transparent Case of Virtuality." *PoLAR: Political and Legal Anthropology Review* 27 (1): 90–113.

Lim, Jie-Hyun, 2010. "Mapping Mass Dictatorship: Towards a Transnational History of Twentieth-Century Dictatorship." In *Gender Politics and Mass Dictatorship: Global Perspectives*, edited by Jie-Hyun Lim and Karen Petrone, 1–22. London: Palgrave Macmillan.

Luong, Hy Van. 1988. "Discursive Practices and Power Structure: Person-Referring Forms and Sociopolitical Struggles In Colonial Vietnam." *American Ethnologist* 15 (2): 239–53.

Lutz, William. 1989. *Doublespeak: From "Revenue Enhancement" to "Terminal Living," How Government, Business, Advertisers, and Others Use Language to Deceive You*. New York: Harper & Row.

Manning, Paul. 2010. "The Semiotics of Brand." *Annual Review of Anthropology* 39:33–49.

Matanle, Peter C. D. 2003. *Japanese Capitalism and Modernity In a Global Era: Re-Fabricating Lifetime Employment Relations.* London: RoutledgeCurzon.

McCann, Leo, John Hassard, and Jonathan Morris. 2004. "Middle Managers, the New Organizational Ideology and Corporate Restructuring: Comparing Japanese and Anglo-American Management Systems." *Competition and Change* 8 (1): 27–44.

McGill, Peter. 2021. "Friend or Foe? Corporate Scandals and Foreign Attempts to Restructure Japan." *Asia-Pacific Journal: Japan Focus* 19 (14).

Mennicken, Andrea, and Peter Miller. 2014. "Michel Foucault and the Administering of Lives." In *Oxford Handbook of Sociology, Social Theory and Organization Studies: Contemporary Currents*, edited by Paul Adler, Paul du Gay, Glenn Morgan, and Mike Reed, 11–38.

Mialet, Hélène. 2012. *Hawking Incorporated: Stephen Hawking and the Anthropology of the Knowing Subject.* Chicago: University of Chicago Press.

Miller, Peter, and Ted O'Leary. 1989. "Hierarchies and American Ideals, 1900–1940." *Academy of Management Review* 14 (2): 250–65.

Minto, Barbara. 2009. *The Pyramid Principle: Logic in Writing and Thinking.* Harlow, England: Financial Times Prentice Hall.

Mitchell, Timothy. 2002. *Rule of Experts: Egypt, Techno-Politics, Modernity.* Berkeley: University of California Press.

Miyazaki, Hirokazu. 2013. *Arbitraging Japan: Dreams of Capitalism at the End of Finance.* Berkeley: University of California Press.

Moon, Seungsook. 2001. "The Production and Subversion of Masculinity: Reconfiguring Gender Hierarchy in Contemporary South Korea." In *Under Construction: The Gendering of Modernity, Class, and Consumption in the Republic of Korea*, edited by Laurel Kendall, 79–114. Honolulu: University of Hawai'i Press.

Moore, Robert E. 2003. "From Genericide to Viral Marketing: On 'Brand'." *Language and Communication* 23 (3): 331–57.

Moseley, Fred. 2002. "Hostile Brothers." In *The Culmination of Capital: Essays on Volume III of Marx's Capital*, edited by Martha Campbell and Geert Reuten, 65–101. London: Palgrave Macmillan UK.

Nakassis, Constantine V. 2016. *Doing Style: Youth and Mass Mediation in South India.* Chicago: University of Chicago Press.

Nelson, Laura. 2000. *Measured Excess: Status, Gender, and Consumer Nationalism in South Korea.* New York: Columbia University Press.

Nozawa, Shunsuke. 2015. "Phatic Traces: Sociality In Contemporary Japan." *Anthropological Quarterly* 88 (2): 373–400.

Nyqvist, Anette. 2015. "The Corporation Performed: Minutes From the Rituals of Annual General Meetings." *Journal of Organizational Ethnography* 4 (3): 341–55.

Ogasawara, Yuko. 1998. *Office Ladies and Salaried Men: Power, Gender, and Work in Japanese Companies.* Berkeley: University of California Press.

Oppenheim, Robert. 2008. *Kyŏngju Things: Assembling Place*. Ann Arbor: University of Michigan Press.

Orlikowski, Wanda J., and JoAnne Yates. 1994. "Genre Repertoire: The Structuring of Communicative Practices in Organizations." *Administrative Science Quarterly* 39 (4): 541–74.

Orta, Andrew. 2013. "Managing the Margins: MBA Training, International Business, and 'The Value Chain of Culture'." *American Ethnologist* 40 (4): 689–703.

Paranque, Bernard, and Hugh Willmott. 2014. "Cooperatives—Saviours or Gravediggers of Capitalism? Critical Performativity and the John Lewis Partnership." *Organization* 21 (5): 604–25.

Park, Joseph Sung-Yul. 2009. *The Local Construction of a Global Language: Ideologies of English in South Korea, Language, Power and Social Process*. Berlin: Mouton de Gruyter.

Park, Joseph Sung-Yul. 2010. "Naturalization of Competence and the Neoliberal Subject: Success Stories of English Language Learning in the Korean Conservative Press." *Journal of Linguistic Anthropology* 20 (1): 22–38.

Park, Won-woo. 2006. *Hanguk timjeui yeoksa, hyeonhwanggwa baljeonbanghyang (Team Structure in Korea: Its Past, Present and Performance)*. Seoul: Seoul National University Press.

Peacock, Vita. 2015. "The Negation of Hierarchy and its Consequences." *Anthropological Theory* 15 (1): 3–21.

Peacock, Vita, and Philip Kao. 2013. "Transcending Structure-Agency in the Study of Organizations." *Anthropology in Action* 20 (2): 1–5.

Philips, Susan U. 1998. *Ideology in the Language of Judges: How Judges Practice Law, Politics, and Courtroom Control*. New York: Oxford University Press.

Plath, David W. 1969 [1964]. *The After Hours: Modern Japan and the Search for Enjoyment*. Berkeley: University of California Press.

Porteux, Jonson N., and Sunil Kim. 2016. "Public Ordering Of Private Coercion: Urban Redevelopment and Democratization in South Korea." *Journal of East Asian Studies* 16 (3): 371–90.

Power, Michael. 1997. *The Audit Society: Rituals of Verification*. Oxford: Clarendon Press.

Prentice, Michael M. 2019. "The Powers in PowerPoint: Embedded Authorities, Documentary Tastes, and Institutional (Second) Orders in Corporate Korea." *American Anthropologist* 121 (2): 350–62.

Rajak, Dinah. 2011a. *In Good Company: An Anatomy of Corporate Social Responsibility*. Stanford, CA: Stanford University Press.

Rajak, Dinah. 2011b. "Theatres of Virtue: Collaboration, Consensus, and the Social Life of Corporate Social Responsibility." *Focaal* 2011 (60): 9–20.

Rakova, Oxana, and Olga Fedorenko. 2021. "Sticky Notes Against Corporate Hierarchies in South Korea: An Ethnography of Workplace Collaboration and Design Co-Creation." *Design Studies* 76:101033.

Rea, Stephen C. 2018. "Calibrating Play: Sociotemporality in South Korean Digital Gaming Culture." *American Anthropologist*.

Redfield, Peter. 2006. "A Less Modest Witness." *American Ethnologist* 33 (1): 3–26.

Reed, Adam. 2017. "An Office of Ethics: Meetings, Roles, and Moral Enthusiasm in Animal Protection." *Journal of the Royal Anthropological Institute* 23 (S1): 166–81.

Reed, Robert Roy. 1990. "Are Robert's Rules of Order Counterrevolutionary?: Rhetoric and the Reconstruction of Portuguese Politics." *Anthropological Quarterly* 63 (3): 134–44.

Reyes, Antonio. 2015. "Building Intimacy Through Linguistic Choices: Text Structure and Voices in Political Discourse." *Language and Communication* 43:58–71.

Rhodes, Lorna. 2004. *Total Confinement: Madness and Reason in the Maximum Security Prison*. Berkeley: University of California Press.

Riles, Annelise. 2004. "Real Time: Unwinding Technocratic and Anthropological Knowledge." *American Ethnologist* 31 (3): 392–405.

Rogers, Douglas. 2012. "The Materiality of the Corporation: Oil, Gas, and Corporate Social Technologies in the Remaking of a Russian Region." *American Ethnologist* 39 (2): 284–96.

Rose, Nikolas. 1988. "Calculable Minds and Manageable Individuals." *History of the Human Sciences* 1 (2): 179–200.

Sahlins, Marshall. 1972. *Stone Age Economics*. Chicago: University of Chicago Press.

Schneider, Mary. 1998. "The Wal-Mart Annual Meeting: From Small-Town America to a Global Corporate Culture." *Human Organization* 57 (3): 292–99.

Schober, Elisabeth. 2018. "Working (Wo) man's Suicide: Transnational Relocations of Capital–Repercussions for Labour in South Korea and the Philippines." *Journal of the Royal Anthropological Institute* 24 (S1): 134–47.

Scott, James C. 1989. "Everyday Forms of Resistance." *Copenhagen Journal of Asian Studies* 4 (1): 33.

Seo, Dongjin. 2011. "The Will to Self-Managing, the Will to Freedom: The Self-Managing Ethic and the Spirit of Flexible Capitalism in South Korea." In *New Millenium South Korea*, edited by Jesook Song, 84–100. New York: Routledge.

Silverstein, Michael. 2003. "Indexical Order and the Dialectics of Sociolinguistic Life." *Language and Communication* 23 (3): 193–229.

Simmel, Georg. 2004. *Philosophy of Money*. London: Routledge.

Son, Chan-Hyun. 2002. *Korea's Corporate Restructuring Since the Financial Crisis*. Vol. 2. Korea Institute for International Economic Policy.

Song, Jesook. 2009. *South Koreans in the Debt Crisis: The Creation of a Neoliberal Welfare Society*. Durham, NC: Duke University Press.

Souleles, Daniel. 2019. "Another Workplace is Possible: Learning to Own and Changing Subjectivities in American Employee Owned Companies." *Critique of Anthropology* 40 (1): 28–48.

Spinuzzi, Clay, and Mark Zachry. 2000. "Genre Ecologies: An Open-System Approach to Understanding and Constructing Documentation." *Journal of Computer Documentation* 24 (3): 169–81.

Star, Susan Leigh. 1999. "The Ethnography of Infrastructure." *American Behavioral Scientist* 43 (3): 377–91.

Strathern, Marilyn. 2008. "Afterword: The Disappearing of an Office." *Cambridge Anthropology* 28 (3): 127–38.

Szymkowiak, Kenneth. 2002. *Sokaiya: Extortion, Protection, and the Japanese Corporation*. Armonk, NY: M. E. Sharpe.

Townley, Barbara. 1993. "Foucault, Power/Knowledge, and its Relevance for Human Resource Management." *Academy of Management Review* 18 (3): 518–45.

Turco, Catherine J. 2016. *The Conversational Firm: Rethinking Bureaucracy in the Age of Social Media*. New York: Columbia University Press.

Turner, Fred. 2006. *From Counterculture to Cyberculture: Stewart Brand, the Whole Earth Network, and the Rise of Digital Utopianism*. Chicago: University of Chicago Press.

Urban, Greg, and Kyung-Nan Koh. 2013. "Ethnographic Research on Modern Business Corporations." *Annual Review of Anthropology* 42:139–58.

Urban, Greg, and Kyung-Nan Koh. 2015. "The Semiotic Corporation: An Introduction to the Supplement Issue." *Signs and Society* 3 (S1): S1–S12.

Vaara, Eero, and Richard Whittington. 2012. "Strategy-as-Practice: Taking Social Practices Seriously." *Academy of Management Annals* 6 (1): 285–336.

Van Vree, Wilbert. 1999. *Meetings, Manners, and Civilization: The Development of Modern Meeting Behaviour*. London: Leicester University Press.

Vogel, Ezra F. 1963. *Japan's New Middle Class: The Salary Man and His Family in a Tokyo Suburb*. Berkeley: University of California Press.

Vogel, Ezra F. 1991. *The Four Little Dragons: The Spread of Industrialization in East Asia*. Cambridge, MA: Harvard University Press.

Warner, Michael. 2002. "Publics and Counterpublics." *Public Culture* 14 (1): 49–90.

Wästerfors, David. 2008. "Businessmen as Folk Ethnographers." *Ethnography* 9 (2): 235–56.

Weeks, John. 2004. *Unpopular Culture: The Ritual of Complaint in a British Bank*. Chicago: University of Chicago Press.

Welker, Marina. 2014. *Enacting the Corporation: An American Mining Firm in Post-Authoritarian Indonesia*. Berkeley: University of California Press.

Welker, Marina, and David Wood. 2011. "Shareholder Activism and Alienation." *Current Anthropology* 52 (S3): S57–S69.

Whitelaw, Gavin 2014. "Shelf Lives and the Labors of Loss." In *Capturing Contemporary Japan: Differentiation and Uncertainty*, edited by Satsuki Kawano, Glenda S. Roberts, and Susan Orpett Long, 135–60. Honolulu: University of Hawai'i Press.

Whittington, Richard. 2006. "Completing the Practice Turn in Strategy Research." *Organization Studies* 27 (5): 613–34.

Whyte, William H. 1956. *The Organization Man*. Garden City, NY: Doubleday.

Wilf, Eitan. 2015. "Ritual Semiosis in the Business Corporation: Recruitment to Routinized Innovation." *Signs and Society* 3 (S1): S13–S40.

Wilf, Eitan. 2021. "Phaticity as a Technical Mystique: The Genred, Multi-Sited Mediation of the Innovation Architect's Expertise." *Journal of Cultural Economy* 1–17.

Wilf, Eitan Y. 2019. *Creativity on Demand: The Dilemmas of Innovation in an Accelerated Age*. Chicago: University of Chicago Press.

Yan, Yun-xiang. 1996. *The Flow of Gifts: Reciprocity and Social Networks in a Chinese Village*. Stanford, CA: Stanford University Press.

Yanagisako, Sylvia Junko. 2012. "Transnational Family Capitalism: Producing 'Made in Italy' in China." In *Vital Relations: Modernity and the Persistent Life of Kinship*, edited by Susan McKinnon and Fenella Cannell, 74–95. Santa Fe, NM: School of Advanced Research Press.

Yang, Mayfair Mei-hui. 1994. *Gifts, Favors, and Banquets: The Art of Social Relationships in China*. The Wilder House Series in Politics, History, and Culture. Ithaca, NY: Cornell University Press.

Yates, JoAnne, and Wanda J. Orlikowski. 1992. "Genres of Organizational Communication: A Structurational Approach to Studying Communication and Media." *Academy of Management Review* 17 (2): 299–326.

Yi, Sohoon, and Jennifer Jihye Chun. 2020. "Building Worker Power for Day Laborers in South Korea's Construction Industry." *International Journal of Comparative Sociology* 61 (2–3): 122–40.

Index

CULTURE AND ECONOMIC LIFE

Diverse sets of actors create meaning in markets: consumers and socially engaged actors from below; producers, suppliers, and distributors from above; and gatekeepers and intermediaries who span these levels. Scholars have studied the interactions of people, objects, and technology; charted networks of innovation and diffusion among producers and consumers; and explored the categories that constrain and enable economic action. This series captures the many angles from which these phenomena have been investigated and serves as a high-profile forum for discussing the creation, evolution, and consequences of commerce and culture.

Black Culture, Inc.
Patricia A. Banks
2022

The Sympathetic Consumer: Moral Critique in Capitalist Culture
Tad Skotnicki
2021

Reimagining Money: Kenya in the Digital Finance Revolution
Sibel Kusimba
2021

Black Privilege: Modern Middle-Class Blacks with Credentials and Cash to Spend
Cassi Pittman Claytor
2020

Global Borderlands: Fantasy, Violence, and Empire in Subic Bay, Philippines
Victoria Reyes
2019